SMART TIMES

Also by the author

Smart Toys: For Babies from Birth to Two

SMART TIMES

A PARENT'S GUIDE
TO QUALITY TIME
WITH PRESCHOOLERS

KENT GARLAND BURTT

ILLUSTRATIONS BY TRICIA TAGGART

1817

HARPER & ROW, PUBLISHERS, NEW YORK
CAMBRIDGE, PHILADELPHIA, SAN FRANCISCO
LONDON, MEXICO CITY, SÃO PAULO, SINGAPORE, SYDNEY

SMART TIMES. Text copyright © 1984 by Kent Garland Burtt. Illustrations copyright © 1984 by Tricia Taggart. All rights reserved. Printed in the United States of America. No part of this book may be used or reproduced in any manner whatsoever without written permission except in the case of brief quotations embodied in critical articles and reviews. For information address Harper & Row, Publishers, Inc., 10 East 53rd Street, New York, N.Y. 10022. Published simultaneously in Canada by Fitzhenry & Whiteside Limited, Toronto.

FIRST EDITION

Designer: Helene Berinsky

Library of Congress Cataloging in Publication Data

Burtt, Kent Garland.
  Smart times.

  1. Play—Handbooks, manuals, etc. 2. Creative activities and seat work—Handbooks, manuals, etc.
3. Parent and child. I. Title.
HQ782.B87 1984   649'.5   83-48938
ISBN 0-06-015287-7   84 85 86 87 88 10 9 8 7 6 5 4 3 2 1
ISBN 0-06-091124-7 (pbk.) 84 85 86 87 88 10 9 8 7 6 5 4 3 2 1

CONTENTS

PART II. TOGETHERNESS EXPERIENCES FOR LOVING TIMES

ACKNOWLEDGMENTS

Special thanks go to the following men and women, who by the fine quality of their own parenting, gave much substance to this book:

Claudia and Robert Amen, Abby and John Bamman, Denise and Steve Boockvor, June and John Burstein, Ann Bush, Jane and Lawrence Caldwell, Kathy and Walter Connor, Bonnie Cunningham, Sandy and Jim Geyer, Pat Grace, Laurie Jones, Caroline and Walter Lippincott, Anne and Bruce Lynn, Clarisse and Doug MacGarvey, Beverly and Peter Millard, Joanne and Steve Otto, Arlene and Joseph Pitts, Debora and Alan Pressman, Cheryl Reade, Jo and Jim Tatum, Alice and Russell Treyz, Kathy and Jacobus Vreeken, Jan and Warren Wehmann, Judy and Norris Wolff, Susan and Harold Woolley.

And grateful appreciation to the following list of professionals consulted:

Mary Craig, Nautilus Early Learning Center (Wilton, Conn.)
Joanne Eager, Colonial Christian School (Georgetown, Conn.)
Mari Endreweit, Bank Street College of Education (New York City)
Jeanna Gollobin, Children's Energy Center (New York City)
Judy Greenfield, Rye (New York) Public Library
Nancy Hansen, Darien (Conn.) Public Schools
Louise Hartwell, The Spence School (New York City)
Enid Hyman, A Child's Place (Westport, Conn.)
Nancy Johnson, Greens Farms Academy (Westport, Conn.)
Diane Levin, Wheelock College (Boston)
Mary Libby, Diller Quaile School of Music (New York City)
Hanna McElheny, Bank Street College of Education (New York City)

Carol McGee, Noroton Presbyterian Nursery School (Darien, Conn.)

Jean Nelson, Saugatuck Day Care Service (Westport, Conn.)

Teri Perl, The Learning Company (Menlo Park, Calif.)

Ann Ramone, Mead School for Human Development (Greenwich, Conn.)

Marcy Raphael, Whitby School (Greenwich, Conn.)

Margaret Skutch, The Early Learning Center (Stamford, Conn.)

Joan Sprigle, Educational Research Center for Child Development (Tallahassee, Fla.)

Michael Temple, Logo Computer Systems (New York City)

Fritze Till, New Canaan (Conn.) Nature Center

Patricia Vardin, Teacher's College, Columbia University (New York City)

Nancy Wayman, Stepping Stones (Westport, Conn.)

INTRODUCTION

Busy parents yearn for quality time with their child. Fifteen minutes or half an hour when there's a meaningful exchange heart to heart, mind to mind, is an experience that is good for a child and good for a parent.

However, once you are poised for this valuable one-on-one time, do you know what to do with it? You needn't trot out that same old storybook you're both bored with. Offer instead an innovative story session, a new lighthearted game, or a creative project. To save you time hunting for a clever idea, this book presents an array of interesting playtime possibilities.

Smart Times contains over two hundred activities designed to put the "quality" element into quality time. These activities promote your child's physical, social, and cognitive skills. They help you enjoy each other's company more. They draw out the best a parent has to give a child and the best a child has to give a parent.

The games are not only entertaining for kids but also pleasurable for parents. In fact, most were invented by parents. Even if you're tired and preoccupied with problems, you can find something you're in the mood for. After a happy interlude with your child, you'll feel brighter. While experts often note the benefits of quality time for the child, they often overlook the emotional, recreational, and spiritual benefits of quality time for the parent.

Parents feel deep contentment and excitement as a result of observing their child blossom during intimate times together. Their various comments describe the rewards: "My son gives my life a special beauty that my career could never afford me." "Parenting makes me feel more complete." "When things go wrong in the real world, my well-developing child is a consolation." "My daughter is good company; she's a thinker."

Understanding of self and others increases. One father says, "I've been reflecting on my own childhood. Seeing how I influence my child, I understand how my parents influenced me. I'm more sensitive to others and understand why they do what they do."

Interactions with their children force parents to grow. A mother explained, "In order to be a better model for my children, I'm bringing my behavior more in line with my ideals." A father said, "In an effort not to pass on my character flaws, I work harder on overcoming them."

As one quality-time experience succeeds another, grown-ups find themselves growing up. They talk about being more tender, patient, sunny, playful, and peaceful. The capacity for unselfish love evolves. As one father put it, "My son is the only person I love with a true love."

HOME CURRICULUM

The recipes for fun and learning in *Smart Times* are planned like a well-balanced menu. Some activities stimulate imagination, some promote close rapport, others educate intellectually. Grouped under the broad headings of Creative Activities for Joyful Times, Togetherness Experiences for Loving Times, and Learning Games for Smart Times, they will bring more joy, love, and intelligence into your lives.

Choices range from cooking, painting, and let's-pretend scenarios to rowdy roughhousing and quiet-in-the-lap play. There are ideas for inspiring a good conversation between parent and offspring. There are suggestions for ways to tuck in a child that make for especially sweet good nights. There are icebreakers to involve everyone when grandparents or cousins visit. Finally, there are educationally sound recommendations for teaching early reading, writing, and arithmetic skills. The subject matter really includes all the important areas of early learning—art, music, fantasy, listening, talking, physical exercise, spiritual development, understanding one another, fine motor skills, beginning academics. Even disks for the home computer are discussed. The book can serve as a kind of home curriculum for the child aged two, three, and four.

EASY-TO-FOLLOW FORMAT

Each chapter starts with a brief overview of a particular category of play, such as cooking. Then a dozen or so specific activities in that category follow. Each of these could be carried out in a half hour or less. Some include mini-activities which might take only five minutes.

To decide which to do, scan the summaries entitled Activity. Go with your own enthusiasms. Or scan the paragraphs entitled Benefits, which follow the explanations of many activities and describe their special boost to your child's development. Then choose the activity which gives the kind of boost your child could use.

The list beside the word Props quickly shows you what materials to gather for the fun. The word Actions begins the instructions for carrying out each activity.

Within each chapter the activities progress from easier to harder. The first few activities are more appropriate for the two- to three-year-old and the later activities more suitable for the three- to five-year-old. References to ages are at a bare minimum, as aptitudes vary widely. Every child is so different that you, the individual reader, need to survey the activities and choose the ones you think are most appropriate for your child's tastes, needs, and current abilities. Your own expertise in an area, such as carpentry, might make it easier for you to introduce a project to the youngest age level.

The book's activities are by no means indispensable prescriptions for preschoolers. They need only serve as samples to inspire readers to invent their own projects and games.

Some parents who are not working outside the home may have more free time with their preschooler. They could pick two or three activities to enliven a day and vary the pace by choosing one from the Creative Activities in the first section of the book, one from the Togetherness Experiences in the second section, and one from the Learning Games in the third section.

HOW TO PLAY

Remember! Whatever area you explore together, your main goal should be to promote your child's self-esteem. It's the crucial factor in fulfilling individual potential. When you focus loving attention on your child and show interest in doing something with him, you are shaping his personality positively. Let warm approval radiate through all your communications. He'll reflect the glow if there's plenty of face-to-face interaction, eye contact, smiling, touching, and praising. Nobody ever gets too many of these signs of affection from those he loves!

Talking should accompany almost all the projects and exchanges. Describing the details of the activities you are engaged in develops your child's intelligence. Talking also fosters social skills. Verbalizing what you and she are thinking and feeling will help her tune in to others and be easy to get along with.

CAREGIVERS, BABY-SITTERS, COUNSELORS, GRANDPARENTS

Day-care-center staff and family day-care providers will find the catalog of activities here a handy source of ways to occupy children constructively. Parents eager to upgrade the skills of a baby-sitter employed in their home might show the book to her. Grandparents, often the favorite baby-sitters, can peruse this book for ideas to add sparkle to their day with a grandchild. Professionals such as parent educators, family counselors, day-care directors, and home teachers in early education projects can share ideas from *Smart Times* during workshops and interviews.

INPUT FROM PARENTS AND EARLY CHILDHOOD EDUCATORS

This book is based on interviews with about fifty parents of preschoolers, almost as many fathers as mothers. They shared specific activities they found nurturing to their children and satisfying to themselves. I also drew on my experiences during the rearing of my own four children. So the activities recommended have all been tested in the "laboratory" of family life.

Finally, I consulted nursery school teachers and directors and other professionals in early childhood education. Their strong contributions are featured mainly in the third section of the book, Learning Games for Smart Times.

I

CREATIVE ACTIVITIES FOR JOYFUL TIMES

· 1 ·

KITCHEN COMPANIONS

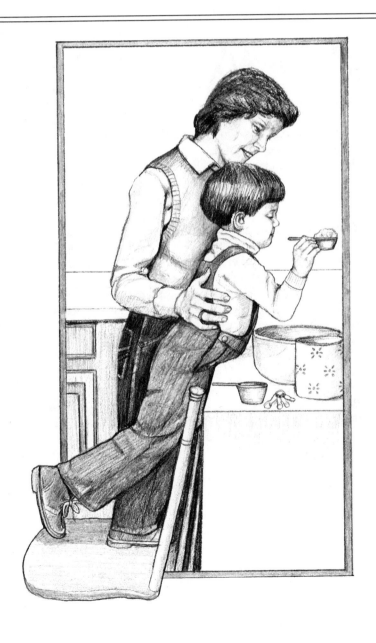

Amajority of one-on-one time with your child may take place in the kitchen. As a suburban parent put it, "John grew up at the countertop." It's an ideal setting. You can freely exchange small talk when cooking doesn't demand your concentration. Focusing on concrete things—food and utensils of all sizes and shapes—is work your child can understand. On days when cooking strikes you as a lot of fun, you certainly have a kindred spirit in your child, to whom cooking always seems like fun. On days when you're experimenting with new concoctions, he can identify with that mood, also. He's been experimenting since day one.

Participation, of course, is the name of the game. No itchy-fingered preschooler is going to perch idly on a stool for long playing the passive role of viewer to your TV chef show. He wants into the act!

Inevitably he's going to slow you down. You may have to choose simpler recipes or prepare fewer dishes in order to give your me-tooer his chance to be a Big Help. You'll need virtues such as forbearance, patience, and playfulness—virtues you may not have exercised during meal preparations before when efficiency was your hallmark. The counter and floor are going to be dirtier, too. That may call for an ounce more elbow grease than hitherto.

Cooking with kids doesn't necessarily mean making gingerbread men or decorating cupcakes with gaudy colored icing. "David gets to do one or two steps of whatever dish I'm fixing," one dad said. Kids want to work on the evening meal. They don't even have to like the food they help prepare. They might hate coleslaw but they'll still love shredding cabbage. It's the process, not the product, that interests them.

Food preparation gives your child many mathematical and scientific experiences. When you are measuring, weighing, counting, and timing, your sidekick is paying attention to numbers. When you're mixing, heating, and chilling various liquid and solid substances, your ever-present observer is learning about physical properties.

Talking your way through preparations gives your child exposure to following a sequence of steps. Out-loud commentary also benefits his vocabulary. Name all the ingredients as you handle them. Name utensils, too, as you use them. Describe your actions, using a rich assortment of verbs: "I'm mashing the potatoes. I'm mincing the garlic. I'm kneading the dough. I'm squeezing the lemon."

The efforts of a novice cook may be clumsy and delay dinner, but your tact in incorporating these efforts into the routine will pay off in all kinds of learning. On the following pages are five activities for noncooking countertop involvement and a dozen recipes your child may enjoy making at first with you and someday on his own.

UTENSILS IN USE

♦ ACTIVITY

Scooping, funneling, sieving, and practicing other simple skills with kitchen implements.

♦ PROPS

Contents of your kitchen drawers: scoop, sieve, tongs, melon baller, funnel, spatulas (rubber and metal), garlic press, grater, sprinkler, eggbeater, egg separator, pitcher, potato peeler, dull paring knife, ice cream scoop, measuring spoons, measuring cups.

♦ ACTIONS

Give your child only one or two of the tools listed to handle at one time. (Then you stretch out the fun and give her time to find many ways to handle one single device.) She can use a utensil to help you with a recipe or, if you want her nearby but not involved with your work, she can use it with any appropriate food that happens to be at hand. Wielding the utensil with different substances or with various containers, she will gradually become more adept.

Utensils become toys, and performing functions with them becomes a form of play. Montessori classrooms stock kitchen utensils to encourage the mastery of hand-eye coordination tasks. The scoop can be used to scoop flour, sugar, or dried beans and transfer these from one container to another. The tongs might be used to pick up tea bags from a commercial cardboard box and put them in a decorative tin. A sprinkler with perforated holes in its screwed-on lid can be shaken to decorate food surfaces with confectioner's sugar or fire-engine-red paprika. A melon baller can be balanced to transfer whole walnuts from one attractive bowl to another (not a usual task, but a challenge to progressing coordination).

A funnel might be used to transfer coarse-grained salt from a box to a narrow-necked container like a salad dressing cruet. A small spatula can be used to level rice in a measuring cup or to level flour in a scoop or in a measuring spoon. A large spatula can be used to flip pancakes, fishcakes, or hamburgers. An eggbeater can be spun in water or chocolate milk just for the fun of seeing the bubbles. An egg separator enables a youngster to really help in some recipes without the danger of mixing yolks and whites.

A decorated pitcher with an easy-to-hold handle can increase the delight of pouring. If your child practices pouring solids first, such as rice or sugar, then you'll both be more confident about him pouring liquids without spilling them. A potato peeler can be managed by a three-year-old to peel not only potatoes but carrots, zucchini, and apples. Some parents allow careful offspring to cut up raw vegetables for salad with a somewhat dull knife.

◆ BENEFIT

Manipulating utensils improves fine-motor skills.

INCREDIBLE INEDIBLES

◆ ACTIVITY

Imitating the cooking process by adding sundry ingredients to a bowl and stirring vigorously to blend.

◆ PROPS

Bowl, large spoon, measuring cups and spoons, flour, sugar, salt, herbs, vegetable oil, water.

◆ ACTIONS

Two-year-olds are blissful just pretending to be preparing a meal. At first they pretend without any realistic props at all. They might use toys or just move their hands in the air as if utensils were there. When they get older, they want real implements and foodstuffs, though not the discipline of a real recipe. If you can afford it, give your child access to the flour, sugar, and salt canisters and to a few old jars of herbs and spices that have lost their oomph. Let her measure out some conservative amounts of flour and sugar and sprinkle in various herbs and ground spices. Add water for a gooey texture. She could toss in some cloves and peppercorns, too. Businesslike stirring can follow each addition. Try a smidgen, at least; it's tastier than mud pies!

♦ BENEFIT

Make-believe cooking satisfies the child who wants to imitate you but who is not yet ready for the precision of following real recipes.

PUSH-BUTTON WORLD

♦ ACTIVITY

Pressing the button of the food processor, switching on the oven, swiveling the knob of the timer, and operating other mechanisms in today's kitchen.

♦ PROPS

Scales, thermometers, timers, coffee grinder and brewer, blender, electric mixer, food processor, can opener, toaster, toaster oven, plate warmer, dishwasher, clothes washer, drier.

♦ ACTIONS

Understand the intellectual fascination a small child has with kitchen machines. All those dials, levers, little red lights, knobs, buttons, and hinged lids beg little fingers to touch. Whir, buzz, ding, vibrate, light up! The kitchen is a circus! Satisfy his attraction when possible, but safety comes first. So supervise those investigative instincts.

Rather than bombarding your child with no's, let him learn how and when to start and stop some of your appliances. Give him opportunities at your side to preheat the oven, set the timer, eject the blades from your electric mixer, place food on the scales, and swivel the knob to grind the coffee beans. You need to take time to teach carefulness (even though preschoolers are more careful than many adults believe them to be).

One four-year-old regularly made his parents' morning coffee, measuring the grinds and water accurately and placing these in the right compartments of the electric drip machine and then turning on the brew button. Oh, the joy of making that red light shine!

SCINTILLATING SENSATIONS

♦ ACTIVITY

Tasting, sniffing, feeling, and looking at food.

♦ PROPS

Various foods in your fridge and cabinets; containers such as an egg carton, a candy box insert, a muffin tin, and an empty ice cube tray.

♦ TASTING ACTIONS

Tasting can take place during all meal preparations. But here's a game to play once in a while. Blindfold your child. Spoon a different food into each section of a muffin tin. Try ketchup, apple sauce, jelly, cream sauce, pudding, gravy. Put a little of each on your child's tongue and ask her to guess what it is. Describe what the taste buds note—salty, sweet, sour, and so on. Then when your spouse comes home, let your child administer the taste test.

♦ SMELLING ACTIONS

Line up a bunch of jars from your spice cabinet. Together, compare smells. Start using some recipes that incorporate certain appealing spices so your child comes to recognize them readily. Can your child smell a raw banana and then recognize it in the fragrance wafting from banana bread hot out of the oven? Can she notice the lack of smell of a raw potato compared to the tempting aroma of a cooked and mashed one? How about detecting a decaying vegetable, some rancid bacon, or turned cream in a neglected fridge?

♦ FEELING ACTIONS

Fingers are for touching, so appreciate a child's instinct to examine the texture of all those wet, dry, gooey, crumbly, and smooth substances within easy reach. Why not wash his hands and together think about the similarities and differences in the feel of various foods? Granola, bread crumbs, and cold cereal flakes are dry and bumpy. Rolled oats are velvety. Raw macaroni is hard and smooth, and listen! It clicks when dropped. Cooked macaroni is soft and sticky and noiseless when dropped. Jell-O is powdery at first, then syrupy, then wobbly, then firm.

Have you ever fiddled with cornstarch? Put a cup of it into a bowl. Gradually add a scant half-cup of water to it, working the water in with your fingers. Queer things begin to happen. Lumps appear. Then the mixture looks like a liquid and acts like a solid. Tap the bottom of the bowl. You feel a solid substance yield to pressure. See what happens when you move your fingers around the bottom of the bowl. Scoop some up in your palm, squeeze and release. Then, with a clean finger, rub your coated fingers for a half-dry, half-wet sensation.

♦ **ACTIONS FOR VISUAL APPEAL**

Sharpen perception by comparing the appearance of various foodstuffs. For display purposes, pick a container with compartments such as an egg carton, candy box insert, or empty ice cube tray. The first arrangement could be just skins or shells—the "gift wrapping" of foods. Save apple and cucumber skins, potato peelings, citrus fruit rinds, nutshells, and eggshells. A second arrangement could be greens: lettuce, celery leaves, spinach, and carrot tops. Fresh and/or dried herbs make another arrangement. Move on to dried beans of various colors and split peas. A display of fistfuls of the cold cereals from the boxes on your shelf might be interesting, too.

CHEMISTRY 101?

♦ **ACTIVITY**

Watching substances change: solids melt, liquids solidify, shapely foods get mashed, shapeless foods get molded.

♦ **PROPS**

Everyday items such as Jell-O, ice cream, garlic clove, pie crust mix, eggs, potato, apple.

♦ **ACTIONS**

Realize how brand new to this world of the kitchen countertop your child is. Like an explorer discovering the flora and fauna of a strange continent, your child is finding out about the myriad fruits, vegetables, meats, and grain products you take for granted. Spend an extra minute to study with your child, say, the lowly cauliflower. Be amazed with her at the way it's composed of dozens of miniature flowerets.

It's natural for a child to examine food. One day a parent realized her child was fussing because she wanted to peel her own banana. After finally breaking through the skin at one end and pulling strips of skin halfway down, the little girl suddenly squealed with delight and kissed the creamy-white fruit she'd unveiled.

With a magician's sense of drama, show your child the crystals from the Jell-O packet, study their transformation upon contact with hot water, then look for quick hardening of the gelatin after a little time in the freezer. Together notice ice cream when it's very hard, then when it's softening, later when it's refrozen, and again when it's whirred in the blender for a milkshake. Be amused by that curvaceous crescent of garlic clove "smooshed" suddenly in the garlic press. Let your child observe the changing texture of the pie crust mix from fluffy powder to moldable dough to flaky baked crust. An egg can take any number of forms—fried, hard- and soft-boiled (and eaten out of the shell with an end trimmed off), scrambled, yolk and white separated, and the white beaten stiff. The appearance is dramatically different each time.

♦ BENEFIT

To your junior scientist, the family kitchen is a laboratory and the nightly meal a chemical experiment.

RECIPES FOR SIDE-BY-SIDE COOKS

♦ ACTIVITY

Preparing real food and cooking with your child.

♦ PROPS

Normal kitchen equipment.

♦ ACTIONS

The following recipes are for parent and child to follow together. All have been tested and enjoyed by both generations. They involve manipulating ingredients in ways that are fun for kids. Almost all the steps of preparation are easy enough to be managed by a preschooler. How you divide the work will depend on your child's age and stage. Once you both have made a given recipe a few times, your role might be only supervisory.

PRETTY PIZZA

Frozen cheese pizza pie
Meats and vegetables for decoration, such as pepperoni
    slices, mounds of ground beef or sausage, onion rings,
    mushroom slices, green pepper slivers, tomato slices,
    shavings of extra cheese

You can slice the decorative foods and your child can position them on the surface of the pizza. Bake according to directions on package.

♦

LEMON ICE CREAM

1 cup milk
1 cup sugar
1 cup cream
Juice of 2 lemons

Mix all ingredients in large bowl and place in freezer till slushy. Remove and stir again thoroughly. Freeze till solid. This ice cream actually tastes better when not too hard. For special occasions, hollow out orange halves and scoop portions into the rind "bowl."

♦

DADDY'S SMILE CAKES

Pancake mix
Drinking straws

Make pancake batter. Suck some batter up a straw. Then blow it out onto the griddle in the form of two eyes, a nose, and a smile. Brown these shapes on both sides. With spatula, arrange them on the griddle like a face. Then pour a circle of batter on top of them. Cook, then flip. Serve face side up, natch! An older preschooler might try his luck with these. A younger one might rather be served and surprised.

♦

PEANUT BUTTER FROM SCRATCH

Bag of peanuts
Oil

Shell the peanuts, using a nutcracker if that's easier or more fun for your child. Pour a little oil into the blender or food processor. Add a handful of peanuts at a time, making sure not to gum up the machine. Mix on low to medium speed. Add salt to taste. If you're not in a hurry, your junior chef might manage everything: taking the lid off, adding more peanuts, replacing the lid, starting and stopping the blender for each addition.

♦

PEANUT BUTTER PLAY DOUGH

1 cup peanut butter (homemade or store bought)
1 tablespoon honey
About 1 cup powdered milk
Raisins

Spoon peanut butter into a bowl. Pour in honey. Add some powdered milk. Let your child mix with her hands. Keep adding powdered milk until it makes a pliable dough. Mold it into any shape or roll it with a rolling pin. Make designs with raisins or cut shapes with cookie cutters. Sculpt and eat alternately.

◆

AUNT JOAN'S BROWN-EDGED WAFERS

½ cup shortening
½ cup sugar
1 egg
¼ teaspoon salt
½ teaspoon vanilla
¾ cup flour

Blend shortening, sugar, egg, salt, and vanilla. Stir in flour. Drop by small spoonfuls onto greased cookie sheet far apart (they spread). Bake in a 350-degree oven until delicate brown around the edges—about eight minutes.

◆

YOGURT SUNDAE

Vanilla yogurt
Trimmings such as sliced bananas, apples, oranges, raisins,
*   nuts, wheat germ, sunflower seeds*
Honey

Scoop yogurt into a dish. Stir in sliced fruit. Add raisins and/or any favorite nuts. Sprinkle wheat germ and sunflower seeds on top. Trickle honey all over.

◆

I-CAN-DO-IT CHICKEN

½ cup flour
1 teaspoon salt
½ teaspoon pepper
1 teaspoon paprika
2½-pound broiler-fryer, cut up
Stick of butter
Currant jelly

Put flour in large plastic bag. Shake in some salt, pepper, and paprika. Drop in each chicken piece one at a time and shake till coated. Melt butter in shallow baking pan over burner or in oven. (Maybe Mom should help here.) Arrange chicken pieces in pan so they nestle together. Bake uncovered 30 minutes at 425 degrees. Then turn with tongs (help, again) and bake 15 minutes more. Serve with currant jelly.

◆

RAINBOW MEAT LOAF

2 eggs
2 pounds ground chuck
2 cups bread crumbs
1 cup assorted minced vegetables, such as green and red
   peppers, onions, parsley, carrots, and celery
2½ teaspoons salt
¼ cup milk
¼ cup ketchup
3 peach halves
½ cup ketchup (for top)

Beat eggs. Mix meat with eggs. Why not use hands? Then add bread crumbs and vegetables. Hands can turn, squeeze, knead, and pinch till ingredients are evenly mixed. Add salt, milk, and ¼ cup ketchup. Stir them in with a spoon. Pack mixture into greased loaf pan. Make three hollows on top and put peach halves in them. Spread ketchup over the top. Bake at 400 degrees for fifty minutes.

◆

Here are three recipes that are more complicated than the previous ones, but guaranteed to please the grown-up palate as well as the child's. In the first two, your child can have fun rolling the mixture into small balls before cooking them. In the last recipe he will dunk cooked muffins in melted butter and then roll them in cinnamon sugar.

SWEDISH MEATBALLS

1 pound ground chuck
1 tablespoon chopped parsley
1 egg
¼ cup fine bread crumbs
⅛ teaspoon salt
⅛ teaspoon nutmeg
pepper and garlic powder to taste
1 to 2 tablespoons shortening or butter
1 cup sour cream

Mix together well the meat, parsley, and egg. Then add bread crumbs, salt, nutmeg, pepper, and garlic powder. Mix again. (Clean chubby hands can plunge in wrist-deep for this step.) Roll into tiny meatballs. (Here have your child cup his palms together. Stick a chunk of meat mixture in between. Now show him how circular movements of his hands can create a little ball.) Fry meatballs in shortening or butter, browning them on all sides. Then pour sour cream over them and baste until meatballs are well coated. Serve hot or chilled.

◆

CHOCOLATE CRINKLES

½ cup vegetable oil
4 squares unsweetened chocolate, melted
2 cups granulated sugar
4 eggs
2 teaspoons vanilla
2 cups flour
2 teaspoons baking powder
½ teaspoon salt
1 cup confectioner's sugar

Mix oil, chocolate, and granulated sugar. Blend in 1 egg at a time until well mixed. Add vanilla.

Measure flour by dipping method or by sifting. Stir flour, baking powder, and salt into oil mixture. Chill several hours or overnight.

Preheat oven to 350 degrees. Now put your child's dimpled hands to work! Drop teaspoonfuls of dough into a bowl of confectioner's sugar. Let him roll blobs in sugar and then shape into round balls. Place them about two inches apart on greased baking sheet. Bake ten to twelve minutes. Do not overbake. Makes about six dozen very pretty cookies.

♦

CINNAMON-SUGAR MUFFINS

⅔ cup shortening
1 cup sugar
2 eggs
3 cups sifted flour
1 tablespoon baking powder
1 teaspoon salt
1 teaspoon nutmeg
1 cup milk
stick of butter, melted
1 cup sugar mixed with 2 teaspoons cinnamon

Mix thoroughly the shortening, sugar, and eggs. Then sift together the flour, baking powder, salt, and nutmeg. Into the egg mixture, stir alternately some of the dry ingredients and some of the milk until all is well blended.

Fill greased muffin cups two-thirds full. Bake twenty to twenty-five minutes at 350 degrees till golden brown. Let cool slightly, just until they're not too hot for your child to handle.

Here's the fun part. Dunk each muffin in a bowl of warm melted butter till coated. Then dip it in a bowl of cinnamon sugar, rolling it around till the grains of sugar cover the whole surface. Lick fingers. Serve warm.

· 2 ·

ART START

A rt is a dramatic means of self-expression. In essence, it consists of a sheet of blank paper, an instrument that applies brilliant color and pattern to the blankness, and a human being who likes to leave a mark!

Our child development experts say preschoolers are interested in "making things happen." Creating something out of nothing fits that bill. Having a just-finished product displayed prominently on the fridge door by an admiring parent imparts self-esteem. Through the early years maturing art projects give a child practice in the creative process—being receptive to ideas that occur to her and translating them into the concrete. Both visualizing skills and manual dexterity develop. Adult artists are often in awe of the daring and direct way little children begin a painting, without a trace of the caution that often hampers grown-ups.

You can facilitate your child's early forays into the world of art by providing easy access to art supplies. Organize a handy cupboard, drawer, or stack of in/out boxes for storing crayons, paints, scissors, paper, glue, and collage materials. Provide newspapers for protecting tables and rags for easy mop-ups so setting up and cleaning up won't be too big an imposition on you. (See Artsy-Craftsy Corner, p. 36.)

The way you talk to your child about her artwork can either make her uptight and stifle creativity or relax her and encourage inventiveness. Never speak disparagingly of her work: "That's rather messy. You can do better." But don't lavish her with praise, either. If you say, "Darling, that's a gorgeous picture!" You put a child under pressure to live up to a reputation of being just as clever when doing the next art project. Instead of using superlatives, simply notice and describe the details of your child's artwork:

>   On color: "Wow! You let the reds and blues slide into each other."
>   On texture: "That section is bumpy. Hmm . . . this one is velvety."

On quality: "This painting looks wet and shiny. That one's all dry."

On lines: "All these lines go in the same direction. Those lines go in different directions. I see some straight lines. Now I notice a curvy one."

On line weight: "That's a big fat line. There's a skinny one."

Never value one aspect over another. Just describe, using a healthy variety of adjectives. Then you'll be teaching terms that will sharpen her perceptions as well as leaving her free to experiment.

ALL-ABOUT-ME ART

The first three activities involve the child's body directly in producing art. One art teacher of preschoolers sees little kids as me-centered. So art that tells them more about themselves is of great interest. If you outline their bodies on a large sheet of paper, they see themselves from a new perspective. If part of the body becomes the tool for producing the art, as it does when they make prints of their fingertips, they enjoy the direct involvement. If the body is the object being decorated, they are entranced. The next few activities cater to this egocentrism.

TRACING MYSELF

◆ **ACTIVITY**

Tracing your child's hands, feet, and body.

◆ **PROPS**

Crayons, typing paper, large piece of brown wrapping paper or a roll of shelf paper, radio.

◆ **ACTIONS**

You and your child are equal participants in producing these primitive "self-portraits," but your roles are different.

Just Hands Lay a sheet of paper on a table or the floor and draw with a crayon around your child's left hand and right hand. Outline each hand first with fingers apart, then together. Now draw around your own hands for comparison.

Just Feet Crayon a heavy line around your child's left foot and right foot. Try it when the feet are apart, then together. Both Mom and Dad can submit their feet to the outlining process, too.

Whole Body Have your child lie down on a piece of brown wrapping paper or a roll of shelf paper. Crayon around his body. Then Dad lies down, too, and Mom and Junior can draw around his taller body. Older children might like to fill in facial features and color in clothes.

Wriggle and Freeze Have your child lie down again. This time turn on some music. Let her wiggle her hips, wave her arms, and flex her legs in time to the music. When you turn off the music, she should freeze. Draw around her limbs and torso in this new frozen position. Can Mom pose in a funny position, too?

PRINTING MYSELF

♦ **ACTIVITY**

Making fingerprints, handprints, and footprints and noticing that everyone's imprint is unique.

♦ **PROPS**

Acrylic paint (or tempera paint with cornstarch), typing paper, shallow baking dish.

♦ **ACTIONS**

You can do each of the three activities here on different days in order to enjoy each one to the fullest.

Fingerprints Squeeze a thin layer of acrylic paint or pour a little tempera paint thickened with cornstarch into a shallow dish. Hold your child's hand and dip each little fingertip into paint. Then press it onto a piece of paper. The impressions should show the lines on the skin. Compare his thumb and pinky prints. Compare your fingerprints with your child's. Make designs composed of fingerprints. "Walk" two fingers across a page.

When comparing your child's fingerprints with yours or an older sibling's, it might be a good time to explain with awe that everyone's fingerprint is special, like no one else's!

Handprints Coat palms of hands with paint and pat them on a nice white sheet of paper. Let your child hold her fingers close together and then opened wide for different impressions. How about a fist print next?

Footprints Put acrylic paint or tempera paint thickened with cornstarch into a shallow baking dish. Working in the kitchen or bathroom, let your child step into the dish and then plant his feet on paper waiting beside the dish. If you've acquired a roll of newsprint, you might unroll a room-length segment and let your son walk along it. He can dip the soles of his feet again whenever the marks fade. Now it's your turn! Sure, it's yukky, but get your feet wet too!

DECORATING MYSELF

♦ **ACTIVITY**

Making paper costumes, headgear, some jewelry, and a mask so your child can cover himself from top to toe with his own artwork.

♦ **PROPS**

Typing paper, colored construction paper, scissors, glue; empty toilet-paper rolls, felt-tip pens; large sheet of brown wrapping paper, brown paper grocery bag; paper plate, popsicle stick.

♦ **ACTIONS**

These projects can be undertaken one at a time and the results set aside. Eventually they can all be worn at once.

Weird Crowns Fold a piece of typing paper or colored construction paper in half the long way. Draw two wiggly, somewhat parallel lines down the length of it. Cut along the lines (through both halves of the folded paper), starting and stopping an inch from the edges of the typing paper. Pulling gently, separate this double strip from the rest of the paper. (The strip will have zigzag or scalloped borders.) As you pull the strip toward you, it will curve into a semicircle. This becomes the band that fits around the back of your child's head, leaving at the front of his head the rest of the paper with the cutout portion as a design. Your child can glue on bits of contrasting colored paper as jewels before or after the cutting process. Make crowns for Mom, your dog (a regal canine), a doll, or Teddy bear.

Jewelry Paint empty toilet paper rolls or decorate them with felt-tip pens or glue and glitter. Cut them into inch-wide rings. String them on a shoelace for a monarch's necklace or an Indian anklet.

Hula Skirt   Tape around your child's waist a large sheet of brown wrapping paper. Fringe it by cutting strips an inch apart from hemline to hips. Show your daughter how to float those arms and wiggle those hips Hawaiian-style.

Cowboy or Indian Vest   In the bottom of a brown paper grocery bag, cut a generous hole for your child's head and neck. On the sides, cut holes for arms. Fringe the top of the bag for decoration around the hips when the bag is turned upside down and worn. Have him decorate it with felt-tip pens or collage materials.

Mask   With this popsicle-stick/paper-plate combo, your child can try on a new face. This type of mask is comfortable for kids who don't like a paper bag surrounding their heads. Cut eyes out of a stiff paper plate. On the bottom side, paint rosy cheeks and a smile or grimace. You can shape the circumference of the plate with scissors to make it more oval than round. For a handle, glue to the chin area a popsicle stick. Your child can hide her face or whisk the mask away to reveal "the real me."

BEFORE BRUSHES

♦ **ACTIVITY**

Finger painting in the bathtub.

♦ **PROPS**

Finger paints in plastic jars (these can be measured in modest amounts from larger commercial containers), finger-painting paper from an art store or paper supplied with a finger-painting kit.

♦ **ACTIONS**

Warm up the bathroom. Strip your child of all clothes. Lay paper on the tub bottom or on the borders (if wide). Place child and the paints in the bathtub. Give him free license to smear paper and, if so moved, the tub, the tiled walls, and his body. When the artistic urge is satisfied, remove the art materials and give your child a bath.

♦ **BENEFIT**

This adventure in color and goo is one of the few ways a child can get happily dirty with approval from the powers on high.

SCRIBBLING TO HEART'S CONTENT

◆ ACTIVITY

Encouraging your child to use a writing tool and experiment with random lines and squiggles.

◆ PROPS

Pencil, ballpoint pen, or crayon. Lots of scrap paper.

◆ ACTIONS

Never tell a child to try to draw a particular something. This can stifle the creative process. Don't say you see a black cloud or a tree in the pencil marks. A scribble is a scribble is a scribble, to paraphrase Gertrude Stein. And your child needs to scribble. In every culture children go through the scribbling stage before they move on to more recognizable shapes or patterns.

A circle is the first form almost all children make and they usually identify it as a face. But don't say, "The eyes should go here and the nose there." Most artists believe there is no right or wrong way to draw anything. Art is an experimenting thought process carried on with a line-making tool and paper. It's the experience of moving one's hand through space across a page.

PLAY CLAY

◆ ACTIVITY

Beginner sculpting with a dough more pliable than clay or plasticene.

RECIPE

1 cup flour
1 cup water
½ cup salt
1½ teaspoons salad oil
dash of cornstarch
drops of food coloring

Combine ingredients and cook in a saucepan, stirring well over low heat until mixture becomes rubbery. Divide the dough and make each batch a favorite shade with food coloring. For a wonderful sensation, start sculpting dough while it's still warm.

♦ ACTIONS

Never urge your child to make some "thing," such as a turtle or a bunny. Also resist the temptation to be clever yourself and shape your pet dog's head. (That would be a hard act for your kid to follow.) Let your child just feel the stuff, fool with it, manipulate it in different ways. Describe some of her actions: "You're rolling the dough, squishing it, pinching it. Now you're poking your fingers into it. Let me flatten it. Now pound it." Later, "I see you've molded some fat spheres, some long ropes, some thin discs." Keep her in the world of the abstract.

This play dough is reusable indefinitely if kept in a tightly lidded coffee can in the fridge.

♦ VARIATION

Using a fork, an old comb, or a shell, your child can make an interesting pattern of indentations in the soft surface. A dull knife and cookie cutters are welcome tools some of the time.

COLOR GALORE WITH TEMPERA

♦ ACTIVITY

Experimenting with mixing colors and producing first simple works of art.

♦ PROPS

Old shower curtain to cover floor.

Man's old shirt to cover child.

Good tempera paints, such as those manufactured by Rich Art. These attractive, strong colors come in liquid form in jars and are preferable to paint in cake or powder form requiring mixture with water. The liquid tempera is brighter and produces more dramatic results. Only buy the three primary colors—red, blue, and yellow. Later buy black and white.

Three to six margarine tubs or frozen juice cans.

Paintbrush with long handle and ½-inch-wide bristles.

Paper 12-by-18-by-24 inches (if you can afford heavy manila, the results are vastly superior to newsprint.)

Coffee can for water.

Sponge (slightly moist) or rag.
Old tray for all tools of the trade (optional).

♦ ACTIONS

Make setting up and clearing up easy for yourself so you'll be able to offer your child this activity often. Put the shower curtain on the floor or on a table. Lay paper on top of it. (Avoid using an easel, as paint dribbles downward, spoiling the child's design with unintentional vertical streaks.) Pour conservative amounts of paint into tubs. If your child's interest wanes quickly, you won't have much paint to throw away.

As soon as possible, teach your youngster to rinse the brush in water when he is finished with one color and wipe it on the sponge or rag before dipping it into a different color. Make up a singsong line such as,

> *Rinse and dry before I try*
> *A brand new color of paint.*

An alternative is to supply a different brush for each container of paint, in which case you need tall containers to hold standing brushes.

Mixing colors soon teaches a young child which two primary colors combine to make a new color. Start by providing just a jar of red, a jar of blue, and an empty jar. Show your child the three-step process: (1) Soak up some red tempera on the brush and deposit the paint in the empty jar. (2) Dunk the brush in water and wipe it on a sponge. (3) Soak up some blue tempera on the brush and stir it into that once-empty jar with the bit of red. Voilà! purple.

After he has mastered working with red, blue, and purple, introduce yellow. He will soon learn that blue and yellow make green, and that red and yellow make orange. Later you can introduce black and white for more subtle gradations of all the colors.

High-quality undiluted paint and high-grade paper make a more striking work of art. The lesson in esthetics may be worth the cost of materials.

♦ BENEFIT

Painting develops sensitivity to the beauty of color and pattern.

NO-FUSS WATERCOLORS

♦ ACTIVITY

Daubing splotches of color in all sizes and shapes on good-quality paper.

♦ **PROPS**

Dime-store set of watercolor paints that come in a row of solid dry cakes.

Quality brush from art store rather than inferior brush in dime-store set.

Various kinds of paper that will provide surfaces of different textures to paint on: cardboard; shiny paper; construction paper; and thick, porous and rough-textured watercolor paper (expensive but worth it once in a while).

Glass of water.

♦ **ACTIONS**

Show your child how to dip brush in just a bit of water, perhaps stroking it across the glass rim so some drops roll off. Then show her how to dab the brush on a cake of paint several times till the brush absorbs the color. Next have her put brush to paper, dabbing or stroking as she's moved.

OUR IN-HOUSE VAN GOGH

♦ **ACTIVITY**

Experimenting with a paint medium different from tempera and watercolors.

♦ **PROPS**

Set of three to six tubes of acrylic paint (the contemporary substitute for the oil-based paints of the old masters).

Large and small sheets of paper. You don't need to buy canvases, as acrylic paints can also be applied to paper.

A large brush and a small one.

♦ **ACTIONS**

The thick consistency of these paints will be interesting after the thin texture of tempera and watercolors. Variety is the spice of a budding artist's life.

Squeeze a little paint from each tube into a tiny dish. These paints are water-soluble, so your child can rinse and wipe off the brush before dipping into a new color. While art teachers usually encourage bold strokes on large sheets of paper, you can occasionally offer your youngster four-by-six-inch paper and a little bitty brush for a quaint minimasterpiece.

◆ **BENEFIT**

Working with diverse media will spur your child's creativity, though opportunities should be rife to repeat trials in the same media.

COLLECT FOR COLLAGES

◆ **ACTIVITY**

Gluing onto a sheet of paper torn-up bits of colored paper, string, and fabric swatches, together with found objects such as buttons or leaves.

◆ **PROPS**

Nontoxic white glue.

Manila or construction paper.

Collection of odds and ends (to be added to continually). Some suggestions: feathers, buttons, bottle caps, wood chips, plastic paper clips, styrofoam squiggles (for packing), fabric swatches, felt, old magazines, greeting cards, wallpaper samples, computer cards, cellophane, tissue paper, doilies, foil, used postage stamps, toothpicks, corks, straws, netting from sacks of fruit, raw macaroni, rice, beans, leaves, shells, bark, yarn, string, ribbon, broken puzzle pieces, toys.

◆ **ACTIONS**

For one little boy, collecting for collages was just as much fun as making them. His expression "Let's go collage-ing" meant "let's go for a walk and collect things." Your child might contain his collection in a plastic organizing box with little compartments (sold at hardware stores for separating nails and screws). Your child will select and arrange items, gluing the back of each one before he sticks it onto the large sheet of paper.

◆ **VARIATIONS**

Occasionally preselect items from just a few categories in the collection—items that your esthetic sense tells you are compatible. They may go together because of color harmony, texture similarities, or subject matter (e.g., paper clips and computer cards). Leave these in three or four cute dishes beside an empty work surface and invite your child to make a collage from these ingredients only.

CRAYON RUBBINGS

♦ ACTIVITY

Forming images of textured surfaces by laying a piece of paper over them and rubbing with a peeled crayon held horizontally.

♦ PROPS

Cardboard, glue, tracing or typing paper, masking tape, crayons with paper wrapper entirely peeled off. Some objects with interesting textured surfaces: keys, comb, coins, metal window screening, burlap, cheesecloth, doilies, swatch of corduroy, tiled floor, slab of slats, woven straw table mat.

♦ ACTIONS

Give your child a shirt cardboard and together collect some thin flat items. Glue these any which way to the cardboard. Let them dry overnight and continue the project the next evening.

Tape the cardboard to a work surface (countertop, table, or floor). Lay a piece of paper over the cardboard, taping it in position. Tell your child he's not going to use the point of the crayon. Show him how to hold a peeled crayon sideways so that its whole length contacts the paper. Your child can rub back and forth and watch the image of the objects underneath appear. Different crayons can be used in different areas of the picture or on top of each other.

THE PRINTING CRAFT

Tots love tools, and printing provides a delightful purpose for using them. The following activities give suggestions for impressing colorful designs on paper with unusual printing devices.

To organize your time, one of the sessions can be simply assembling the materials necessary for your project. At another get-together time, your child might simply prepare her printing device—the engraved styrofoam board or the string-decorated toilet-paper roll. Then at the third session your child applies paint to her tool and stamps out numerous designs.

PRINTING WITH TIRE TREADS

♦ ACTIVITY

Producing colorful imprints with the tire treads of toy trucks.

◆ PROPS

Miniature trucks, printer's ink or tempera paint thickened with cornstarch, shallow dish, paper.

◆ ACTIONS

Run trucks through a thin layer of ink or paint in a shallow dish, then drive them in all directions across a piece of paper. The tread marks will make a jazzy design. Doing this outdoors on a very long strip of paper can be especially enjoyable.

PRINTING WITH CARDBOARD ROLLS

◆ ACTIVITY

Creating prints with a decorated empty toilet-paper roll dipped in ink or paint.

◆ PROPS

Empty cardboard toilet-paper rolls, thick string, glue, water-based printer's ink or tempera paint thickened with cornstarch, paper, and pencil.

◆ ACTIONS

Your child cuts string into short lengths, then spreads glue along each length and sticks it to the roll in a wiggly line. He can either wrap each length around the cylinder, spacing them one-half to one inch apart, or he can lay each length in a wavy pattern along the width of the roll. Let glue dry thoroughly.

Roll the cardboard tube in a dish of thinly spread printer's ink or tempera. Now roll it across some paper. The strings will transfer the paint in curvy colored lines onto the page. If some of the roll gets coated, it will add intriguing smudges to the design.

PRINTING WITH STYROFOAM

◆ ACTIVITY

Making impressions on paper with a styrofoam board that has been engraved with a pencil point.

◆ PROPS

Styrofoam trays (from supermarket meat department) of various sizes.

Brayer (a black rubber roller with handle, available at art-supply stores).

Water-based printer's ink or tempera paint thickened with cornstarch.

Wide shallow dish.

Pencil.

Paper.

♦ ACTIONS

Your child scribbles on the bottom of the styrofoam tray, digging in her lines with a not-too-sharp pencil point. Then pour the printing ink or tempera into a shallow dish. Your child coats the brayer with the ink and then rolls it across the surface of the styrofoam board. Then she presses the board on a piece of paper. Her design of lines shows up as the white of the paper. The rest of the surface is a color.

· 3 ·

ORGANIZE IT

Y ou are the designer of the environment your child plays in. How you define the space and organize her belongings determine, to some extent, the nature of her play and the extent of her learning. Certain floor plans and storage facilities can spur on the fun and provide better educational experiences.

A child's bedroom and playroom have to be planned for flexibility. Children outgrow pieces of furniture, arrangements of furniture, and decorative touches. Be prepared to change things around often to keep pace with emerging interests and abilities.

You might imitate the open-classroom system of organizing materials in various centers. Divide toys in categories and assign each category a special shelf, cupboard, or box. With your child, look over her belongings and see if they fit into the following categories: stuffed animals; books, records, and tapes; musical instruments; cars and trucks; art supplies; puzzles; construction toys; dolls; punch-out cardboard books and workbooks; costumes and playhouse equipment.

Grandma's axiom "A place for everything and everything in its place" makes sense. Little children like things to have special places and will take pleasure in arranging them "just so" every night.

Keep the setup simple so your child can take care of it herself. Maintain a happy medium between museumlike order and junk-shop chaos. If a room is kept too neat, your child may feel inhibited about getting involved in a project. If a room gets too messy, she cannot find the materials she wants to develop a project.

Don't exclude using an end of your living room or half of the family room as a location for play equipment. You may have to surrender your standards of interior decorating for the cause of your child's developmental needs. Don't apologize to friends, but rather explain how these accommodations for your child foster harmonious playtimes and promote family togetherness.

The following activities enable you and your child to design together an environment that is conducive to joyful play and creative projects. Be sure to get your child's input. Then she will be more likely to test the various areas and use the storage facilities she thought up or made.

BOXES AND BASKETS

◆ ACTIVITY

Providing containers for the orderly stowing of many-piece toys.

◆ PROPS

Some or all of the following: shoe boxes; coat or suit box from a department store; gift boxes left from a holiday, birthday party, or wedding; five-gallon containers from an ice cream store.

Cloth tape or strapping tape.

Colorful Contact paper (optional).

Brown paper grocery bags and staple gun (optional).

◆ ACTIONS

With your child, identify the toys or games that are composed of several or many component parts. Hunt down every missing piece in each incomplete group, if possible. For each of these toy conglomerates, select an appropriate box. Line or stack boxes on shelves, tucking a few out of sight for a rest. If you have a toy chest, you can arrange the smaller boxes in it.

A child might want to color-code the shoe boxes—red stripes for little cars, green stripes for paper-doll clothes. Tape around torn or weak corners of boxes or lids. If you'd like all the boxes to match, you could cover them with cheerful contact paper.

One mother, who said she has "a high sense of order which has been drastically disrupted by growing twin girls," uses a row of sturdy grocery bags to keep the parts of each plaything together. First, she cut a three-inch-wide strip off the top of each bag. Then she folded these in thirds to make firm handles. Next she folded down the top edge of each bag twice to make a one-inch cuff. Then she curved the handle over each bag and stapled it to opposite sides of the cuff.

◆ VARIATION

Other containers for corralling scattered toy components are wooden salad bowls, plastic or metal mesh plant pots, plastic food storage containers, and large cylindrical cracker or pretzel tins. You might find these and other possibilities at tag sales.

SHOWING OFF WITH SHELVES

◆ ACTIVITY

Constructing shelves to display the latest educational game purchased or a fresh arrangement of some old favorites.

◆ PROPS

Three or six planks about 15-by-48 inches, made of particle board or wood.

Eight or 16 cement blocks, sometimes called cinder blocks.

Paint (optional).

◆ ACTIONS

Saw or buy planks whatever length is appropriate for the size of your child's room. Talk to him about their position. You can place the shelves out in the middle of the room for a central work surface or line them against the wall. If they're in the middle, a child can approach them from both sides.

Place one plank on the floor in your chosen position, for a bottom shelf. Put two cement blocks on top of each other at both ends (or toward the ends). Lay another plank on these blocks for a middle shelf. Then stack two more blocks at both ends of the second plank. Lay a top shelf on these blocks. Repeat this process if you are making two sets of shelves. Place them in an L shape if that suits your room design.

If they are painted, the planks should be a neutral color such as gray, tan, or white to set off the vibrant colors of toys displayed on them. A light should be provided nearby to illuminate the area. Arrange just a few materials at a time on this smooth work surface, such as some Lego pieces, a jigsaw puzzle, and a set of math materials such as the colorful Cuisenaire rods. Like a store manager merchandising the goods he wants to promote, you can arrange materials in such an inviting way that you elicit your child's involvement. Some nights, after he's gone to sleep, you might clear the decks and bring out of the closet some materials he hasn't seen for a while. To surprise and stimulate a new game, group together some toys that don't usually get combined.

◆ BENEFIT

An attractive presentation of educational materials can be the key to your child's interest in them.

TABLETOPS

♦ ACTIVITY

Building a table for the playroom to provide a large, smooth work-play surface.

♦ PROPS

For large rectangular table: hollow-core door, 11 feet of quarter-round molding, set of 11-inch-high table legs, paint, polyurethane, and brushes.

For small rectangular table: substitute 2-by-4-foot piece of plywood for the door and buy 8 feet of the molding.

For semicircular table: a semicircle of plywood (18-inch radius) and two L-shape brackets.

Small chairs.

♦ ACTIONS

If you have room for a table the size of a door, a hollow-core door makes a wonderfully generous activity surface, especially appropriate if you have more than one child. Nail molding to three sides as a border to prevent spilled water or paint from running off. Leave one long side free for sponging off spilled liquids. Paint the surface with primer and a top coat of a neutral color. Then brush it with several coats of polyurethane to protect the surface from moisture.

Support the door in a horizontal position with a set of table legs. These are sold with steel bases. You screw the bases into the underside of the tabletop, then screw the legs into the bases.

Your child should be able to kneel in front of the table and find its height comfortable. A two-year-old loves a chair her size to pull up to a table. She feels businesslike and in the mood for a Very Important Project you might dream up together. Add another little chair for a friend. If you buy a sturdy one (without arms), you can perch there, too.

If your child's room or the family room isn't big enough for a long table, provide a small rectangular one of plywood. Even less space is necessary if you attach a semicircle of plywood to the wall a foot or so off the floor. Apply L-shape brackets to the wall and the underside of your semicircular tabletop. This table doesn't need legs. Your child will enjoy being apprentice in these carpentry efforts on her behalf.

ARTSY-CRAFTSY CORNER

♦ ACTIVITY

Designating a cupboard, closet, shelf, or drawer as a resource center and filling it with as many art supplies as you can afford or scrounge.

♦ PROPS

Items listed can be stored as grouped:

PAPER GOODS

Jumbo pad, rolls of plain white newsprint, craft paper, or all-purpose paper.
Construction paper of various colors, white typing paper.
Good-quality paper for watercolors.
Scrap paper, including envelopes, old greeting cards, old magazines and newspapers, napkins, paper towels.
Shirt cardboards, empty toilet-paper and paper-towel rolls.

DRAWING IMPLEMENTS

Crayons; felt-tip pens; tempera, watercolor, and finger paints; paintbrushes.

CRAFT TOOLS

Scissors, ruler, nontoxic glue or paste, masking and cloth tape.

SCRAP MATERIALS FOR COLLAGES AND CRAFTS

Fabric swatches, wallpaper samples, styrofoam packing material, ends from lumberyard, colored yarn, pipe cleaners, rubber bands, popsicle sticks, toothpicks, paper fasteners, string, ribbons, foil, various dried beans and split peas, peanut shells.

CONTAINERS FOR STORING COMPLETED ARTWORK

Large envelopes, blanket storage box.

♦ ACTIONS

Don't pack all this stuff out of reach. Your child's freedom to help himself to any material on a whim will develop artistic talent. Judge how few or how many of these things your preschooler can cope with. A very young child would need less available at one time but would benefit from access to a limited amount without having to ask a parent. If especially compatible materials were sometimes organized in dishes near his work surface, he could initiate his own art projects when he felt in the mood.

Low on the wall, mount a giant holder for a roll of newsprint similar to the device at a store gift-wrapping counter. You could also supply a low bulletin board for exhibiting artwork.

To save precious artwork for posterity, one father acquired huge manila envelopes such as those used at advertising agencies. Another dad bought drawer-size storage boxes from a discount store—the kind used for storing blankets or out-of-season clothes. Showing saved artwork to a spouse who travels a lot or to a visiting grandma can be done with a lot of hoopla. The most appreciative audience of early masterpieces, however, will be your own child six years hence!

BOOK NOOK

♦ ACTIVITY

Arranging a cozy area for looking at picture books and reading.

♦ PROPS

Something soft to sit or sprawl on: rocking chair (adult- or child-size), hammock, window seat, shag rug, cushions, or bean-bag chair.
Bookshelves, plus rope or a 2-by-4 (optional).
A lamp.

♦ ACTIONS

You and your child choose a spot near a window where good light will fall on the pages of books. Otherwise provide a lamp that your child likes, perhaps one with a storybook character at the base or that has a quaint shade. Together decide on a chair or comfy surface for your bookworm to curl up on. An area rug might help define the nook.
The bookshelves should be low down and not too crowded. A clever way to display books to encourage reading is to stand them with their colorful front covers facing forward. The appealing jacket designs invite a child to reach out and examine them. To keep these books from toppling, attach a rope across the front of a shelf or use a two-by-four horizontally as a bar, nailing the ends of it to the sides of your bookcase. The rope or two-by-four is centered halfway between the top and bottom of the shelf area.

♦ BENEFIT

A lovingly planned book corner may compete successfully with the couch in front of the TV.

UPS AND DOWNS, INS AND OUTS

◆ ACTIVITY

Designing an innovative environment that offers your child a raised platform to climb up to and an enclosed recess to crawl into.

◆ PROPS AND ACTIONS

To build from scratch a really interesting play space with a loft, ladder, ramp, and peek-a-boo enclosures, you would need all the tools and materials of the carpentry trade. You may want to consult a local builder or an interior designer. Browse through decorating magazines, looking especially for loft beds and loft play areas and other ways of doubling the space available in tiny apartment bedrooms. Read toy manufacturers' catalogs and brochures advertising equipment for nursery schools and day-care centers and copy the structures you like best. One father copied a commercial crawl-through by building a set of homemade plywood boxes open at two ends. He drilled portholes in the sides.

There is an organization that can be commissioned to custom-make home indoor play areas. For information, write to Open Connections, 312 Bryn Mawr Avenue, Bryn Mawr, Pennsylvania 19010. For ideas to execute on your own, send for their book *Spaces for Children: Learning/Play Structures for Home and School* ($5 plus postage).

Meantime think what materials you already have at home or in the homes of extended family. For ups and downs: a raised platform could be an unfolded convertible couch, the top deck of bunk beds, an indoor slide with a platform, an outgrown playpen, a balcony overlooking a two-story room, or a stair landing. These elevated places convert easily in children's imagination to a castle, a fortress, a ship, an island, or a plane. In one family an older child safely built towers in an idle playpen while his boisterous baby sister crawled around able to see, but not touch, his precarious constructions. The necessity for private space becomes the mother of invention.

You can devise pro-tem ins and outs with materials at hand. Drape a blanket over the piano, dining room table, or folding card table for a hideout. Put a "roof" over the passage between twin beds. Enclose the alcove under a staircase with some cheap paneling or a bulletin board leaning against the side of the staircase. Put an unused baby gate in front of a closet. Beg, borrow, or steal an enormous carton in which an appliance was transported. Cut peepholes in it. Partition one corner of a room with a decorative folding screen.

◆ BENEFIT

The child may covet private space for solitude, but he will enjoy creating it *with* you.

NEAR-YOU NEEDS

♦ ACTIVITY

Gathering some favorite playthings and placing them in a cabinet near the spot where you spend most of your time.

♦ PROPS

Spare drawer or cupboard, basket.

♦ ACTIONS

Ask your child where she thinks you spend most of your time. If your joint conclusion is a room you use as a home office, give her the bottom file drawer. If the conclusion is the kitchen, assign her a low cabinet. If storage space is at a premium, think about wall space. A homemade easel or chalk board can lean against a wall with crayons, felt-tip markers, or pieces of chalk at hand.

A free basket with a handle might be kept at the ready for transporting a few toys to a spot you work in infrequently.

Choose fresh items for these places often. The more inspired your choices, the more absorbed in activity your child will be, and the freer you will be to get on with your work.

SWITCHEROO

♦ ACTIVITY

Stashing away toys your child is bored with and ferreting out of the closet toys he hasn't seen for a while.

♦ PROPS

A new toy or piece of equipment that combines well with some old playthings.

A new piece of furniture or innovative structure on which to display old toys.

Containers that combine parts of old toys in fresh ways.

♦ ACTIONS

Survey the clutter in your child's room. Having too many things discourages in-depth play with one or two quality games. Decide with your child which items to put away. See what's left and then hunt for some forgotten toys that might be appreciated again.

An old toy might be combined with some current favorites. For instance, perhaps your child recently acquired an animal puzzle that's still a challenge to put together. What about those old Noah's ark three-dimensional animals he used to stand in a row as a toddler? Put the puzzle and the plastic animals side by side. How many are the same? Now bring to the scene a child's animal encyclopedia. Looking in it for pictures of animals that are in the puzzle and in the ark can be lots of fun.

Even totally outgrown infant toys can be used in make-believe play. Your daughter could open a store and sell infant toys. Or she could run a day-care center, supplying each of her dolls with a rattle or a mobile. Or she could make miniature crib toys with craft materials for her dolls, using an old toy as a model.

♦ BENEFIT

A child with maturing interests and skills finds new ways to play with old belongings.

CLEANUP-TIME TACTICS

While sane parenting necessitates tolerance of clutter much of the time, good dispositions are preserved by intervals of order. A light touch and an inventive spirit rather than a power struggle can help families over the tedious routine of tidying up.

A preschooler can actually conceive of cleaning up as fun, which means you'll have all his energy at your disposal. Also a two- or three-year-old has a natural fascination with order. So capitalize on these inclinations.

GETTING PSYCHED

♦ ACTIVITY

Arousing enthusiasm for putting away toys by song, slogan, team spirit, and logical reasoning.

♦ PROPS

Records with lively music.

♦ ACTIONS

Parents I interviewed have devised various strategies. One put on a record with lively music to spur her child on—marches, Broadway show tunes, nursery songs. Another parent made up suitable poems to chant, such as:

No more work
No more play
Time to put
Our things away.

A third parent "tucked in" toys with her child. "The blocks have to go to bed now. Soon the animals are going to sleep. Let's tuck in your lotto games next." Still another parent emphasized the logical reasons for cleanup. "Now no one will trip over your ball tonight. It's a good thing these plastic teacups won't get stepped on and broken. You might have lost that puzzle piece for a long time if you hadn't checked under the sofa. Somebody might have thought those empty cereal boxes were garbage instead of produce for your pretend store."

One dad's slogan was "Let's team up to clean up." Another dad made a sign:

Neat and tidy
From Friday to Friday

A third dad at the end of a weekend commandeered all able bodies for a *blitzkrieg,* defined by Webster's dictionary as "a war [in this case, on disorder] conducted with great speed and force."

OVERCOMING RESISTANCE

♦ **ACTIVITY**

Offering a democratic choice after an autocratic decision that your child must join in the routine tidying.

♦ **ACTIONS**

Since you are not offering a choice between picking up and not picking up, you may dissolve reluctance by offering a choice on which area of the mess she will pick up. Ask your child, "Do you want to put away the indoor or the outdoor toys?" or "Would you like to store the big things or the small ones?" Try: "You may choose a certain color. How about picking up the blue and green things while I pick up the yellow and red? Oh? You want yellow and red? Okay."

You can sometimes beat your child at the baby game by some comical role-playing of a stubborn toddler. Whine in your best high-pitched voice, "I don't wanna," or "I'm too tired." This can turn your child into a coaxing parent, setting a good example for you while you're hamming it up as the reluctant kid.

FREIGHT TRAIN

◆ ACTIVITY

Providing a game format for picking up scattered toys and parts of toys.

◆ ACTIONS

Sort room clutter into piles, perhaps one for art equipment, one for books, and one for clothes. Make a train of people—Mom, toddler, and older sibling, perhaps, each placing hands on the waist or hips of the one in front. Make train sounds: "Chug-a-chug-chug! Toot-toot!" Shuffle around the room a few times. Then come to a grinding halt at the first pile—art stuff. The last "car" (read "person") is hitched off to pick up at that stop. He chugs back and forth from pile to art closet, then rejoins the train. The complete train circles again and the next "car" is dropped off at the second pile—books. This family member shuttles from pile to bookshelves. Soon the train merrily reforms to pick up clothes freight to be hauled upstairs.

STUFFED ANIMALS: PRESENT AND ACCOUNTED FOR

◆ ACTIVITY

Grouping stuffed animals for fun, for decoration, and for neatness.

◆ PROPS

The various and sundry furry friends received as gifts and purchased (sometimes in a weak moment)—some cute, some garish, all beloved.

◆ ACTIONS

If they are not controlled, these invaders from the animal kingdom can take over a room. One father spoke of his daughter's ten Teddy bears, including his own thirty-year-old favorite with the missing ear.

Your child's entire collection of creatures might be corralled from all corners of the house by you suggesting one of the following special events:

Story hour at the library—sit them in a semicircle and place a book in the lap of one.

TV watching—sit them in front of a carton with a TV drawn on it.

A birthday party—sit them in a circle with paper plates and fake food in front of each.

CLEANUP CONTESTS

♦ **ACTIVITY**

Making up competitive games with the goal of restoring order.

♦ **PROPS**

Clock or stopwatch.

♦ **ACTIONS**

Present a challenge: "Let's see who can clear the floor of a room the fastest. I'll take the kitchen. You take the family room." Appeal to pride: "Who can make the neatest pile of newspapers?" Go for quantity: "Who can gather the greatest number of objects off tabletops?"

With your eye on a nearby clock or stopwatch, occasionally time how long it takes your child to put the pieces of a puzzle back in its box. Jot down the number of minutes. Have your child compare this time with how long it takes you to put away the ingredients of a recipe or your gardening tools. You could time your child several nights in a row on a particular tidy-up chore and see if she can beat her own record. Or time your child at picking up a variety of games, comparing a pickup of the farm animals versus the puzzle pieces.

You might contrast the time it takes to put away toys in a special arrangement and the time it takes to throw them in a box any old way. For instance, how long to stack the blocks in matching sizes? How long to toss them into different containers according to size? How long to throw all sizes onto the closet floor?

MR. FIX-IT

♦ **ACTIVITY**

Pretending to be repairmen while putting back together the take-apart toys.

♦ ACTIONS

You can make believe you and your child are a pair of workers repairing an appliance for an imaginary customer or boss. Even though you're snapping colorful plastic toys together, talk as if you had a household problem. Refer to the parts, the repair tools, the working conditions, the finished product, and the wish for a coffee break.

· 4 ·

LET'S PRETEND

Children's abililty to lose themselves in let's-pretend games is one of the most captivating aspects of early childhood. The first signs of a two-year-old's imagination at work might be talking to Grandma on a toy telephone or tucking a doll into bed.

You may be surprised at how fertile your child's imagination is. But if it needs stimulation, you can facilitate make-believe episodes by being director of or fellow actor in a scenario. You may have to lose your own inhibitions and be willing to be a bit silly or overly dramatic—the way you might behave when playing charades at an adult party.

One father improvised a blanket tent in the living room, and together he and his two-year-old son "went camping." They hid inside while bears roamed outside and then went to sleep when the coast was clear. It was a simple plot but satisfying to that little boy for seemingly endless nights.

With a three-year-old, another father enriched the living room camping site with a real backpack, canteen, camera, compass, whistle, telescope, binoculars, and field guide. Through realistic dialogue during make-believe outings, the little boy soon learned a lot about wilderness experiences.

Role-playing is a good way for your child to enjoy his blossoming ability to speak well. When you play, too, you can increase his vocabulary and, of course, his knowledge by introducing new concepts, such as the use of a compass on the trail. An occasional prompting from you— "Uh-oh, we're getting fogged in"—can cause an interesting turn of events in the plot.

Of course, your involvement can be tedious, too. One mother says, "I've been everyone—Mickey Mouse, the Wicked Witch, Mary Poppins. My son keeps the dialogue going and going. I have to say, 'During lunch today I am *not* Snow White.'" Your child's obvious pleasure at your participation is sometimes irresistible, but you'll have to suggest another activity when you reach your limit.

When friends aren't available, your child may invent an imaginary playmate. Possible scenarios for your child to enact increase when she can pretend to be interacting with a friend. Also, relating to another, even in make-believe situations, is a way of practicing social skills. A child is often unconsciously rehearsing for future encounters with peers.

In fantasy play your child may fuse people and events she encounters in real life with characters and events she finds in storybooks and on TV. They may get all mixed up in play as she makes free associations among all the resources stored in her mind. This is an early expression of creativity. Combining characters and events in a simple dramatization is an exercise in the creative process. Rather than restraining a child because of an unfounded fear that she may lose touch with reality, you should encourage fantasy play.

Role-playing can be therapeutic also (see Rehearsing Sad and Scary Situations, p. 52). Some feelings a child couldn't tell you about directly may come out in pretend play. Advice your child might not take from you without resistance may be acceptable if you voice it through a character in your game.

You can also learn about your child's experiences when you are absent, for instance, how the baby-sitter treats him. Try this for openers: "Now you be the baby-sitter, and I will be you. I say (whining), 'Mrs. Smith, I don't want to go to sleep yet. . . .'" Your child will reflect back to you how Mrs. Smith usually fields that comment!

The following activities will help you encourage your child to enjoy the colorful world of make-believe.

◆

THE HAT TRICK

◆ ACTIVITY

Putting on one of the hats in a collection and instantly becoming the character it suggests.

◆ PROPS

A few or a dozen hats such as a knight's helmet, a pirate's bandanna, an Indian headband, a cowboy hat, a sailor cap, a hard hat, a desert head covering, a derby, a straw hat, a firefighter's hat.

Accessories such as a sword, bow and arrow, and rope are nice but not essential. (One couple found a 5-foot length of rope, ½ inch in diameter, the most versatile prop in their child's collection.)

A cape, vest, or full costume—extra fun, but not needed.

Makeup, on occasion.

♦ **ACTIONS**

Wrap a bandanna around your child's head, hand him a sword (a strip cut from a cardboard carton?), and watch him become magically transformed in soul and body. He may jump all over the bed, which is now his ship, challenging the air with sword thrusts. Aid and abet the fantasy with dialogue: "Well, me hearties, it's time to make the prisoners walk the plank." Or, "Look yonder! A mermaid stranded on the shore. Rescue her, sail her into the deep, and release her into a wave."

An interest in knights or pirates can be enhanced through picture books, a children's encyclopedia, or visits to a museum with an armor exhibit or a harbor with a historic sailing vessel.

♦ **BENEFIT**

Imaginary games are an outlet for new knowledge and pique curiosity.

FAIRY-TALE DRAMAS

♦ **ACTIVITY**

Listening to a fairy tale such as Goldilocks or Hansel and Gretel over and over again, then acting out the story.

♦ **PROPS**

None. A child imagines settings and movement vividly and doesn't need real bread crumbs or ovens. Your Gretel can twitch fingers as if to drop crumbs and "see" a trail of them or push a witch into an oven that is simply not there. It doesn't even have to be symbolized by a piece of furniture.

♦ **ACTIONS**

After you've read a fairy tale many times and your child is very familiar with it, act out the story with her. She'll easily recall key lines, such as, "This porridge is too hot!" Throw yourself into the part and have fun giving a vivid characterization. How gruff can you sound when you ask, "Who's been sleeping in my bed?"

♦ **VARIATIONS**

Act out the fairy tale again, switching roles. You play Goldilocks and she'll become the bears. After you've acted out the story a few times as it's written, improvise a different version. Your child may be the first to take liberties with the plot, but if not, propose a different ending. In the middle of a rendition suggest, "Let's say the witch wants to be a good woman, and Hansel decides not to push her into the oven." Then see how your child creates a new final scene. Your budding actress may naturally become Hollywood director for moments, letting you know of changes in the story line. Cooperate and see where her fertile imagination goes.

ON THE JOB

♦ ACTIVITY

Role-playing an adult at work, such as a car-wash attendant, hair stylist, flight attendant, shopkeeper, child caregiver, businessperson, architect, trail guide, librarian.

♦ PROPS

Your old clothes, belts, scarves, and jewelry. Unwanted clothes from a grandparent's attic.

Household objects or basement junk to be substituted for tools of the trade required in the role your child adopts. (An upside-down colander on the head can be a beauty salon dryer. A cup can be an oxygen mask being demonstrated by a flight attendant. A broken TV can be the businessman's video terminal.)

♦ ACTIONS

When you go out with your child, encourage him to observe people at work. Then he'll have a rich source of material for imitation of adult behavior.

Enter into his fantasy and talk to your child as his pretend business partner, client, or boss. Sometimes suggest situations and describe the professionals who would be found in the workplace. For instance, you could say, "I'm coming to your travel agency to buy a ticket. I want to go to Puerto Rico. You look up a plane time on your video terminal, then write out my ticket. Telephone to reserve my hotel room. Here's my credit card. Stamp it for your records."

♦ BENEFIT

Your child picks up vocabulary as well as new knowledge if you enrich fantasy with pertinent conversation.

CALL ME JENNIFER

♦ ACTIVITY

Calling your child by a different name (upon her request) and relating to her as if she were someone else.

♦ ACTIONS

Your child may want to pretend that she is someone she knows at nursery school or a character she's seen on TV. Perhaps she wants to try on for size some different personality traits. Maybe she's fantasizing that she is someone she admires. By taking this request seriously and not resisting the nuisance it may be to you to remember who your child is at the moment, you may learn about inner yearnings or perplexities.

IMAGINARY PLAYMATE

♦ ACTIVITY

Indulging your child's penchant to do everything with an unseen friend.

♦ ACTIONS

If your child develops an imaginary playmate who, he claims, is with him while he is eating meals, playing in the yard, picking up his toys, why not feed the fantasy? You can enhance your son's enjoyment of his buddy by matter-of-factly including the invisible boy in your conversations. "Does Jimmy want to hear the story, too?" you might ask. "Well, let's make room for him on the couch. Now he can see the pictures, too."

If your child is alone a lot, it may be helpful to teach sharing and taking turns by including the imaginary peer. How you treat Jimmy when he's good or naughty may reveal to your child more about your attitudes and style of child rearing.

♦ BENEFIT

Your child practices socializing and gets ready for having a real friend, and for being one, too.

PUPPETEER AND CHARMED AUDIENCE

♦ ACTIVITY

Putting on puppet shows with stuffed animals, dolls, or hand puppets.

♦ PROPS

Hand puppets representing animals and people. These can be bought or easily sewn from patterns in a library book. (See page 144 of *Smart Toys: For Babies from Birth to Two* by this author.) A puppet has a hollow head for your index finger and a cloth-bag body for your hand. Puppets are much easier for little children to manipulate than marionettes with strings.

A puppet theater. This can be made by cutting out a rectangle from one side of a huge box. Your child stands inside the box and moves puppets around this cutout stage. Or a big armchair can substitute for a theater, allowing your child to hide behind it and walk the puppets along the top of the chair back.

♦ ACTIONS

A child sometimes needs a lot of help from you in making up a story for puppets to act out. You can crawl into the theater, too, manipulate and talk for one of the puppets. You could just start a skit, leaving it unfinished, and suggest your child make up the ending. Or, as audience, you can interact with the puppet, asking it questions or petting it, thus adding substance to the plot.

Your child might do a takeoff on a "Sesame Street" scene or on a story from a book. Sometimes the plot and dialogue are irrelevant to the actual puppet characters. A puppy puppet can serve as a dinosaur and a policeman puppet can understudy for an astronaut.

A good audience is important to a theatrical entrepreneur. Perhaps a visiting aunt can watch, too. If you have a baby, bring him to the production and save a seat for Teddy Bear. Then the live audience can react with terrified gasps or rolling in the aisles, depending on the tragic or comic nature of the act. Enthusiastic applause is always appreciated by amateur puppeteers.

♦ BENEFIT

Making up skits exercises a child's imagination. Acting out relationships aids the recognition of feelings. Providing dialogue gives practice at talking.

HOME AS NEIGHBORHOOD PLAYHOUSE

♦ ACTIVITY

Going to a play for children put on at a local theater or school and then acting out your own very informal version at home.

♦ PROPS

Some, if you wish. This is not really staging a play but acting out the basic plot and taking unlimited liberties with it.

♦ ACTIONS

When you know a certain play is coming to town, read the story if it's a well-known one like Snow White and the Seven Dwarfs. Read several versions of it to your child from different books, if possible. Note the discrepancies.

After the play, talk with your child about how it was different from what she thought it would be like. Ask her which version she liked best— one you saw or one you read. Now choose one of the versions to do at home with Mommy and Daddy and an older brother or sister.

The family who suggested this activity was lucky enough to live in a town that had a series of productions for children every summer.

♦ BENEFIT

Borrowing from and rearranging elements from others' art forms is an aspect of creativity expressed here.

REHEARSING SAD AND SCARY SITUATIONS

♦ ACTIVITY

Letting your child act out scenes that relate to past, present, or future situations he might find troubling.

♦ PROPS

Things appropriate to the setting or objects to "stand in" for the real things.

♦ ACTIONS

If your child is soon to attend a day-care center or nursery school, you can role-play the new experience together. "Robbie, let's pretend you are going to school for the first day. I will say, 'C'mon. Get in the car.' Now we're driving and chatting and maybe singing songs. Then I walk you to the door, like this. You *see* a friend. Your teacher says, 'Hi, Robbie.' And I say, 'Goodbye.'" One little boy at this point asked his mother, "You come back?"

"Sure, I go to the office. At noon I look at my watch and say, 'Mr. Goodnow, I have to stop showing houses now and pick up my little boy at school.' Then I drive back to school, and into the car you hop."

This kind of improvisation works well in advance of a visit to the dentist or doctor, too.

Sometimes a child who's going to school will role-play his teacher and/or a peer. One mother said she finds out this way exactly what kind of morning it has been. By entering the fantasy as teacher, parent, or another child, she discovers how her child is reacting to events and personalities around him.

♦ BENEFIT

These rehearsals often work a kind of catharsis for your child. They bring fears to the fore and offer a chance to practice dealing with them (with some help from you), and thus relieve tension.

ADVENTURE SCENARIOS

♦ ACTIVITY

Helping your preschooler and a playmate lose themselves in an adventure fantasy.

♦ PROPS

T-shirts of superheroes such as Darth Vader, Batman, Wonder Woman, and Astro Girl.

A box of old clothes for dress-up.

A garage or playroom to convert into a spacecraft, palace, or island tree house.

♦ ACTIONS

While you may not be involved actively in the scenario if your child has a playmate, you may be responsible for the initial suggestion and support for launching the kids into their world of make-believe. The cast of characters might include cartoon superheroes, TV or movie space fiction personalities, or just kids leading an adventurous, romantic life as poor people on a farm, orphans in an old mansion, princes and princesses in a palace, or a shipwrecked family on a desert island.

Perhaps their imagination has recently been captured by a current

TV series or a comic book you have read aloud. Appoint them roles or activate their interest with some old clothes or a piece of equipment you were about to take to the thrift shop. If they choose a space fantasy, you might offer to play a planet inhabitant if their rocket ship crew conquers its adversaries, survives assorted catastrophes, and lands.

◆ **BENEFIT**

A way to avoid passive TV watching when a friend visits is to encourage imaginary escapades based on past shows viewed.

· 5 ·

MASTER BUILDERS

As you tiptoe respectfully around your child's tallest-ever tower or longest-ever bridge and then nearly trip over a stray plastic thingamajig, you may rue the day you ever supplied her with the raw materials for these architectural masterpieces. Nevertheless, erecting three-dimensional structures or laying out elaborate communities of animals and people (or humanoids) is a perennial pastime of the under-six set. Why so?

If you think back on your child's first two years, you will recall how much time she spent examining and manipulating small toys and found objects. She developed a huge repertoire of manual skills: she could pick up, put down, hold, release, turn upside down, fit through openings, fit together, take apart, pinch, screw, unscrew, stack, line up, open, close, et cetera. Now what activities are going to make all that learning worthwhile? Constructing things—yes, constructing colorful, interestingly shaped, complex structures and scenes. Such work is play that shows off the old skills and cultivates even more sophisticated eye-hand coordination abilities.

Your child is getting increasing exposure to the real world. Her expanding observations have an expressive outlet in re-creating this world in miniature. The many new images in her mind have a nice counterpart in the concrete toys that simulate in plastic form houses, apartment buildings, and people. By arranging scenes of adults working in shops, children playing in amusement parks, and animals dwelling in barnyards, she participates in these spheres in fantasy.

One way a child enhances her own interest in these miniature scenes is by endowing the animal and people figures with personalities and talking for them. Often such dialogues, imitative of conversations overheard, are rehearsals for the real thing. You can assist her active imagination by happily role-playing one or two of the characters. In keeping up the conversation and occasionally introducing words that are not yet part of her vocabulary, you further her language development. Also by drawing on your own knowledge of life on a ranch (however limited) if she has a ranch set-up, and sharing such concepts as branding a steer, you widen her horizons.

Children from two years of age on start showing pride in personal accomplishments. They desire to make products that are praiseworthy. However all-absorbing the *process* of construction is, the end *product* is also important. They seek approval for it and, when they get it, this reinforces their efforts to build higher, more precisely, or more intricately. Constructing things is a good way for your child to demonstrate her capabilities in a tangible way. Recognition makes for self-esteem. Heap on the praise for things well done. Soft-pedal it when the product isn't up to your child's current potential. Occasionally building together with your child will give her more technical know-how and add to her proficiency with the construction medium, whatever it is. The following activities indicate that there are a lot of things besides blocks that can be used for building operations.

◆

JUNIOR ARCHITECT

◆ ACTIVITY

Building, with an extensive set of blocks, towers, houses, bridges, tunnels, roads, and whatever else the imagination devises.

◆ PROPS

Hardwood unit blocks available at school supply stores. Buy close to a hundred, if you can afford them. They come in various solid geometric shapes. The term "unit" means they are mathematically proportionate to each other, that is, two small blocks equal the size of one large block. For mail order purchase, write for a free catalog to Community Playthings, Rifton, NY 12471. They also sell a mobile cart for storing the heavy blocks.

Two other options: corrugated cardboard blocks, sometimes available in kit form for do-it-yourselfers at a discount store; or giant hollow blocks available at school supply stores. The latter are for building child-high playhouses.

◆ ACTIONS

One long-time nursery school teacher thought hardwood blocks, even though they are expensive, were the most important toy that could be purchased in the preschool years. Perhaps a relative could share the cost, or you could plan on reselling them in a few years. The expense is mitigated by the fact that interest in blocks lasts over a long period, from two years of age to over six. Also a set of blocks is not really just a single toy; it is the equivalent of a dozen toys. A child can transform a structure of blocks into a fire station, a rocket launching pad, a gas station, or a community in outer space.

Facilitating your child's play with blocks will find you playing one or all of three roles: instigator of an architectural idea, co-worker, approving surveyor of finished construction. As instigator, you may propose with some excitement a new idea—a condominium for Grandpa or a replica of the Great Wall of China (to stretch the length of the living room). As co-worker, you'll get down on the floor next to your child and partici-pate in the style most appropriate to his age and temperament. You might do most of the work, an equal share, or simply be an idle observer, occasionally straightening a tower or constructing a clever support device. It's your companionship during the building process that will be impor-tant.

In the third role as surveyor, you enter the scene during the final stages of construction. You scan the work attentively and comment thoughtfully on certain details—the dizzying height of the skyscraper, the sturdiness of the bridge, the practicality of the carport for Grandpa's condo. Your appreciation of the accomplishment increases your child's pride in his work.

◆ BENEFIT

There is no one right way to play with unit blocks. What a relief! A child needs toys that are open-ended.

FITTING AND CONNECTING OPERATIONS

◆ ACTIVITY

Sprawling on the floor with your kid amid countless tiny compo-nents of a Lego box or Erector set and connecting one piece to another until an engineering marvel has been constructed.

◆ PROPS

Any of the commercial toys designed to build shelters, vehicles, or machines: Lego (and Lego Preschool for two-year-olds), Lincoln Logs, Tinkertoy, Erector sets, Fishertechnik, and cardboard toys such as Flex-agon. Some of these may not be designed for preschoolers, but if an eager parent enjoys working with them or if an older child is using them, kid sister aged three or four would enjoy some novice-level participation.

♦ **ACTIONS**

When you first buy these multipart toys, you might introduce only a third or half of them to your child. You might even cover the picture on the box and sketches on the instruction sheet. An initial attitude of laissez-faire will enable your child to examine the materials without pressure and explore ways that occur to her to play with them. If you can wait before building one of the complicated structures on the box lid, it would be better for your child to form simple structures of his own devising.

Building sets have surefire ingredients for fun. The materials often intrigue you as well as your child. The units are colorful, variously sized and shaped, and feel good in the hand. Often the fitting of one piece to the other is just enough of a challenge to your child to be interesting, but not so big of a challenge as to be frustrating. If both your skills develop to the point that you can motorize a structure, this will have a lot more educational value than pushing the button on a ready-made electronic vehicle.

One of the beneficial extras of this kind of activity is the talk that accompanies it. Describe what you are doing and describe what your child is doing, using as many specific words as you can. "I'm holding each square gray piece and wedging it onto the bumps on the green platform. At each corner you build a tower of the rectangular red pieces." Point out trouble spots. "That bridge is weak in the middle." Then show your child how thinking about a solution and then trying alternatives corrects the problem. "How shall we strengthen that bridge? We have to think about that. Shall we prop it up in the center? Or shall we take it down and make it shorter? Let's try a supporting column in the center."

TABLECLOTH ROADMAP

♦ **ACTIVITY**

Crayoning a network of roads on a paper tablecloth and routing small cars and trucks over them.

♦ **PROPS**

Plain paper tablecloth, crayons or felt-tip pens, toy vehicles.

♦ ACTIONS

Spread a paper tablecloth on the floor or on a dining room table. Draw a couple of roads, one straight, one curving, that meet at an intersection. Let your child propel his toy car along them. Another day your child can add more roads. Red and green circles can indicate a traffic light. Perhaps you could sketch in a gas station and label it like the one you frequent. If the idea takes hold, your child can keep adding roads and vehicles till he has created a massive traffic jam.

♦ VARIATION

You could enter the play one day as a helicopter-borne observer of rush-hour traffic conditions reporting to your radio station. "A collision on the red road is snarling homebound commuters. They are being diverted to the blue road." Your child will enjoy hearing you describe the patterns he's creating.

STYROFOAM CASTLES

♦ ACTIVITY

Finding material around the house slated to be thrown away and using it for building projects.

♦ PROPS

Styrofoam packing material in rectangular boxlike forms used to protect during transport new appliances such as a coffee maker, stereo speaker, or typewriter. Ask relatives or friends (newly marrieds are good sources) to save them for you.

♦ ACTIONS

The two of you can create interesting structures by taping together various boxlike forms with flat and convex panels. Help your child cut out see-through holes in his castles for miniature soldiers. He can paint or color with felt-tip pen on the white styrofoam surface.

♦ BENEFIT

A child can learn to make use of household resources as raw materials for constructions instead of begging for a toy to be purchased.

COIN STACKS

♦ ACTIVITY

Piling up coins to create architectural structures, an activity for older preschoolers.

♦ PROPS

Dozens of quarters or tokens saved for meters, fares, or tolls; or a piggy bank full of pennies.

Paper or cardboard.

♦ ACTIONS

Stack coins in four equal columns about two inches high. The heights of the stacks can be matched exactly by counting or by judging visually with an eye-level squint.

Place each column in one corner of a rectangle about the size of a piece of typing paper. Place the paper on top of the columns for one story of your house. Now stack more coins in columns on top of the first columns to create a second story. Place another piece of paper on top of these for a roof. This pastime is recommended as an amusing challenge for children who are already nimble-fingered.

TOOTHPICK HABITATS

♦ ACTIVITY

Building a geodesic dome and other modern habitats incorporating triangle and diamond patterns.

♦ PROPS

Plastic toothpicks, tiny marshmallows.

♦ ACTIONS

Place a bunch of toothpicks and a half-bag of tiny marshmallows on a tray. Have your child stick one end of a toothpick into a marshmallow. Stick the other end into another marshmallow. Now stick into one of the marshmallows a second toothpick at a 45-degree angle to the first toothpick. Clap a marshmallow on the other end of the second toothpick. Complete the triangle with a third toothpick stuck at each end into the marshmallows in your assemblage. Together with your child continue to add toothpicks at 45-degree angles, anchoring the ends in marshmallows until you have formed a geodesic dome.

These materials combine like Tinkertoy parts, but they are easier for some little tots to manage. Sometimes their small hands are not strong enough to wedge Tinkertoy sticks into the holes of the Tinkertoy wheels.

For safety, closely monitor your child's handling of the sharp toothpicks.

PAPER CUTOUTS

♦ ACTIVITY

Cutting or punching out a prefabricated barnyard, dollhouse, school, or village, with appropriate animals or people.

♦ PROPS

The paper-doll type of booklets from variety stores.

Children's magazines such as *Sesame Street* (Children's Television Workshop) and *Wow* (Scholastic). These have stiff pages with perforated lines around drawings of figures, buildings or parts of buildings, furniture, and other equipment.

♦ ACTIONS

Stiff paper or cardboard is a much cheaper material than plastic for construction projects. It makes a nice alternative to building with blocks. Whatever you assemble won't last as long and perhaps can't be taken apart and stored for reuse, but the essential pleasure of giving shape to the shapeless exists. Once your child masters the punching-out or cutting-out process, she will enjoy the variety of characters and habitats available in the medium of paper.

Once the assembling of the characters and scene is finished, you can prolong your child's interest by talking for some of the characters. You can carry on a conversation with the paper dolls like a ventriloquist talks with a lap doll. Your child will catch on and develop a range of voices and personalities for the little people.

♦ BENEFIT

Since paper materials are not bulky or heavy to tote, they can be worked on anywhere—in the car, in bed, on the porch, on a tiny table at a friend's house, or on a board on the lap.

RECYCLED DOLL HOME

◆ ACTIVITY

Turning stacked cartons into a multistory dollhouse and converting throwaway household objects into furniture (an activity for sons as well as daughters).

◆ PROPS

Cartons, perhaps disposable diaper boxes.

For wall decor: paint, gift wrap or Contact paper.

For furniture: construction paper, shirt cardboard, tape, little cosmetic boxes, and cans, food jars or boxes. Other possibilities: lids, plastic-bag twisters, cheesecloth, broken hardware.

For upholstery: Contact paper, foil, fabric swatches, wallpaper samples, carpet trimmings.

For people: pipe cleaners or three-dimensional flexible dolls (purchased, not made).

◆ ACTIONS

Don't work for artistry or perfection. These furnishings can be crude approximations of dollhouse furniture. They should be partly done by your three- or four-year-old with no pressure for skilled craftsmanship. Leave a lot to the imagination, which covers a multitude of flaws.

Glue two or three diaper boxes together, stacking them to make a multistory house. Or use heavier cartons. Paint the insides or cover walls with Contact or gift-wrap paper.

Make tables and stools out of the little boxes cosmetics come in. Cover the writing with brightly colored cloth tape, construction paper, or a piece of fabric glued on.

Fold part of a shirt cardboard into a thin rectangular box. Cut and tape at the corners. Then draw shelves and books on it. Stand it upright like a secretary desk or bookcase. Cover a cube shape with white paper for a stove and glue buttons on the surface for burners.

You can get ideas from a library book on dollhouse furniture, but skip the complicated designs or adapt them for a preschooler. Your furnishings are not for showing off but just for having fun together.

Buy dolls with bendable limbs and torsos so you can move them into a standing or sitting position. Or create some stick figures with pipe cleaners.

◆ BENEFIT

Your child sees you adding decorative touches to your home. Having a house to work on too makes him happy.

ALL ABOARD!

♦ ACTIVITY

Controlling model electric trains on tracks surrounded by realistic miniature scenery.

♦ PROPS

HO-gauge track and trains: these are expensive scale models of various types of train cars—a box car, a refrigerator car, a coach, a caboose, a diesel, a long car, a coal hopper. Adding to the collection of a beginning hobbyist is part of the fun.

HO railroad accessories are exact copies of the real thing, for example, a Warren trestle bridge, a plate girder bridge, a signal bridge, a water tower, and buildings such as a miniature station house and a school.

An engineer's cap for your child.

♦ ACTIONS

Although the manufacturer states that these trains are for children five years or older, some parents can't wait until their children get to that age. These expensive trains are not left out for a preschooler to play with on her own but brought out at night or on a rainy weekend when Dad or Mom is available.

An oval course of track can be nailed to a large rectangle of plywood to eliminate the process of linking sections of tracks. Or for easier storage the oval track can be divided and half of it nailed to one board and the other half nailed to another board. The boards can be stored upright. When you are ready to play with them, the boards can be laid on the floor and the tines of the track connected at the points of division. Although you miss the fun of connecting each strip and building the course anew, this is time-consuming. You and your child will probably play with the trains more frequently if the track is fixed. Then your child can concentrate on selecting and connecting certain cars in the collection to form the train, setting up scenery—a village, a mountain with a tunnel, bridges—and working the controls.

You can build on your child's interest by going for a real train ride and noticing the signal lights, bridges, and other real-life corollaries to the scale models. Sharing a little information about the history of each locomotive type might appeal to a four-year-old.

♦ BENEFIT

This interest can last well into the middle years of childhood. Also it is one of the few parent hobbies that can delight small children.

SCRAPBOOK FOR MEMORIES

♦ ACTIVITY

Collecting mementoes and pasting them into a scrapbook as they are acquired.

♦ PROPS

Scrapbook, nontoxic glue, scissors.

All kinds of mementoes: circus ticket stubs, matchbook covers, menus or place mats from restaurants, snapshots, theater programs, movie ads, favors from birthday parties, brochures from amusement parks or zoos, postcards, souvenirs from a day with Grandma.

♦ ACTIONS

Let your child glue the mementoes one or two to a page. Compose picture captions together, or note the date of the experience. If your child can write, have him letter the captions. If he gets bogged down by the writing and loses momentum in adding to the scrapbook, you do the captions and let him color in page-edge borders or frames around the items.

♦ BENEFIT

This is a creation that is a re-creation. Looking at it again and again enables you to talk about the past happy, sad, or exciting times.

· 6 ·

MAKING MERRY
WITH MUSIC

Have you given your child a "musical bath" today? That is, have you sung some catchy tunes or played some Mozart or Gershwin in order to surround her with the joy and harmony of beautiful music?

Don't be misled by the term "born musician." An ear for music, talent with an instrument, and, most basic of all, love for music can all be cultivated. They're not inborn.

The value of exposure to good music in the early years has been promoted widely by Dr. Shinichi Suzuki, a world-famous Japanese master violin teacher. His success in teaching three- and four-year-olds to play the violin competently has astonished many. His main objective, though, is not turning out prodigies but finer people; people with more sensitivity and inner beauty.

The benign effect of classical music even on babies has been noted. In one study babies who had listened regularly for four months to Mozart's "Eine Kleine Nachtmusik" looked markedly different from other babies. Their eyes were more radiant, their facial expressions more mobile and their actions livelier. Suzuki proponents believe that listening to complex music in early childhood leads to preferring it in adulthood.

Maybe this is the time to start or expand your own collection of classical records and enjoy them while you're carrying out some of the menial chores involved in running a home or caring for children.

Of course, music composed and recorded especially for children goes straight to their hearts. They respond readily to it by singing along or dancing or by simply shaking a petulant mood and reflecting a sunnier disposition.

Libraries have record and tape collections that include nursery rhymes set to music, folk songs, sing-along or dance-along tunes with a friendly narrator, lively songs in foreign languages, and good stories with a lot of musical accompaniment.

Many parents give their children a cheap record player or tape recorder soon after the age of two-and-a-half so that they can work it themselves. Singing some of the recorded songs with your child after the audio device is turned off continues the musical education.

Various approaches to music appreciation at a tender age are discussed on the following pages.

◆

OLD FAVORITES

◆ ACTIVITY

Spontaneous rendering anytime, anyplace, of summer camp songs, college football numbers, folk songs, your favorite top-forty radio hits, or school chorus semiclassical standbys.

◆ ACTIONS

Sing a lot, even if you don't have a great voice. Songs help create a happy atmosphere, perking up a tired, ill, or moody child. They may even chase *your* blues away. You can sing to your child while you're dressing her in the morning, driving in the car, picking up toys, cooking dinner, bathing her, or tucking her in at night. Be willing to give frequent encores of songs she seems to respond to most. And try to muster the enthusiasm you'd bring to an onstage amateur talent show.

Your child will hum along, sway to the rhythm, or sing snatches of the song with you. Often she'll pick up the words to the whole song and perhaps the whole melody, too. But don't discourage her if she doesn't carry a tune. She'll improve.

Sometimes you can imitate your teenage idols. One child loved her dad's rendition of that old rock 'n' roll number, "Ba-ba Ba-ba Barbara Ann."

Tunes that your parents used to sing to you can be amusing to pass along to the newest generation. "I'll be down to get you in a taxi, honey" has an ending that one little girl just loved. Her mother belted out the last word, "B . . . A . . . double-L . . . ball!" and the daughter always grinned.

◆ BENEFIT

Your own enthusiasm for music can prepare a child for some kind of formal musical training at a young age.

HANDS MARK THE BEAT

◆ ACTIVITY

Tuning in to a song with finger movements synchronized with the beat and descriptive lyrics.

◆ PROPS

A book of songs or rhymes with instructions for accompanying finger movements. Any such book will probably contain "The Itsy-Bitsy Spider," the best known ditty of this type.

A piano, if you play.

◆ ACTIONS

Following is a song that has descriptive words that will keep little fingers busy. In the first verse children alternate stretching out their fingers with making fists. In the next three verses they wiggle them, running them up their body from their toes to their shoulders, chin, and eyes. In the last verse the hands revolve around each other.

O-pen, shut them, o-pen, shut them, give a lit-tle   clap.

O-pen, shut them, o-pen, shut them, put them in your lap.

> Open, shut them; open, shut them
> Give a little clap.
> Open, shut them; open, shut them
> Put them in your lap.
>
> Creep them, crawl them; creep them, crawl them
> To your shoulders high.
> Let them like the little birdies
> Fly up to the sky.

Creep them, crawl them; creep them, crawl them
Right up to your chin.
Open wide your little mouth
But do not let them in.

Creep them, crawl them; creep them, crawl them
Right up to your eyes.
Cover up so very tight [silent pause]
Then peek-a-boo, surprise!

Spinning, spinning; falling, falling
Almost to the ground,
Quickly raising all your fingers
Twirl them round and round.

♦ BENEFIT

The *visual* attraction of the moving hands enhances a child's enjoyment of her *audio* experience.

MOVING TO MUSIC

♦ ACTIVITY

Singing songs that invite body movements, especially with the legs and feet.

♦ PROPS

Your own voice and a songbook or record.

♦ ACTIONS

You can often take a basic melody and alter it to fit the words you are making up as you go along. The song that follows is a takeoff on "Here We Go Round the Mulberry Bush." As the child does the specified movements, he gradually learns to synchronize them with the beat. Slow up for the last line each time to allow for a dignified bow in contrast to the vigorous actions. Start the first verse with your child's name.

Linda likes to jump and jump,
jump and jump, jump and jump.
Linda likes to jump and jump.
Linda likes to bow down.

Now use a friend's name or an imaginary playmate's name:

> *Scottie likes to run and run,*
> *Run and run, run and run.*
> *Scottie likes to run and run.*
> *Scottie likes to bow down.*

Now a parent's turn:

> *Mommy likes to gallop and gallop,*
> *Gallop and gallop, gallop and gallop.*
> *Mommy likes to gallop and gallop,*
> *Mommy likes to bow down.*

Use a doll's or bear's name for hopping, skipping, swaying from side to side, or spinning. Continue singing, using one of these verbs per verse.

◆ VARIATION

Play a record of marches and a record of waltzes. Strut about in straight lines for one, pirouette with the other. Get your child used to responding differently to different types of music. Sometimes let your child copy your motions; other times you copy her.

◆ BENEFIT

Children take to music naturally if they can throw their bodies into the arena and not just sit and listen.

UP AND DOWN THE SCALE

◆ ACTIVITY

Singing or playing on a piano or xylophone the simple nursery tunes that stay within the first five notes of the scale.

◆ PROPS

Children's songbook.
Xylophone or piano (optional).

◆ ACTIONS

The first five notes of the scale provide a comfortable range for a child's singing voice. And there are plenty of tunes that stay within that range. Familiarity with a melody enables two- and three-year-olds to

Down by the river in a little bitty
Pool lived three little fishies and a
mama fishie too. "Swim," said the
mama fish, "swim if you can," and they
swam and they swam all over the
dam.

Boom, boom, diddle, daddle, watum chu
Boom, boom, diddle, daddle, watum chu
Boom, boom, diddle, daddle, watum chu
and they swam and they swam all over the dam.

keep a tune. So sing or play a song over and over again. Repetition is what kids love and repetition is how kids learn. So grin and bear it! Sometimes it's not so hard to suppress boredom when you see what a kick your child is getting out of the song.

Here is an old song sung often in the primary class at the Diller-Quaile School of Music in New York City. During the nonsense verse, every time the teacher hits the syllable "chu," she pops a raisin onto the tip of a child's tongue. Each line starts on middle C and works up several notes to G. The last line goes from G down to middle C.

Boom, boom, diddle, daddle, watum chu
Boom, boom, diddle, daddle, watum chu
Boom, boom, diddle, daddle, watum chu
And they swam and they swam all over the dam.

INSTRUMENT TUNE-UP

♦ ACTIVITY

Listening together to a melody, hearing the beat, and tapping or shaking a percussion instrument in time to the music.

♦ PROPS

Two or three of the following: drum, tambourine, jingle stick, triangle (with handle to suspend it), maracas, sleigh bells, sand blocks, wood blocks, finger cymbals.

♦ ACTIONS

When you sing, listen to a record, or watch a song being performed on TV, get out the rhythm instruments. Help your child tune in to the melody and catch the tempo. On the downbeat have him tap his instrument or shake it in the air. He could also strike a tambourine or jingle stick against his shoulder, elbow, or knee on each downbeat.

If Dad plays the piano or guitar, your child can "jam" with him, using a percussion instrument.

A mother-child pair can take turns being dancer and musician. You can whirl while your son shakes maracas or your son can step lively while you emphasize the rhythm.

SHOW BIZ

♦ ACTIVITY

Encouraging your child to imitate the singers you and your spouse regularly listen to on stereo and TV or go out to hear in concert.

♦ PROPS

Stereo, radio, or tape recorder with recordings of your favorite performers.

For costumes: Mom's half-slip can be a strapless dress or full-length skirt; nightgowns have pizzazz; Dad's vest can be decorated with jewelry to look like a rock musician's.

Large mirror.

Cylindrical box with string attached to look like a microphone.

♦ ACTIONS

Start the ball rolling by enthusiastically mimicking a star you love. One family I interviewed are operagoers, and their daughter did melodramatic renditions of Verdi-style arias. Clad in ruffled negligee, she studied her performance in a full-length mirror. A three-year-old whose mom was a soap opera actress and whose dad was a choreographer sang "Tomorrow" from Annie like a pro.

As audience, you can play exhilarated fan to your child's song-and-dance acts. Standing to clap and call "Bravo" doesn't hurt occasionally. However, the accent doesn't always have to be on performance, especially performance that you imply has to be rehearsed for a homecoming parent. Singing and dancing for each other is best as a spontaneous form of sharing your mutual pleasure in music.

EXERCISE TIME

♦ ACTIVITY

Practicing the warm-up exercises learned at dance or physical fitness class (your child's or yours) in time to music.

♦ PROPS

Exercise mats, plenty of floor space, background music (both lively and slow).

♦ ACTIONS

If you've ever taken modern dance or ballet lessons, review some of your old warm-up exercises and invite your toddler to copy. Or if your child is taking lessons, observe and, at home, practice your child's exercises with him. Otherwise a library book on stretching, limbering, and strengthening exercises might start you off.

If one of your TV channels has a morning exercise show, you might watch it together. Your child and you can do some of the exercises with the TV personality. Then you can do more later without the TV, when you can go at his pace, choosing just the exercises he likes best. Work on performing the movements in time with the music. Pretend to be the TV personality while your child is an audience participant. Then switch places and let your child run your at-home exercise session.

Your child learns not only by copying your actions but also by hearing you describe both your own and his movements. "I see you're stretching your arms over your head. Now your legs are straight as can be. I'm pointing my toes. If you curve your feet, you will point your toes too." Matter-of-fact description rather than judgmental praise or criticism keeps exercise time low-key.

DANCE RECITAL

♦ ACTIVITY

Dancing that is inspired by carrying a prop or wearing a costume accessory.

♦ PROPS

A large silk scarf that floats and flutters.

A skirt that swirls.

A pair of boots for a Cossack or cowboy dance, a Teddy bear for a square dance partner, a sword for a fencer's or a pirate's dance.

A straw hat and cane for a soft-shoe routine.

A balloon to encourage leaps and jumps.

A wand and soapy liquid for blowing bubbles (to encourage graceful movements with adagios).

A broom for a clown dance.

Records or tapes from your local discount record store.

♦ ACTIONS

Little kids are so marvelously unselfconscious. Turn on just the right music, hand them one of the props listed, and see if they don't swing into action. Be an attentive audience, or, if you feel like shaking out the kinks, all the better: Let the solo become a duet.

Your child may try to duplicate a performance she's seen at the circus or on TV. Through pantomime or dance she can reenact a theatrical experience. Or she might put into dance form aspects of nature she's observed—flowers opening, leaves falling, squirrels scurrying, swans gliding. She could also compose a dance based on the movements of people she has seen—passengers jiggling and lurching on a bus; window washers reaching and wiping in circular movements.

♦ **VARIATION**

At intervals, turn off the music and have your child freeze in the exact position she was in when the music stopped.

DISCO AFTER DINNER

♦ **ACTIVITY**

Dancing with your spouse to the music you courted to, and then taking turns partnering your child.

♦ **PROPS**

Records from your collection.

♦ **ACTIONS**

Turn the lights down low, roll back the rug, and turn up the stereo. Do you like ballads for slow dancing, country music, rock 'n' roll, or the hustle? Get out your Elton John, Billy Joel, Bob Dylan, and reggae albums. Play whatever used to get the two of you out on the dance floor when you were dating.

After you've warmed up and given your child a demonstration, invite him to join in the fun. One of you can pick him up or just dance opposite him. It's amazing how quickly youngsters pick up a beat and imitate the fluid body movements of adult dancers.

VIOLIN FOR PRESCHOOLERS

♦ **ACTIVITY**

Listening to classical music and practicing the violin together (if your child is enrolled in Suzuki violin lessons).

♦ **PROPS**

A very small violin (a real instrument, not a toy) one-sixteenth the size of an ordinary violin.

A violin-type object such as a spaghetti box and a bowlike object such as a ruler, just to practice holding and coordinating the two.

An adult violin.

♦ ACTIONS

If a teacher of the Suzuki method gives classes in your area, you might consider enrolling your child. Two ground rules are especially interesting. The child should be listening to music as well as striving to play. The parent should be practicing a violin along with the child.

Suzuki proponents urge that children be exposed to classical music from birth. The same way a child picks up a foreign language by hearing it spoken, he will recognize classical music if he hears it played over and over again. Suzuki teachers encourage parents to play tapes during meals or at bedtime. Certain pieces are recommended for each age. For two-year-olds, Bach Minuets 1, 2, and 3 are considered appropriate.

Before the first lesson at age three, prospective pupils hear recordings of the five pieces they will learn to play in Level One: "Twinkle, Twinkle, Little Star"; "Lightly Row"; "Song of the Wind"; "Go Tell Aunt Rhody"; and "O Come Little Children."

If you enroll, you will attend lessons with your child in which you are taught too. Then you practice with him at home. When you pick up your violin and play your child's piece, this has the effect of drawing him to the practice session right away. Dr. Suzuki has observed that a strong, loving child-parent relationship produces the best learning. His wise prescription for practice sessions might have connotations for other activities—"two minutes with joy, five times a day." He advises finding things to enjoy and approve of in your child's playing at all times. No matter how many mistakes he makes, Dr. Suzuki believes, there will always be something to praise. Again, sound advice for other areas of life as well.

♦ VARIATION

Some Suzuki teachers give piano instruction.

♦ BENEFIT

This successful method of early musical training has developed pitch, a sense of timing, and rhythmical skills in many pupils, as well as qualities that are not strictly musical—sensitivity, concentration, perseverance, and memory.

· 7 ·

"WE'RE WORKERS!"

P lay with toys? No, that's for babies! Often when you're working around the house, your child would rather do what you're doing. He aspires to be like Mommy or Daddy, so he relishes behavior that gives him the illusion of achieving that similarity. He feels important doing adult things. The belief that he's helping raises the mercury of self-esteem. If you recognize the contribution, your eager beaver becomes even more industrious.

Camaraderie develops when you tackle a job together and triumph. Suppose everyone's been complaining about a fallen towel rack. Your "gofer" fetches the screwdriver (even choosing the right size) and holds the rack in place while you insert the screws. Voilà! The broken now functions again. One child, exulting during a repair, exclaimed, "Mom, we're workers!" A successful partnership is heady stuff.

A child has to believe that his appointed task is a genuine part of the job, not a meaningless activity you've given him just to keep him out of your hair. When possible, break down a project into many little steps and arrive at a few your child can do—washing paintbrushes, handing you nails. Of course, this task delegation will slow you down. One father of twins who was adding a garage onto his house said, "I outline my expectations for a Saturday and then cut them in half."

One of the time-consuming factors may be establishing safety precautions. With a rank beginner as an apprentice, you have to be careful where you put down your tools or set your cans of wood stain. However, most parents I talked to were surprised by how careful and obedient their tots were. Of his three-and-a-half-year-old, one handyman-dad said, "I trust Devin. If I tell him not to pick up something, he doesn't." But supervision is needed even with the most trustworthy kids. The child who tags along a lot with a parent doing mechanical chores gets very adept at mechanical skills—too adept! He may unscrew things he shouldn't.

With certain projects you may not be able to think of any related tasks you can assign to a preschooler. To satisfy his eagerness to be on the scene, you may have to set him up in some parallel activity. A photographer gave her son a broken camera to cock and click as she worked. A parent typing at his desk gave his child an old typewriter. A mother disconnected one phone and let her child push its buttons while she made calls on another phone.

To a young child, your work is his idea of play. Being near you is another plus. Meantime, his absorbent mind is taking in all the how-to's of accomplishing tasks, including use of tools, resources, and general attitudes, such as forethought, carefulness, and patience.

◆

GROOMING TASKS NOT HO-HUM

◆ ACTIVITY

Letting your child watch and imitate the transforming processes that constitute your grooming routine.

◆ PROPS

Dad's: razor, shaving cream, shampoo, blow dryer, shoe polish, cloth. Mom's: curlers, brushes, combs, makeup jars, cotton balls, tweezers, etc. Your child's: toy replicas, empty bottles, or unwanted products.

◆ ACTIONS

Jobs you do every day, such as shampooing, shaving, or making up—jobs that may be utter bores to you—are fascinating exhibitions to your offspring. If you appreciate the novelty to a two-year-old of these ordinary actions, you'll be more tolerant of his being underfoot while you're trying to get on with it.

Ongoing commentary enhances the show. "Feel those prickles! Now I'm going to spread this foam over my chin and cheeks. I scrape it off like this. Now when the water drains, look at all those little black stubs. I'll let you sponge them away." The highlight of one little boy's day was maneuvering his own toy razor across his face while he chitchatted with Dad.

The makeup routine seems to combine all the elements of fun that your child has already known in water play, painting, and small-object manipulation. You'll have to find a way to protect your carpet and fabrics from amateur experiments. Fair warning!

Don't miss the expression on your son's or daughter's face the first time you put polish on teeny toenails. The sight of those ten red ovals is hypnotizing.

BIG HELP WITH CHORES

♦ ACTIVITY

Giving your child domestic tasks to do with you and instructing him in the needed skills.

♦ PROPS

Your own household equipment most of the time.

♦ ACTIONS

A preschooler has a penchant for helping with chores. So make hay while the sun shines. Even though you could do the work twice as fast on your own, encouraging a child's zeal pays off. Break down a chore into small steps, assign him a simple operation, and show him exactly how to do it. Graduate him slowly to more complicated tasks, and you'll soon have a surprisingly effective helper.

Domestic jobs involve the kinds of mechanical actions that are truly interesting to kids' minds. Some chores include various fill-and-dump movements, at which little kids are pros: stuffing dirty clothes in a hamper, dropping peelings in a disposal, flinging dry towels out of the dryer, pouring water out of a watering can. Previous practice with fitting toy shapes into openings makes them good at sliding forks and spoons into the dishwasher silverware basket. Instead of sorting toy shapes by colors, children can happily separate the whites and the coloreds for the laundry. Instead of matching lotto cards, they can have just as much fun matching pairs of socks.

Kids like seeing changes in physical objects. This accounts for their pleasure in making dusty tables clean, a sticky counter smooth, the tarnished silver shiny. An ardent desire to work mechanisms can be satisfied by chances to turn appliances on and off.

Of course, doing chores together will soon enable a child to do some jobs on her own. One toddler was very proud of being able to open the apartment door, pick up the newspaper, and bring it to her parents' breakfast table every day.

♦ BENEFIT

The best spinoff of shoulder-to-shoulder work on household chores is not learning manual skills but learning the satisfaction of pitching in and cooperating.

TO REPAIR IS TO CARE

♦ ACTIVITY

Examining broken toys and repairing them when possible.

♦ PROPS

A box for broken toys or torn clothes, mending equipment such as glues, tapes, needle and thread.

♦ ACTIONS

There is less crying over broken toys in homes where one spouse has a reputation as a handyperson. One little girl rarely shed a tear over a mishap but calmly proclaimed to friends, "Daddy fix dat!"

You may not have the time or energy to fix a toy the minute it is broken. But rather than appear uninterested, you might keep on a high shelf (for safety) a special box labeled Save for Repair. This could be taken down at intervals for mending sessions. One parent (or grand-parent, perhaps) could set aside time with the child twice a month to examine the problems. You should think out loud as you explore remedies. If a toy can be fixed, your child will enjoy watching the process. If not, part of the toy might be salvaged and used in a different way. If it is beyond repair and there are jagged edges or other dangerous aspects, you can explain why it has to be thrown away. Your interest and thoughtful attention to the situation will soften the blow of the loss.

A DAY OF DECORATING

♦ ACTIVITY

Providing equipment for your child to imitate you when you're plastering, painting, or wallpapering.

♦ PROPS

Play dough, spatula, empty paint can, old paintbrush, wallpaper samples or old magazines, scissors, paste, cartons, mugs, stool.

♦ ACTIONS

If you're washing walls in preparation for painting, your child can sponge off the baseboards or the doors. If you're patching cracks, your child could smear his play dough on an acceptable surface with a spatula.

After a little initial resistance to not being allowed to dip into the real paint, your child may be content with an old paint can full of water. He can "paint" all the tiles, the toilet, and the tub in a bathroom near where you're applying paint.

During the ticklish job of wallpapering, you may not welcome an apprentice. But there's a chance of total absorption in a sideline activity if you set your child up with old magazines or a sample book of discontinued wallpapers. She can cut out pages and paste them to the insides (or outsides, if easier) of cartons. These could become dollhouses or storage boxes.

FIRST WORKBENCH

♦ ACTIVITY

Pounding with a wooden mallet, fitting pegs in holes, and joining slats with nuts and bolts.

♦ PROPS

Toy pounding bench with board of holes, wooden mallet, pegboard and pegs for finger-fitting plastic or wood nuts and bolts, accompanying slats with holes for bolts, small metal wrench.

♦ ACTION

You can prepare a two-year-old to be a knowledgeable co-worker by giving him hammering practice on a toy pounding bench. This has a board with holes into which your child pounds pegs with a wooden mallet.

Shop around for another toy that provides pegs of different sizes and a pegboard with holes of varying dimensions. Your child will learn to press each peg into the matching hole with his fingers, not a hammer.

If you can't find a good nut-and-bolt toy, use real nuts and bolts. Provide some sanded wooden slats with holes drilled in them the size of your bolts. Help your child twist the bolt into the nut. Together, hold the wrench. As you perform the tightening actions with your hand over his, he will gradually get the idea.

♦ BENEFIT

These experiences provide a child with woodworking tasks when you cannot include him in your own carpentry projects.

REAL TOOL KIT

♦ ACTIVITY

Assembling a few lightweight, inexpensive tools so your child can work on your and her own carpentry projects.

♦ PROPS

Tack hammer, hand drill with ¼-inch chuck and ¼-inch bit, small screwdriver, small adjustable wrench, pliers, flashlight, self-coiling measuring tape, sheet of sandpaper with block to wrap it around, masking tape, T-square, pencil, acrylic adhesive (from art supply store), metal box with handle (like fishing tackle box).

♦ ACTIONS

You might start with a shiny gray metal box and only two of the tools listed. Gradually add others. If you have spare tools, give them to your child. If not, you may find inexpensive real tools for the same price as toy tools (which are only good for pretend play).

Your child can learn the functions of each tool better if as you work you describe your actions. "I'm keeping my eye on the nail head as I hammer. I'm fitting the end of the screwdriver into the groove. I'm twisting this wrench to tighten the nut." Also using correct labels for objects and descriptive verbs for actions will make her surprisingly articulate.

Your child may not want to hang in for a whole morning of carpentry work, but toting her own toolbox to the work site, opening it, choosing an appropriate tool, and participating in a few tasks for a while will be pleasant for both of you. When your job gets too intricate, she may glide easily into a make-believe scenario of carpentry tasks.

WOODWORKING EXPERIMENTS

These woodworking experiments—tack-hammering, nailing, sanding, and gluing—get progressively more difficult. Your child may repeat one of them quite a few times before going on to the next.

EXPERIMENT I

♦ PROPS

Tack hammer, long-stemmed colored thumb or carpet tacks, short lengths of wood 2 by 2 inches.

♦ **ACTIONS**

Show your child how to hold the hammer. Hold each tack in place for him. Help him tap firmly till he can do it on his own. Suggest he make a design on the wood with the colored tacks.

EXPERIMENT II

♦ **PROPS**

Tack hammer, roofing nails, 2-inch-thick scraps of lumber, strips of lath or tongue depressors.

♦ **ACTIONS**

Watch out for splinters. Roofing nails are easier for a novice carpenter to hit than common nails. Have her lay a length of lath or a tongue depressor on top of the thick piece of scrap. Then let her drive in nails to fasten the two together.

EXPERIMENT III

♦ **PROPS**

Sheets of medium-grade and fine-grade sandpaper, two blocks of wood, each about 2 by 3 by 1 inch, masking tape, a bag of lumber scraps and cutoffs.

♦ **ACTIONS**

Wrap each kind of sandpaper around a block and tape it in position. This becomes a tool to rub the lumber scraps with until they are smooth. Your child should use the medium grade first, then finish off with the fine grade. Show him how to handle the scraps carefully so he doesn't pick up splinters. Do some scraps for him to build up his collection. When he gets a nice pile of sanded pieces, you are ready for the next experiment.

EXPERIMENT IV

♦ **PROPS**

A bag of sanded lumber scraps with cutoffs (2-by-4-inch end pieces, turnings, and bits of molding); a pine or plywood square about 8 by 8 inches; acrylic adhesive and acrylic paint (art store items).

♦ **ACTIONS**

Your child can make an interesting abstract sculpture by gluing odds and ends of wood on top of each other but nicely askew. Start with the plywood square for a base. Point it, if desired. Glue some scraps here and there on the base, then erect asymmetrical towers from these, letting parts of the towers touch or be connected by wooden strips.

BUSINESS PARTNERS

♦ ACTIVITY

Offering your child desk space and a few interesting desk accessories to inspire work that imitates your own.

♦ PROPS

Pencil, pen, pencil sharpener, bottle of correction fluid, nontoxic glue, stapler, staple remover, letter opener, paper clips, ruler, calculator, scissors, rubber bands.

Order pad, ledger paper, old envelopes, check register, old checkbook, typing paper, carbon paper, old stamps, Christmas cards, obsolete office memoranda, computer printouts.

♦ ACTIONS

Introduce the props a few at a time. Some of your partner's jobs might be for real and some just pretend. For instance, she can stuff, stamp, and seal envelopes; open letters; and perhaps staple papers together for a mailing. When you run out of tasks you can trust your child with, let her imagination take over.

She can play office by making a design of paper clips or staples or pasting together a collage of used stamps. More realistic actions might be scribbling on each page of an old checkbook, tearing them out, and stuffing them into envelopes (with your former address on them). She might make an X in a specific corner of each check stub. Occasionally facilitate her game by asking for a flow chart, a memo, or some profit-and-loss calculations. She can put her own interpretations on these terms: for example, drawing lines with a ruler or making a row of As (if that's the first letter of her name), and then brushing every other letter with correction fluid. Executive nods, gestures, and sporadic grown-up comments in solemn office tones can prolong the parallel play.

If you have a personal computer, perhaps you can bargain for an extra half-hour of labor before you both break to play one of the learning games on her diskette.

♦ BENEFIT

If you are operating a small business out of your home, it is nice for both you and your child if she can occupy herself contentedly in your office at times.

· 8 ·

FOSTERING A CREATIVE BENT

L ittle children are naturally creative. Many adults envy the fearless, joyful way children launch projects.

Creativity isn't mysterious. It has been analyzed and found to include various skills that can be learned, such as modification, metaphorical thinking, and tolerating the unpredictable. Children practice these skills instinctively.

Before the age of two, a child concentrates on concrete objects and people within view. Out of sight is out of mind. After two, imagination starts to develop. A child can visualize objects and scenes mentally. Then she brings out her ideas in the concrete world of play materials. Playing with the same toy in different ways, erecting various structures with building materials, rearranging nursery furniture or doll collections, combining parts of two games to forge a third, making up stories and songs, taping together sundry junk items into a whimsical contraption—these are active ways of exercising creativity.

Through the mental environment you establish, you can either stifle or nurture this quality of thought. Easy self-expression will occur when a child feels so loved and valued that she's convinced she has a self that is worth expressing. Accept a child's feelings and ideas. Find specific aspects of her products to praise. Don't be harshly critical if you don't think these products are especially clever. Don't get angry if, by your child's exploring or experimenting, something in your house gets broken. In order to discover, she needs freedom, which will involve her making some mistakes. Also your ability to put up with clutter will help. An active child making a mess is a lot healthier than a passive child not knowing what to do with materials.

Try playing different games with her during a given week, not the same old game every night. If she begs for the same old game, play it, but invent a slightly new twist. If you set up patterns of play and then, like a composer, invent variations on each theme, your interactions with your child will steadily promote creativity.

The activities in this chapter are designed to help you strengthen your child's creativity. As you cause hers to blossom, you may at the same time revitalize your own talent for invention.

◆

INVENTING GAMES

◆ ACTIVITY

Facilitating your child's natural tendency to think up games to amuse himself when bored.

◆ PROPS

Sometimes you, the parent, become the prop. (A child might jump back and forth over your outstretched leg.) Other times *any* object in your child's surroundings (pebbles, rubber bands) might get incorporated into a game.

◆ ACTIONS

Here are some sample games tots have invented. Their parents caught on to the game idea developing in their child's mind and, by cooperating, enabled them both to have a jovial few moments. The point is not to teach *these* particular games but to give you an understanding of how to let similar ones evolve in your home.

Pushover   Melissa, a toddler, sat on a piano bench. Her mother sat down, too. The little girl pouted and pushed her mother away. Perhaps the toddler had intended to be alone on the bench. The mother decided she needn't take the pout or rejection seriously. She pretended to fall off the bench. The pout was replaced by a look of surprise. When the mother sat down again in the same position, the toddler smirked and pushed her again. The mother exclaimed and seemed to tumble off the bench a second time. The toddler giggled increasingly as the mother's clowning continued.

Reachout   This game is best described by the advertising slogan "Reach out and touch someone." Meghan placed her low chair in the middle of the living room and stood on its seat. She extended her left hand toward her dad sitting in an armchair. She couldn't reach him, so he obligingly extended his arm. Their hands touched. Meghan oohed with delight. Then she held out her right arm toward her mom in another chair. Even when her mom stretched her arm out all the way and leaned forward, their fingertips couldn't touch. Meghan climbed down and ran out of the room. She came back with a towel. Up on the chair again, she held outstretched hands with her dad and then flapped the towel toward her mother. Her mother grabbed the end of it. Meghan looked from one to the other, beaming over the unity she had created.

Butterfingers   A two-year-old rediscovered his old fill-and-dump milk bottle. After stuffing plastic snap-on toy parts and puzzle pieces down its neck, he emptied them. Then suddenly he stood and tried to drop the pieces into the open bottle standing on the floor, but they missed the opening. The game didn't work. His observant father gave him a large refrigerator storage box instead. Now when the child dropped the pieces, they landed in the box. Then the father unfolded a brown-paper grocery bag and stood it also at the child's feet. The child dropped some pieces in one container and some in the other. Then the child gave himself a challenge. He stood on a low stepstool and dropped the toys in from this higher position. When this worked well, the child collected other containers and arranged them in a circle around his stool. Bombs away! Just as his interest was fading, his dad suggested he drop just the blue pieces in one container, the plain wood pieces in another, and the red pieces in a third. The fun was prolonged. The game was replayed for months in this format.

Naughty Words in the Dark   Josh and Sarah's dad tucked them in for the night. He walked to the door and flicked off the light switch. A child blurted out, "Woggie-doogie." The dad with mock severity scolded, "I heard a bad word. Are two children saying a naughty word? No one is allowed to say that. I'm going to call the police!" Giggles. He turned on the light and walked to the beds. The children's eyes were closed. "Hmmm, these children are sound aleep. I must have been mistaken." Again he turned out the lights and, of course, Josh and Sarah exclaimed shrilly, "Woggie-doogie" or made up another nonsense word that seemed even more hilarious. The good-humored father played out his scolding role again.

In these examples a seemingly insignificant series of actions culminated in a "happening." They were improvisations dependent on a certain time, place, mood, and the objects in the immediate surroundings. But often such a game can be repeated constantly for a week or more.

Observe your child and be sensitive enough to realize when a little game is forming out of some random actions. You might lend your hand, your foot, or a nodding head to help launch the game. Or you might introduce just the right physical object that causes a game idea to crystallize in your child's mind.

♦ **BENEFIT**

By participating you show your child that you respect his inventiveness.

TALL TALES

♦ **ACTIVITY**

Making up stories together or asking provocative questions that develop a story line forming in your child's mind.

♦ **ACTIONS**

Several parents testified to their children's fertile imagination. Courtney's interest was witches. She invented many spooky variations on that theme. John spun out incredible adventures, such as, "A policeman came to the door and said, 'There are robbers in your neighborhood. Stay inside your house.'" David noticed people by the side of the road and made up their life stories.

The parents of these children tended to listen closely or ask clarifying questions, thus plowing the ground of the fertile imagination. Sometimes they tried to downplay the negative scenes and accent the positive.

Parents can either encourage or discourage the making up of stories, depending on their own temperament. A little boy had been dragging a branch to a brush pile. When he came inside, he said, "That stick was chasing me. It wouldn't let me go." A parent inclined toward realism might say, "Were the twigs hooked onto the yarn of your sweater?" A parent inclined toward fantasy might say, "Didn't it want to get thrown into the brush pile?"

If you wish to encourage creativity, make up simple stories and ask your child for input: "What do you suppose the giant said to the little elf?" Wait for a response. Then interweave the response with your tale. You can also build a story to a climax and then suggest that your child finish it.

Devin and his parents did a lot of joint storytelling and would take turns advancing the plot.

DEVIN: A little bear looked out the window and saw . . .
DAD: It was a very foggy day. He decided to . . .
DEVIN: Go for a walk in the woods.
DAD: A gigantic genie came out of the fog and said, "Ask me whatever you want."
DEVIN: The bear said, "Show me the way to the magic lake."

THE SILLY FACTORY

◆ ACTIVITY

Gathering some odds and ends at random from around the house and constructing a toy, musical instrument, or nonsensical machine.

◆ PROPS

Kitchen utensils, safe bathroom equipment, desk accessories, workbench hardware.

◆ ACTIONS

Pretend you are workers in a factory. Let your child hand you three or four items, and invent a toy or machine with them. Then gather some things and let your child come up with an invention. The devices can be quite silly and useless. Consider, for instance, this cotton-stuffer: use a pencil to stuff cotton balls through the hole of a large funnel. Or how do you like this button-pusher?: press a paper clip against the edge of a button (tiddley-wink style) and make it slide along the table.

◆ VARIATION

The factory motif can be extended to apply to the making of more useful toys. "If you want your child to be creative," one anticonsumerism nursery school teacher said, "don't buy too many toys. After all, necessity is the mother of invention." She suggested kids make a doll crib out of a shoebox, a doll poncho out of a dustcloth, or a train out of a series of cosmetic boxes.

◆ BENEFIT

Combining unrelated items is a skill many creative people have.

MAKING UP SONGS

◆ ACTIVITY

Ad-libbing with popular songs, folk songs, or children's songs, or generating all the lyrics yourselves.

◆ ACTIONS

Substitute your child's name in a song. "Polly, put the kettle on" becomes "Lindsey, put the kettle on." After your child has enjoyed that rendition, insert a friend's or a baby brother's name. Another kind of substitution that goes over well is a preposterous word: "The itsy-bitsy spider crawled up the water spout" is changed to "The itsy-bitsy ele-phant crawled up the water spout."

For the most fun, teach your child the original verse first, singing that often. Then introduce variations on it. You can change whole lines. "We all live in a yellow submarine" can become "We all live in a big apart-ment house." Or update the old favorite: "Over the river, and through the woods, to grandmother's house we go." Today's generation will un-derstand: "Over the highway and into the plane, to grandmother's house we go." You don't have to revise the whole verse, just a couple of lines, for laughs. Children love this kind of humor, creating deviations from the norm, because they feel so smug about knowing the original.

You can take a favorite tune and improvise whole sets of lyrics just describing what you're both doing. "I've got the dishpan blues," crooned one dad on duty at the sink one night, "just scraping and rinsing all the time."

If you and your spouse fool around with such parodies often, your child will also play whimsically with words and music.

♦ BENEFIT

Finding an alternative for the way something has always been done is a creative technique.

ARTFUL COMBINATIONS

♦ ACTIVITY

Taking two unrelated games or toys (or parts of them) and combin-ing them to invent a new game or toy.

♦ PROPS

Items from your child's present collection of toys.

♦ ACTIONS

Instead of coming home with a wrapped-up brand-new toy to present, rack your brain during the commute and devise a brand-new way to play with an *old* toy. Your child may do this more easily than you. One little boy combined a fine-motor toy with a gross-motor toy. He took his box of hand-painted Noah's ark animals and climbed to the top of his indoor slide. He stood each one on the platform and then released it. He watched it slide down the ramp. Then he slid down himself, gathered the animals in the box, and climbed to the platform again.

♦ **BENEFIT**

Creativity includes the ability to see a relationship in usually unrelated things.

REVISED EDITION

♦ **ACTIVITY**

Becoming "author" of a picture book and retelling familiar stories.

♦ **PROPS**

Picture books and storybooks.

♦ **ACTIONS**

When you get a bunch of books out of the library, take turns reading to each other. Give your child the books with more pictures than text. See what characters and plot the pictures suggest to her, letting her invent the story as she goes along. Even after you've read the real story aloud, she can "re-read" it to you, using her own words and taking license with the plot.

After your child knows a story well, you can change a word or a line just for fun. For instance, in Goldilocks you could say, "This porridge is too mushy" instead of the classic line. She'll probably catch your "mistake" right away. She might resist any change. She might want the story line-for-line the same old way. Or she might appreciate the revision and laugh, begging you from then on, "Read it funny."

MYSTERY COLLECTION

♦ **ACTIVITY**

Exercising a freewheeling imagination by thinking up off-the-wall purposes for bizarre objects.

♦ **PROPS**

During a month-long search, find some rather unusual objects or gadgets, even ones your spouse might not recognize. Secretly store them away. Hardware and gift shops are good sources. Some possible curiosities might be a tea infuser, a strawberry huller, a vanilla bean, chopsticks, an eye mask, a seed pod, an old-fashioned toy, an antique kitchen utensil.

◆ ACTIONS

Both parents and child can take turns guessing the function of each item. After you know the real purpose for something, dream up a fantasy purpose. The chopsticks could be an elf's stilts, the seed pod a fairy's ball collection.

◆ BENEFIT

Thinking up fantasy purposes stretches the imagination to see old things in a new light.

HOMEMADE JOKES, RIDDLES, AND MAGIC TRICKS

◆ ACTIVITY

Encouraging your toddler to make up jokes, invent silly riddles, and fool baby sister with some clever magic tricks.

◆ PROPS

Some joke and riddle books for children, books of nonsense rhyme, dime-store magic tricks.

◆ ACTIONS

Once a child learns to do something the right way, he finds it riotously funny to do it the wrong way on purpose. When Wendy's mother held her pajama top in front of her with the two sleeves dangling, Wendy learned to insert her hands into the correct armholes. After she'd mastered this, with a mischievous gleam in her eye, she thrust her left arm into the right-arm sleeve. "Hey!" her mom protested, "that's the wrong way."

"Wrong way!" Wendy echoed and broke up with laughter. This farcical shenanigan was repeated night after night, and Mom obligingly cooperated by playing the straight man.

Slapstick comedy is soon followed by the cracking of purely verbal jokes. You will endear yourself to your child if you catch them and laugh along with him. For instance, Jamie's mother put a bowl of soup in front of him and sat down. There was a plate of crackers in the middle of the table. Jamie eyed them. Suddenly he grinned and warned her of a coming joke: "I'm going to make a goof. I say, pass me the *cookies!*" Then he slid down into his high chair to show how overcome with giggles he was.

Jamie's mother said, "You silly! You mean pass me the *crackers.*" And she laughed hard too. Discovering he had an audience in the palm of his hand, he went on. "I make 'nother goof. Pass me the—the—telephone!" This naming of ridiculous things to pass went on and on as his eyes roved the room. His mother flattered him with her laughter until the end of the meal.

When your child is four, you may be able to find some juvenile joke books he'll enjoy or books with nonsense verse. Tell jokes your child can grasp, such as this one: There was a mama hummingbird and a baby hummingbird. One day the baby hummingbird was getting real big. (Hold your fingers an inch apart) His mama decided it was time for him to fly. So she pushed him nearer and nearer the edge of the nest until finally he fell out. But he didn't fly. He just fluttered all the way down into the tall, tall grass. Now do you know how a teeny-tiny hummingbird calls his mom? (Ask this in a whisper.) He says (now boom it out), *"Hey, Mom!"*

See if your child will compose a story to make you laugh. Explain that a surprise, the unexpected, makes for a good punch line. They may be pretty bad jokes at first, but they may get more artful as your stand-up comedian gets experience.

Try some easy-to-read riddle books. Then make up real-life questions that sound like riddles. "What's white, creamy, and smeared all over tomatoes?" (Mayonnaise.) "Who is tall, handsome, and kisses Ashley good night every evening?" (Daddy.)

A basic magic trick can involve things disappearing and reappearing, or a new object being substituted for the disappeared one. Go to a magic show or watch a magician on TV. Support your child's efforts at doing a takeoff on a magician's act. Perhaps you can buy an easy-to-perform magic trick at a novelty store.

WHY DO YOU ASK WHY?

♦ ACTIVITY

Answering your child's questions.

♦ ACTIONS

Draw a deep breath, summon all your mental energy, and resolve to answer all "why" questions for ten minutes. This can be an intellectual workout, but it gives your child your stamp of approval on her spirit of inquiry. One mother, tired of interrogation, thought of a humorous way to call a halt. The dialogue went like this:

"Why are you wearing those dirty jeans?"

"Because I'm going to garden now."

"Why?"

"Because it's springtime."

"Why is it springtime?"

Et cetera.

The mother, with a twinkle in her eye, finally stemmed the incoming tide of questions by responding, "Why—why—why do you ask me 'why?'" The intelligent daughter was momentarily at a loss for words and giggled, understanding that the tables had been turned.

Sometimes questions may be simply a ruse for keeping you engaged in conversation. But they reflect an inquisitiveness underlying your child's approach to life at this stage. Tax your brain a bit and answer all you can. When you don't know the answers, you might want to look them up together in reference books.

BRAINSTORMING SESSIONS

♦ ACTIVITY

Generating a lot of ideas without judging their merit.

♦ ACTIONS

The traditional brainstorming session is a meeting of a group of people who come up with as many ideas as possible to solve a problem. The cardinal rule is nobody is allowed to criticize anyone else's idea. Evaluation is deferred until later.

Even little kids can learn to brainstorm if you pose hypothetical problems that interest them. It's a creative skill worth cultivating in your child. Ask a question—not a yes/no, right/wrong kind of question but an open-ended one. Then you, your child, and perhaps your spouse, too, can generate answers. These answers can be unrealistic, impractical, even outlandish. The point is to strive for a quantity of alternatives. One idea triggers another by association. Here are some exercises in brainstorming.

Strange Uses for Ordinary Things See how many ways you can think of to use the following objects: an ashtray, a pillow, mittens, a piece of chalk, a shirt cardboard, an earring, a belt. Let imagination, not logic, prevail. For instance, an ashtray could be a dish for kitty's milk, a holder for barrettes, or a bowl to float a flower in. A pillow could be a stool to reach something high, an infant seat for a baby, or a supply of feathers for an Indian headdress.

Gift from the Zoo Pose a mind-boggling question like this: What are all the things you could do with a pet giant panda, a monkey, an owl? Get the panda to pull your little red wagon, curl up next to the panda when you're cold, give your friends a ride on the panda's back, et cetera.

Wild Speculations   Sit still and just wonder with your child. Stretch each other's imaginations beyond the evidence presented to the five physical senses. You can initiate the wondering process now and then with such questions as these: I wonder what would happen if . . .

> we moved to the country (or city) or moon
> we bought ten cats
> houses didn't have roofs
> we owned a plane
> you were as tiny as a doll
> you went to work and Daddy stayed home to play
> all your toys had wheels on them

Fellow Problem-solvers   Apply the brainstorming technique to a family problem. "Recently Mom has been late to the office every day. Let's think of all the ways Dad and you can help her leave on time." Or try this one: "The kitchen floor gets dirty so fast. Let's think of ways to keep it cleaner." Include farfetched ideas—never wear shoes, have mops attached to the bottom of our shoes, have hose squirters built into the walls. Sometimes a crazy suggestion leads to a practical solution.

II

TOGETHERNESS EXPERIENCES FOR LOVING TIMES

· 9 ·

ROUGHHOUSING ROMPS

Tickling, tossing, tousling, chasing, grabbing, wrestling, snuggling—these are the vivacious interactions with parents that kids adore. And why not! They mean excitement and affection—an unbeatable combination.

Webster's makes plain what this chapter is all about. The dictionary defines *roughhousing* as "boisterous play among occupants of a room." Games often evolve spontaneously during the daily routine. The animated spirit with which parents describe them show that this sort of activity is a bright spot in the day for both parent and child. Parents obviously enjoy throwing somber maturity to the winds and becoming silly and playful. The children enjoy their parents' willingness to tune in to childhood.

A key reason for the popularity of the rough-and-tumble moments is the lively physical action. Kids like to be in motion. Preschoolers have only recently learned how to run, skip, climb, somersault; and they revel in demonstrating their increasing agility. They want to use their bodies in as many different ways as they can. They welcome every opportunity to acquire new motor skills. Mastering some of the stunts listed under Circus Acrobats (p. 110) will fill them with pride.

Fathers seem more inclined toward roughhousing than mothers. They also kid around a lot with mock tough talk. One mother complained that her spouse said to their son, "I'm going to punch your lights out, Midget-face." But this was just an opener for a merry chase. Another father said, "I'm going to sell you," "trade you in," or "give you away." Of course, his daughter knew he was kidding, but she'd double-check occasionally by asking, "Are you really?"

Many parents think their child is very physical or hyperactive. Their judgment may be colored merely by their own preference for nonphysical or nonactive games. Or they may be just plain tired after a day on the job. Their child's level of energy and zest for motion may, in fact, be quite normal.

The following pages suggest some happy and constructive outlets for your child's ebullience. Hopefully, you will get caught up in the fun, too, and get a second wind for all the encores your child may beg for. When you're both exhausted, try a quiet activity from the next chapter, In the Lap.

♦

APPLE TURNOVER

♦ **ACTIVITY**

Covering a child with a quilt and then dramatically uncovering her.

♦ **PROPS**

Large quilt or blanket.

♦ **ACTIONS**

First announce, "Now I'm going to bake a delicious apple turn-over." Spread out your quilt on the floor. "There's my pastry dough. Now where's the apple for inside my turnover?" Pick up your child and place her in the center of the quilt. Fold the corners of the quilt over her. "Now let me smear some nice melted butter over this pastry." Stroke your hands along the quilt so your child underneath can feel the pres-sure. "Next into the oven you go." Pick up your child and plop her bouncily onto the bed. Pause. Then say, "All done. Let's eat this deli-cious turnover." Pick up one end of the quilt and roll your child out into the open. "Yum yum!"

♦ **VARIATION**

A quilt makes a nice hammock. You and your spouse can pick up opposite corners of the quilt and sway your child back and forth.

THE CHASE AND THE CATCH

♦ **ACTIVITY**

Parent chasing a scampering child in mock hunter-prey fashion.

♦ **ACTIONS**

Almost all parents play this game with a child in some form or other. It's a favorite with two-year-olds. Here are several variations.

In a Circle A parent chases a child in a circular pattern around the dining room table or around a center stairwell in a house where traffic can flow from front hall to dining room to kitchen to living room and back to front hall again. The parent declares, "I'm going to catch you. You better run." The mood can be merry or scary, whichever the child prefers. You can build suspense by coming closer, then falling back (even far enough so he loses sight of you), reappearing hard on his trail, then gaining on him till you catch him. The capture can include not only grabbing him but holding, tickling, tossing, hugging, and kissing him.

Round two can include an additional element of excitement. After you've been chasing for a while, reverse your direction and trap your child running around a corner and right into you. This can provoke gales of laughter, as surprises usually add to the fun. But be prepared for glum disappointment or anger. With two-year-olds you have to second-guess their preference for the way a game should be played, since they can't explain their expectations.

Teams   In Sandy's house, Dad and Sandy sometimes formed a team. Dad carried Sandy while they pursued Mom or Mom pursued them. Another night Sandy and Mommy made a team, holding hands as they ran.

Wild Animals   In one family where there are four boys, a father devised a game to give his wife a respite. He began with a sudden command: "Look out the window! There's a tiger lurking out there. C'mon, let's get him!" Then they dropped to all fours. Out the front door they all crawled. "Sh! You gotta be quiet." Along the edge of the shrubbery they went, occasionally flattening themselves out so as not to be detected by the imaginary tiger. They waited, not moving a muscle, then continued crawling stealthily until the climax, when they pounced on a shrub or a riding toy or discovered (dismayed) that the beast had wandered off into the jungle. This silent sneaking up on something or someone is a variation on running after prey.

The Getter and the Saver   This game was invented for a Sunday-morning romp on a king-size bed. One parent is the "getter," the other is the "saver." The getter goes after one of the children, perhaps a daughter, who wriggles to a far corner of the bed. "I'ma gonna get you." The saver tries to protect her from being pounced on. If she is caught, the prisoner might be tickled. The saver may then rescue the child from her captivity. Then the getter can pursue the other child or the parents can switch roles.

HIDERS AND SEEKERS

♦ **ACTIVITY**

Child hiding, parent seeking and finding.

♦ **ACTIONS**

This is one of the most common of all games. It provides suspense followed by reunion for the child and a captivating show of childish charm for the parent. Here are a few versions of the game described by various couples.

Hamming It Up   A pair of twins dispersed. One lay down under the glass coffee table; the other stood behind a door that was ajar. The mother, in mock distress, cried, "Oh, dear, Meghan is lost! Where can she be? And Molly has disappeared too." She looked in all the nooks and crannies, moaning and sighing melodramatically. (The twin under the glass coffee table felt quite hidden even though she was in plain view.) When the mother finally spotted them both, she was overjoyed. Her exaggerated display of relief went over very big with the two-year-olds, who could "see" how much they meant to their mother!

A dad hammed it up by mocking anger. "When I get that boy, I'm gonna really scold him. Is he under the pillow? Is he in the closet? Is he behind the drapes?" He kept mentioning different places (a good vocabulary lesson) and going to them. By also naming improbable places—"Is he in the ashtray?" he provoked muffled laughter. At last he spied the boy and jumped on him with an "Aha! Gotcha!" A little wrestling fast turned to snuggling.

Sometimes little ones, unable to handle the suspense, may burst out of their covert spot and "find" the seekers!

Early Warning   Sometimes the process of hiding is more significant than the moment of hands-on discovery. A highlight of Sarah's day was to hide just before her dad came in the door at night. As soon as he entered, he hunted for Sarah. "Did Santa Claus take her away?" "Did she ride a rocket to the moon?" At the peak of the game's popularity, a few times he arrived before expected. Sarah dissolved in tears, crushed that she wasn't ready. To prevent this, she began hiding too far in advance of her father's homecoming. Her parents, not wanting her to crouch too long behind a sofa, developed an early warning signal. Her mother was able to say, "Okay, Sarah, Dad's on his way. Now run and hide."

Bee Game   A father of a four-year-old and a baby invented this game. The older child chose a hideout. The dad pretended to be a bee.

He made a buzzing noise and held one arm outstretched, fluttering his fingers in imitation of an insect in flight. With his other arm he carried the baby sister. The dad scurried from one possible hiding place to another like a bee investigating flowers. Both baby and older sibling were equally amused. The game had a postscript: One day when the baby was a year old, her older brother made the bee sign and sound. Remembering the old game, she toddled away to do the hiding herself.

TUB FOR TWO

◆ ACTIVITY
Parent and child sloshing in the bathtub together.

◆ PROPS
Floating toys, plastic pitcher, empty shampoo bottles, bubble bath liquid or powder, spray attachment.

◆ ACTIONS
Enliven the fun of your child's water play by hopping into the bathtub, too. Shove boats back and forth. Scoop up and pour water out of various containers. Spread suds over shoulders and arms. Trickle water onto each other's hands and feet by wringing out washcloths or emptying pitchers. Put your face in the water and blow bubbles. Encourage your preswimmer to copy you and get used to the feeling of water in his face. Pull your child through the water from one end of the tub to the other. Draw the shower curtain and splash each other gently. Help your child trigger the spray attachment and squirt himself and you.

◆ BENEFIT
Even though water play may get rowdy, it can be more tranquilizing than roughhousing on terra firma.

ROW YOUR BOAT

◆ ACTIVITY
Interacting in a lively physical way based on an imaginary situation, in this case an oarsman-swimmer relationship.

◆ PROPS
Waterbed or conventional mattress.

♦ **ACTIONS**

A mother and her daughter, Sophie, developed this game. The mother lay on her back. Sophie, facing her, sat astride her mother's tummy. They held hands. Her mother pushed and pulled her in a rowing action so that the little girl would lie back and then sit up alternately. "Row, row, row your boat, gently down the stream," Mom sang. When she finished the verse, she rolled the child over onto the mattress and exclaimed, "Oh, you've fallen into the water. It's freezing! You're shivering. The boat is drifting away. You've got to swim, swim, swim to get back to the boat." Sophie made overarm swimming motions, then climbed back on her mother's tummy. "Ah, safe at last!"

ARMCHAIR TUMBLEBUG

♦ **ACTIVITY**

Somersaulting into a soft armchair.

♦ **PROPS**

Upholstered easy chair, stool (optional).

♦ **ACTION**

After you have taught your child to somersault on the floor, help him accomplish this more daring forward roll. Place a stool behind the back of an easy chair. Your child climbs up and leans his tummy over the back of the chair. Then he dives head first onto the cushioned seat of the chair and flips over, landing on his feet on the floor in front of the chair. Guide your child at first, making sure all his landings are happy. Then applaud when your tumblebug, with increasing agility, performs the feat on his own.

♦ **BENEFIT**

Countless repetitions work off excess energy.

TOREADOR

♦ **ACTIVITY**

Child charging like a bull, wheeling about, and charging again.

♦ **PROPS**

Sweater or jacket.

♦ ACTIONS

Stand in front of your child, holding to the side of your body a dangling sweater or jacket. Like a toreador flicks a satin cape, shake the sweater. Coax your child to run toward it, in fact, right into it. She will push it out of the way as she runs behind you. Then have her wheel around. She can lower her head and point two index fingers as horns. You turn around, face her, and dangle the sweater temptingly. She can charge into it again and again.

For a surprise that will make her laugh, jerk up the sweater one time just before she contacts it so she ends up charging the air. From then on she won't know whether you're going to let her fingers and head touch the sweater or not.

When the merriment dies down, try another variation. As she's charging through, drop the sweater on her head. You will both chuckle anew.

♦ BENEFIT

This is a running game that can be played in a small room.

CIRCUS ACROBATS

♦ ACTIVITY

Practicing simple tumbling and stunts with your child in an imaginary circus setting.

♦ PROPS

None necessary, but one of the tricks requires a plank of wood about 6 feet long. It could be narrow. Another trick requires a plank of wood of similar length but about 18 inches wide.

♦ ACTIONS

To get into the spirit, imitate the awe-inspired voice of a ringmaster. "Ladies and gentlemen, children of all ages, welcome to the greatest show on earth! Mary and Joe Stone (your names) now present their son, Tim, the youngest acrobat on the block. Da-dah!" Imitate drumbeats and trumpet fanfares. "Tim will now perform a forward somersault from a crouching position on the rug."

Following are a number of stunts. Help your child master them gradually with you and stage the circus act when you and he have three or four in your repertoire. A second parent can be the announcer. A single parent can both announce and perform.

Wheelbarrow Hold your child upside down so his hands touch the floor. Don't let him put much weight on them. Your left hand is grabbing his left ankle and your right hand his right ankle. Hold on as he walks forward on his palms. Ad lib your narration.

Whirlybird If you have plenty of space, hold your child's hands and swing him in a circle, feet off the ground. Announce, "Watch now as Tim is whirled in the air, held only by his hands!"

Daddy Ladder Stand facing each other. Hold your child's hands. Let him climb up your legs until his feet are higher than his head, and flip him over backward.

Airplane Lie down on your back. Your child stands in front of your feet. Grab his hands, touch the soles of your feet to his tummy and lift him off the ground, holding his hands. Balance him in midair. He may be able to let go of your hands and stretch his arms like the wings of a plane. Announce, "Look at this human airplane! Tim is actually suspended in midair by his father's two feet!"

Lower the Anchor Drape your child over your shoulder with his head hanging down your back and his feet hanging down your chest. Lower him down your back headfirst, holding onto his legs, then his ankles with one hand. As his head and shoulders near the floor, reach one hand through your legs and whisk him forward by the wrists. When you get proficient, announce, "Now an act unparalleled in circus history: Tim descends his mother's back upside down!"

Pyramid Your child climbs up your body, and you hoist him to a sitting position or a kneeling or standing one (if you are both very coordinated). Promenade around the room with care.

Bareback Rider Trot around the room carrying your child piggyback. Drop to all fours and let your child sit astride your back. Could she stand on it as bareback riders stand on a horse? Perhaps she can with your spouse's help. Can she step or crawl from Dad's back to Mom's back if you both get down on your knees?

Balancing Act Place a plank on the floor or place one-inch-thick books under each end to raise it slightly. Help your child walk the balance beam, perhaps saying into your pretend mike, "High above the circus arena, the one and only Tim Stone attempts to walk the balance beam."

If you have a wide board, put one end on the couch and hold the other end. Then you have a horizontal board a foot and a half off the ground. Encourage your child to "walk the plank" from couch end to you. Your spouse might walk beside the balancer.

Backward Flip   Your child should stand with her back toward you. Then, bending way over forward, she reaches her hands back through her legs. Her head is now close to the ground. You grab her hands and pull up on them, flipping her in the air. She lands standing on her feet, now facing you.

Double-Whammy Flip   This stunt is very tricky and requires well-coordinated parents. Practice it first with a large doll, teddy bear, or pillow before you do it with your child. One parent holds the hands of the child, the other parent holds the feet. The child is facing upward. You swing your child from side to side like swinging a hammock: one . . . two . . . three. . . . At the agreed-upon moment you both turn around in place, Dad turning toward his left shoulder, Mom turning toward her right shoulder. Your child's body goes up and around the way a jumprope held by two people would.

♦ **BENEFIT**

Your child's pride in body control plus the desire to romp with you finds a good outlet in these games. Your child will hear some rich vocabulary words if you describe the tricks like a ringmaster.

· 10 ·

IN THE LAP

I n contrast to the energetic games in the last chapter, this chapter offers tranquil activities. They may fit the bill if you are dead tired or if your child is weary. Or perhaps your child is in too boisterous a mood. By settling her into a stationary position and involving her mentally, you can tone down the rowdiness. In any case, this chapter and the next give you a balanced menu of one-on-one times to choose from.

Just before naptime (for either of you) you may want to lie down in bed together or gather your child onto your lap for a little duet of daydreaming. We tend to overprogram ourselves these days, and our children as well. We offer them numerous lessons—gym, dancing, swimming, and skating—even at three and four. Or we shuttle them between home, day-care center, or school and Granny's.

We should schedule time just to look out the window together and watch the clouds float by. Or don't even look out the window. Don't *do* anything. Just *be:* be together, enjoying your togetherness. Kids need periods of your undivided attention. This attention should be suffused with the light of appreciation and gratitude for their wonderful selves. Time in your lap may meet this need.

The following activities are an assortment of personal interaction games. Some involve finger play or using your hands for some unusual handshakes, hand signals, or sign language. Others are word games. Two activities are ways to cultivate the art of conversation between you both. One game invites you to compose a special kind of song for your child's ears only.

To enhance the value of intimate time as a pair, make a habit of really looking at your child a lot. Look deep into her eyes. Maintain eye contact. Then you read her thoughts. You discern her feelings. You move in sync. You come to understand each other better. You teach your child ways of building a good relationship.

Laps are for cuddling kids in, so put yours to good use often.

SHAKE A LEG

♦ ACTIVITY
Jouncing your child on your lap while reciting a rhyme.

♦ ACTIONS
Little ones like being jiggled on your lap in a high-spirited way as well as being held ever so serenely. Here are two rhymes that may have been chanted by your great-grandparents. Follow the instructions for arm and leg movements, which should accompany the reciting of the lines.

Topple Back   Your child sits on your lap facing forward (not face to face). Grasp his ankles. Cross one of your child's legs over the other alternately for the first three lines (left over right, right over left, left over right). At the fourth line lift both of your child's legs so he topples back on your chest.

> *Leg over leg*
> *As the dog goes to Dover,*
> *When he comes to a wall,*
> *Jump! He goes over.*

Trotting to Boston   This rhyme has a surprise ending occurring when your lap caves in. With begged-for repetition, the surprise ending is no longer a surprise but an eagerly anticipated joke. Your child sits astride your lap, facing you. Bounce your legs up and down like a trotting horse. On the last line, while holding your child's hands, open your legs so she slips down between your knees almost to the ground. Scoop her up and place her back on a newly formed lap, and try the rhyme again.

> *Trot, trot to Boston*
> *Trot, trot to Lynn.*
> *Be careful when you get there*
> *You don't fall in!*

FINGER PLAY

♦ ACTIVITY
Reciting a rhyme and making your finger movements act out what the words are describing.

♦ **ACTIONS**

Your fingers put on a little show for your child to watch at the same time as he's listening to your poem. He'll soon want to learn the finger movements, too. If you memorize these poems, you can maintain eye contact with your child as you say them.

> *Here's a ball for Baby—big and soft and round.*
>> [Cup your hands to make a sphere]
>
> *Here is Baby's hammer. Oh, how she can pound!*
>> [Fist your hands, hold one over the other, make the
>> upper one pound the lower one]
>
> *Here is Baby's trumpet. Root-toot-toot-toot-toot.*
>> [Hold a fist to your mouth]
>
> *Here's the way that Baby plays at peek-a-boo.*
>> [Cover your face with your hands, then uncover it]
>
> *Here's the big umbrella, keeps the baby dry.*
>> [Curve one hand like an umbrella top, hold the other
>> under it stiff like a handle]
>
> *Here's the baby's cradle. Rock-a-baby-bye.*
>> [Fold your arms and pretend to rock a baby]

In the next poem you are touching your child's face. Later, when she learns the actions, she can touch your face while you continue to say the words that guide her actions.

> *Knock at the door.*
>> [Tap her forehead with your fist]
>
> *Peep in.*
>> [Hold her eyelashes and lift her closed eyelid]
>
> *Lift up the latch.*
>> [Tilt her nose gently upward]
>
> *Walk in!*
>> [Stick two fingers in her open mouth]
>
> *Chin-chopper, chin-chopper, chin.*
>> [Pinch her chin and wobble it.]

♦ **BENEFIT**

Children respond readily to the rhythm in poetry.

GIVE ME FIVE

♦ **ACTIVITY**

Greeting each other with different kinds of handshakes.

♦ ACTIONS

A street-wise dad from New York City amused his daughter with this handshake and warmhearted greeting. With a smile and gusto, call out your child's name and say, "Maria, give me five." Stretch out your hand stiffly with the five fingers straight, palm upward. Tell your child to offer her hand, fingers straight, palm downward. Then slap your hand against hers. (Of course, not too hard.) Next, turn your hand over so the palm is down, and have her turn her hand over also so her palm is up. Then she should slap your hand. "How ya doin'?"

♦ VARIATIONS

Call out, "Give me a high five!" You and your child hold up your hands vertically, level with your head. (She's on your lap, remember.) Palms meet in a rhythmic greeting, slapping each other. Another time call out, "Give me a smooth five!" Hold out your hands horizontally. Palms meet and graze across each other in a slow stroking motion as they withdraw from each other. Then you and your child turn your hands over and let the backs of your hands touch and slide across each other.

GESTURES AND SIGNALS

♦ ACTIVITY

Showing your child hands signals such as those used by referees, military personnel, movie directors, traffic officers, charade players, and the deaf.

♦ ACTIONS

Because of your job or special interest, you may be familiar with a variety of hand signals. Show them to your child gradually and tell him what each means. Help your child copy the position of your hands. Here are some suggestions:

> Move your finger across your throat for "cut it," as in the world of cinema.
> Circle your finger near your head to indicate "he's crazy."
> Put your three fingers to your forehead for the Boy Scout salute.
> Make a cross over your heart. This means "I promise."
> Give your child the thumbs-up signal. Give her the thumbs-down signal.
> Curl and uncurl your index finger, to mean "come here."
> With pointed index finger, move your hand in the shape of a cross

as a conductor would to direct his orchestra. Do this in time to some music.

Hold up two fingers in the shape of a V for victory or peace sign.

Sports fans will be familiar with referee signals. Cross your arms in front of your legs to indicate a player is safe. Throw your right thumb over your right shoulder: the player is out. Hold your hands in the shape of a T for "time out."

Hold a fist in the air to symbolize power or strength.

If you make a gesture as if you were pulling taffy by spreading your hands apart from each other, this means "slow down the pace" in the theater. If you use both hands in a beckoning motion, this means "pep up the pace."

♦ BENEFIT

When you are sitting somewhere without access to toys, hands become very convenient props for a game.

SNUGGLE READING

♦ ACTIVITY

Settling into a cozy position so you can cuddle your child as you read.

♦ PROPS

A book of stories or poems.

♦ ACTIONS

Snuggling and reading go together automatically, according to one parent. As in the song about love and marriage, "You can't have one without the other." Pick your favorite chair, a nice wing chair by the fire or a modern tilt-back one. (When you fall asleep, your child will gently nudge you to finish the story.) Nestle your child comfortably in your lap. What you read is not always important. The chance to be close is what counts on some occasions. Much more than the reading of a story is going on. What is really happening is you are enjoying the feeling of a soft, warm, chubby creature all your own on your lap, and your child is reveling in the feeling of being encompassed by a peaceful, cheerful, loving parent.

♦ BENEFIT

This experience is particularly treasured if you have been apart all day.

AMANDA SONGS

◆ ACTIVITY

Singing a song to your child about herself.

◆ ACTIONS

An actress said she made up songs about how wonderful her daughter was or about what had happened to the little girl that day. You can make up a tune. It doesn't have to be especially clever; no music critic is listening. You might rather use the tune of a favorite popular song or folk song. The main idea is to use your child's name in the lyrics. Mention how much and why you love her, or describe the qualities she expresses. You could adapt a love song, changing the words a little to individualize it for your child.

◆ BENEFIT

Singing can lift the spirits and calm tensions.

I SPY

◆ ACTIVITY

Guessing the identity of an object described.

◆ ACTIONS

Look about the room where you are sitting with your child in your lap. Decide silently on some object. Use descriptive adjectives to help him pick it out as he looks around. Suppose you choose a brass drawer handle. Say, "I spy with my little eye something that is bright and shiny and hard." If your child doesn't guess it, give larger hints. "I spy with my little eye something that is made of metal . . . that fits in my hand . . . that helps me open a drawer." When you reverse roles, help your child if he can't desribe his object. Ask him, "Is it soft? Is it long?"

◆ BENEFIT

This game makes your child more observant and teaches a lot of great adjectives.

WORDS BIRDS

♦ **ACTIVITY**

Thinking of words that rhyme.

♦ **ACTIONS**

You can start by mentioning a word such as *mug*. Then both you and your child try to think of a word that rhymes. Pause to see if your child will come up with one on her own. If not, you could say, "Oh, I have one—*hug*." Start listing them aloud. *"Mug, hug . . ."* Then perhaps your child will chime in: *"Bug."* If she can't think of a real word, a nonword like *nug* is fine. The approach should be one of witty play with words. Children's literature is full of nonsense verse that may improve your child's skill at this game.

When it's your child's turn to start the rhyming chain, she might pick a word like *curly*. Perhaps you can only think of a difficult word such as *burly* to rhyme with it. No harm in saying it and explaining, "That means a big strong man like a lumberjack." Your child will then ask, "What's a lumberjack?" You may find yourself digressing from the rhyming game to the great game underlying many parent/child interactions—the tell-me-all-about-my-world game. What better pastime is there when your child is ensconced in your generous lap!

TV DATES

♦ **ACTIVITY**

Watching a show for kids with your child.

♦ **PROPS**

TV set and comfortable chair.

♦ **ACTIONS**

Plan ahead with a program guide for a special program that both you and your child would enjoy. Watch the show with your child on your lap. (No sewing allowed or any activities that distract you from concentrating on the show.) You are expressing an interest in his interest. It will make him feel good inside that you too can enjoy what he is enjoying. If no one else is in the room at the time, all the better. Your child will relish the exclusivity.

You may choose to watch a children's program with your child regularly. Then you can talk about it for a few minutes afterward. Ask him questions about the plot. Ask his opinion of the characters. Tell what you like and why. Tell what you didn't like and why.

MIND EXPLORATION

♦ ACTIVITY

Having leisurely conversations with your child during which you draw out perceptions of objects and events.

♦ ACTIONS

Conversation may be the best lap game of all. Sometimes kids have charming misconceptions about objects, scenes they observe, and experiences they have. For instance, a little boy who had gone to the airport to see his grandfather arrive for a visit, then depart, and then arrive again asked him, "Grandad, how do you like living in the sky?"

One of the delights of dialog is finding out such misconceptions. They're usually good for a smile. Often they're worth relaying to your spouse or your parents. Occasionally a child's comments are so poetic and innocent as to be positively inspiring.

A child who is learning to talk at age two loves having you draw her out in conversation. Explore her mind with gentle questions. A three- or four-year-old, perhaps superconfident about her speech, is flattered at your curiosity about her views. You may have to hide your smile at her quaint expressions lest she try to be cute on purpose.

· 11 ·

THE WHOLE FAMILY

Having a family reunion? Step-children spending the weekend? Friends and their kids visiting? Of course you're hoping all will go smoothly. It isn't easy to arrange an event that will involve everyone. Here are some recommendations for activities that should unify a diverse group of people in a way that caters especially to your two-, three-, or four-year old.

Children love an activity in which everybody they know and love is participating. They don't want to be shunted to the other end of the house so the adults can talk. They may crave interaction with a favorite aunt or uncle. Adult relatives who haven't seen each other for a long time can benefit from the icebreaking nature of a planned game (remember college orientation?). Entertaining the youngest family member is the perfect excuse for an organized event during the afternoon.

A little advance planning, including the gathering of the materials, may ensure the success of an activity. Before the reunion scan the following activities for one that is appropriate to your clan. You might want to rehearse some of the activities, such as Party Games for Big or Small Families (see p. 131), in advance of the big event so your youngster will be better able to keep up with older cousins.

Perhaps no members of your extended family live near enough to permit get-togethers. If you have friends who are like family to you, you might propose some of these activities to them. In these days of smaller families, there's occasional hunger for "the more the merrier" times.

Not all the activities in this chapter require a large group. You might adapt some to a parent-child duo or trio.

♦

FAMILY ON PARADE

♦ ACTIVITY

Marching exuberantly through the house to celebrate a patriotic holiday, someone's birthday, or a family reunion.

♦ **PROPS**

Cake pans and wooden spoons for drums, saucepan lids for cymbals, old party hats, last New Year's Eve horns, and rhythm instruments if you have them.

♦ **ACTIONS**

Everyone—grandparents, parents, aunts, uncles, cousins—lines up, each holding an instrument. Plan a route for your parade starting in the front hallway, weaving through the living room, wandering upstairs in and out of a couple of bedrooms, and ending back at your starting point. Try a long corridor if you're in an apartment house. Hum your favorite football band tune. The leader can think up some parade-ground maneuvers for the followers to copy—high-stepping, about-face, quickstep. You can rotate leaders. Encourage everyone to ham it up.

♦ **BENEFIT**

Marching is a way of moving in a lively way through somewhat cramped quarters. Any number can join in.

AROUND THE DINING ROOM TABLE

♦ **ACTIVITY**

Everyone contributing something to the meal, either preparing food or decorating the table.

♦ **PROPS**

Construction paper, solid-color paper napkins, felt-tip pens.

♦ **ACTIONS**

The host mom and dad can do most of the cooking, but Grandma might want to prepare a family favorite. Children can make a dessert. Grandpa can build the fire in the fireplace for hors d'oeuvres time. An uncle can be assigned the arranging of an original centerpiece. A visiting aunt can make place cards out of construction paper with the children. Then the children can go around to family members and watch each one sign his or her name on a place card. Children can decorate the paper napkins, an older cousin perhaps individualizing them by depicting each family member's interests.

After the food is served and just before digging in, there is a nice silent way to acknowledge a happy family reunion. All can hold hands in a circle around the table. Whoever is sitting at the head of the table squeezes the hand of the person on his left. Then that person squeezes the hand of the person next to her. The squeeze is passed around till it reaches the head of the table. Children enjoy this invisible sign of unity.

BIRTHDAY CARD BOOK

♦ **ACTIVITY**

Making a permanent collection of birthday cards received.

♦ **PROPS**

Colored construction paper, yarn.

♦ **ACTIONS**

If a child has a birthday party, he may receive a lot of cards. When all the fun and games are over and favorite toys have been played with, Granny and the now-three- or four-year-old could make a date for a quiet time together. They could look over each card, read the messages again, and discuss their meaning. Then they could talk about the people who sent them and their relationship to the child.

To make a booklet of the cards, paste each one on a color-coordinated piece of construction paper. Punch holes in the edges of the paper and bind them together with bright yarn. If photos were taken at the party, paste a photo of all the guests on the last page.

GRANDPARENTS AS AUDIENCE

♦ **ACTIVITY**

Showing off new skills and possessions to interested grandparents.

♦ **ACTIONS**

Some grandparents are playmates, others are observers. Both types make a good audience for a child's latest "tricks"—that is, evidences of advancing motor skills such as hurdling the back of the sofa, skipping, or sliding down a slide. Grandparents tend to appear a lot more enthusiastic about these feats than parents because they witness them only occasionally.

One parent prompted her child, "Show Gammy how you can jump down the last two steps." Melanie mounted the two steps and then looked at Gammy to check if, in fact, she was giving this performance her undivided attention. Then she took a deep breath and jumped. She looked up at her grandmother again to drink in the way she was smiling, clapping her hands, and saying, "Whee!" She then strutted off proudly to a soft rug where she could give an exhibition of her nimble somersault.

Grandparents also make excellent listeners for an at-home show-and-tell time. In a special place labeled For Grandma, children can save their artwork, found objects, efforts at writing, or books they can read or have memorized. When relatives visit, children can bring out these treasures one or two at a time. The showing of such miscellany helps break the ice and loosen a shy child's tongue. Listeners can ask leading questions to stimulate the tell aspect of show-and-tell time.

LONG AGO AND FAR AWAY

♦ ACTIVITY

Encouraging grandparents to tell stories about their childhood.

♦ ACTIONS

Invite Nana and Gramps to reminisce about events from their past. "There was the time I got left behind in the park after a nursery school outing . . . There were goldfish in a little pond in my neighbor's backyard . . . We had an old Indian guide when we went fishing in Canada . . . An organ grinder with a monkey used to walk up our street and I put grapes in the monkey's little cold paws."

You need to establish the right atmosphere and crack the reserve. A few leading questions may jog the memory and uncover a host of anecdotes.

What games did you play on the playground in elementary school? Who was your favorite teacher? Would you sing a song your mother tucked you in with? What was *your* grandmother like? Did you ever win a prize? What was the achievement you were proudest of before the age of ten? Did you have a pet? What kind of mischief did you get into when you were little?

If a tape recorder would not make your parents too self-conscious, you could record their stories as they relate them. Such a permanent record of these oral histories would be a great addition to your library.

♦ BENEFIT

Grandparents often delight their own grown-up sons and daughters with these stories more than the little ones they're supposed to be entertaining.

GRANDMOTHER'S ATTIC

♦ ACTIVITY

Examining precious memorabilia and listening to grandparents relate details of their origin.

♦ PROPS

A decorative box, evening purse, or traveling jewel case. Family mementoes.

♦ ACTIONS

When you are going to visit your parents' home or before they come to visit yours, coax them to hunt around in special drawers, closets, or boxes in the attic for souvenirs from the past: an old jackknife, a great-grandfather's ring, a sorority or fraternity pin, medals or trophies that you won in childhood but your parents kept.

Once these items are collected, behind the scenes one or two could be placed in the decorative box. After dinner ceremoniously bring out the box. Explain to your child that you are going to look at and perhaps examine very carefully some delicate, breakable objects that you and Granny value a lot. Create an air of awe and mystery. Let your child open the box and draw out the item to handle under supervision. Let your parents reminisce about the circumstances connected with the acquiring of the object. Then tuck it away. The child can look forward to seeing a different object the following night.

♦ BENEFIT

This experience can teach your child respect for sentimentally valued or fragile objects.

FIGURING OUT KINSHIP

♦ ACTIVITY

Finding a way to explain to little tots that grandparents are a parent's mommy and daddy.

♦ ACTIONS

A young child soon learns that grandparents are adults with a difference. They feel the special warmth of kinship and gradually they understand the unique relationship. Here's the way it happened in one home.

A grandfather put his arm around his grown-up daughter, who was the mother of three-year-old Sheila, and said, "Sheila, this is my little girl."

Sheila giggled at what she thought was another one of Grandpa's jokes. "That's not your little girl," she retorted gleefully. "That's my mommy!"

"No, no," he persisted. "This is *my* little girl."

It turned into a great game. Sheila thought herself rather clever that she didn't let her grandfather convince her of such a ridiculous phenomenon. To her, mommies just couldn't have been little girls.

At a later visit the mother and grandfather acted out the past for the grandchild. "This is the way it used to be, Sheila." Dropping to her knees, the mother looked up at her father and said in a high-pitched voice, "May I have a cookie, Daddy?"

"Not till you've had your lunch, dear," he answered. Sheila watched quizzically, gaining a new level of comprehension.

Of course, old photos tell it all. But tots won't recognize the individual they know in photos taken thirty years ago. Nevertheless, an occasional review of old albums, with accompanying anecdotes, will hold their attention. One day, in a flash, they'll understand.

FAMILY TREE

♦ ACTIVITY

Mounting photographs of grandparents and great-grandparents to illustrate your child's genealogy.

♦ PROPS

Posterboard or large sheet of good-quality drawing paper, felt-tip pen, family photographs.

♦ ACTIONS

When grandparents are coming to visit, ask them to bring pictures of themselves (individual photos, if possible) and their parents. Gather around when you are all assembled and work on this project together.

Draw a tree trunk near the bottom of the posterboard. At the top of the trunk before it arches into branches, glue a picture of your offspring. Above your child's photo and slightly to the right and left of it, place photos of you and your spouse. Above each of you, paste pictures of your sets of parents. Then toward the top of the page, position photos of their parents. Write names under each photo. If you have no pictures of some relatives, draw a square and just write in their names. Now connect the pictures with lines that become the branches of the tree.

◆ BENEFIT

This concrete explanation helps your child grasp how he is related to other family members.

◆ VARIATION

If this project seems too complicated, ask visitors to bring any photos of themselves doing things in their own hometown. A self-appointed committee could assemble these and make an informal photo album of extended-family members. A child who enjoys lettering could write each one's name.

POLAROID WEEKEND

◆ ACTIVITY

During the visit of relatives, taking pictures that are not portraits but candid shots of your child doing things with various family members.

◆ PROPS

Instant camera, flashbulbs, film.

◆ ACTIONS

Make a photographic record of what your child does with each grandparent as the weekend or week-long visit progresses. Show them eating out together, going to the zoo, reading books, cooking together, and playing with a pet or toys. If cousins are on hand, keep snapping shots of their activities, too. Toward the end of the stay, have fun together mounting all these in a scrapbook. Either give it to Grandma to take home with her and cherish, or let your child keep it to remind him of the happy times together.

◆ BENEFIT

Photographs of loving interactions keep a relationship strong during absence from one another.

BIG PILE ON DADDY

◆ ACTIVITY

A physical-contact game to liven up the group get-together, especially suitable for an extroverted daddy or uncle and a bevy of idolizing little nieces and nephews.

♦ ACTION

This game was invented by a family with two older children and one sturdy three-year-old tyke. The original locale was Mom and Dad's big bed. When the older children woke up, they tiptoed to the door of their parents' room. If they were invited in, they shrieked, "Big pile on Daddy!" Then they ran across the room and dove for the bed, flinging themselves on their father. When the baby became a toddler, he joined in the free-for-all.

The game was then extended to the television room. When they were all watching TV and commercials came on, it became customary for someone occasionally to call out all of a sudden, "Big pile on Daddy!" or "Big pile on Mommy!" Then everyone pinned Dad or Mom to the couch or floor, somewhat like football players tackling a quarterback. Sometimes the dog participated by stepping on limbs and barking.

When the toddler became three, he wanted a chance to be underneath, too. So one day the others conspired that someone would call out "Big pile on Dougie!" Then they all carefully braced themselves so as not to put their full weight on him when they covered him with a stack of bodies.

Any family who developed this game could easily include visiting cousins if everyone could be trusted not to be too wild or rough.

PARTY GAMES FOR BIG OR SMALL FAMILIES

♦ ACTIVITY

Using traditional children's party games to cause all the adults and children in a group situation to interact.

♦ ACTIONS

Let down your hair and swing into action. Staid parents are no fun. Little kids love to see Mom, Dad, and grandparents, too, if they will, enter into the spirit of these party games. Adults can be even better playmates for little kids than other kids because they're not as competitive. They pace the game so even the slowest or clumsiest has a good time.

There's no reason the classics such as Ring Around a Rosie, Musical Chairs, Drop the Handkerchief, or Pin the Tail on the Donkey have to wait for somebody's birthday to roll around. They can serve as vehicles to get everybody involved with each other. Here are several more games, so you have enough for future occasions. With slight modification some of these could also be played by a small family or even a parent-child pair.

Potato Race You'll need one or two potatoes and spoons of different sizes. Divide into teams (or forget competition and line up as one team). To enable your child to hold a potato without dropping it too often, give her a big kitchen spoon for ladling. When she improves, give her a soup spoon from your tableware set.

One parent starts carrying a potato from one end of the living room to the other and then transfers the potato to a child's spoon. The child carries the potato across the room and gives it to a second parent or sibling. You can clown it up and drop the potato once in a while to amuse the kids. If you are all one happy team, time yourselves. For the second round, see if you can beat your record.

The Mystery Bag You'll need an opaque bag and several household objects such as a sponge, a spool of thread, measuring spoons, a key, a roll of stamps, a tie clip, a credit card. One of you collects the objects and keeps them out of sight. Put one object in a bag and give it to a child. He reaches his hand into the bag and feels the object. You can teach the properties of objects, using descriptive adjectives as you give him hints. "Is it round on the edges? Is it rough? Is it flat on two sides? That's right, a sponge." If a child cannot guess the object, pass the bag along to the next family member. Include a few bizarre items to challenge the adult player.

Bright Eyes Players can be only one adult and one or two children. You'll need to collect some small, delicate possessions (perhaps from your bedroom drawers) in a little box, such as a pair of manicure scissors, a pendant, a thimble, and a half-dollar. Show them to the children. While they close their eyes, find some interesting hiding places in your bedroom for the objects. Then send off the children with the empty box to find the chosen objects.

Spot the Dot Use circular stickers from the stationery store, the labels with peel-off backs. Stick them onto pieces of furniture, only partially concealed if your child is very young. For an older child, you could stick them under tabletops, on the inside of table legs, on the edge of a cabinet door, or underneath an ashtray. The child or children can peel them off the furniture and bring them back to you. Count before you begin and you will know if they found them all.

Scavenger Hunt Here the adults form a jury for found objects that the children have scavenged for in an attic, a basement, a garage, a backyard, or a shed. After a hunt, children display forgotten curiosities they have uncovered in old cedar chests, the back of the garden shed, some unlabeled boxes. The adult judge or panel of jury members awards each item with a title similar to these: the most beautiful, the most colorful, the most unusual, the most mysterious, the ugliest, the dirtiest, the most useful, the most useless.

Thinker's Treasure Hunt You'll need paper and pencil for written clues and sugar cookies for a prize. You can play this alone with a child or with a coterie of cousins, one of whom reads. In advance, place some sugar cookies on, say, the washing machine. Then think of four or five other spots in the house to plant simple written clues. On each piece of paper, describe in riddle style these spots. For instance, on the first clue, which you should hand to your child, write, "Go to where the guests come into the house." When your child figures out that first clue, she will be at the front door. There she picks up the next clue, which might say, "Go to where the cat fills his tummy." In the cat dish, you plant the next clue. The last clue should read, "Go where dirty clothes get cleaned." This takes your child to her sugar-cookie treasure.

You have to set up all the clues first with your child out of the way. Then start the game when you hand her and any teammates the first clue. A child who figures out riddles is on her way to becoming a problem-solver.

· 12 ·

BEDTIME SOFT TALK

‘ ‘ **B** edtime is special to us,” said one mother. And so it is for many. Tucking a child into bed for the night is a simple ritual with profound overtones.

The early years are the most formative of a child's personality, and the bedtime hour can include some of the most formative moments in those early years. This significant opportunity to impart love, happiness, and guidance should not be wasted. Your style in this intimate exchange leaves lasting impressions on your child. At night parents can be their most noble selves and children can be at their most beguiling. Or, of course, things can go sadly awry. Parents may intend to be gracious and supportive but be stretched beyond their limits of patience by a restless offspring. The challenge of settling down a child peacefully builds character in you.

Sensitivity is required to allot the proper amount of time to the tucking-in process. Circumstances may conspire to give you the feeling you must rush the routine. (It's getting late. You have to go to a meeting. Your spouse's and your dinner is about to be overcooked.) Sometimes you can get away with haste; kids are amazingly tolerant. Other times the effects of a rush job are disastrous. Then the unsettled wee one requires more of your time than you normally give to make up for the initial cursory treatment.

Parents I interviewed reported some distinct advantages to that half-hour preceding lights out. One exhausted mother said, “It's the only time my child will sit still.” Another mom with a literary bent said, “It's the only time I can read to him.” A working mother felt it was her best time to have a real conversation with her three-year-old. A father noticed that his son was more receptive to his words of wisdom then.

Some other parents felt the whole scene—the homecoming of the working parent or parents, the winding down of scheduled events, the drawing together before separation for the night—was especially conducive to the expression of affection. Each family had its own way of conveying their devotion to each other. Some of the ways mentioned are included in the activity called Love Chants. Adults who find it hard to say

136

"I love you" spontaneously find it easier to say at the end of a letter, the end of a phone call, or, in person, at the end of a day. For children, this reassurance of their parents' love is comforting.

Reflecting on many years of raising three children, one father said, "I always lay down next to them at night to talk. Removing the height differential facilitated sharing. They told me things they never would have otherwise." In semidarkness private thoughts are easier to express. The other person doesn't see your feelings surfacing in your eyes or the expression on your face, so you feel protected. This habit of sharing at the sandman hour is most easily started when your child is two, three, and four. Then keeping it up right into the teenage years would be ideal. This way you have a good chance of being your child's confidant, at least some of the time.

◆

SANDMAN ON TIPTOES

◆ ACTIVITY

Lightly touching your child with your fingertips, both to soothe and gently tickle her.

◆ ACTIONS

Start a story about the sandman. "A little old man with a big sack of sand on his back goes to all the little boys and girls every night at bedtime." Start walking two fingers along the crib rail, down a slat, across the blanket until you contact your child's foot. Then run your fingers up her leg and torso. "This little man creeps along your bed and heads in the direction of your face." Tap your way up and down her arm and then across her shoulder to her neck. "He wants to make you sleepy, so he drops a few grains of sand in each eye." Walk your fingers up your daughter's neck and along the edge of her cheek. "When he gets to your forehead, he puts down his bag of sand, reaches in and takes a few grains. Then he sprinkles them in the corner of each eye." Dance your fingers in place on her forehead and then tap the inside corner of each eyelid. "Now this little girl will go sound asleep," he says, "while I scurry away to the next child." Reverse your steps and run your fingers down her body across the bed and up to the crib rail.

LOVE CHANTS

♦ **ACTIVITY**

Expressing affection verbally in the same special way every night.

♦ **ACTIONS**

Parents develop individual ways of expressing their love for their child in a way he can understand. The verbal exchange becomes an imperative part of the bedtime routine. The following are some of the ways to get your deep feelings across.

Jamie was tucked into bed every night with a variation on a Ringo Starr song, "Goodnight, Jamie, goodnight," his dad crooned. With a couple of love pats, his mother delivered the same simple four-line poem for several years.

> *Good night*
> *Sleep tight*
> *Pleasant dreams*
> *And I love you.*

Sarah and her mother had a boisterously loving time adding different adverbs to those three words *I love you.*

"I love you."

"I love you more."

"I love you most."

"I love you really."

"I love you honestly."

"I love you *dishonestly.*" Sarah liked to crack a joke and get rambunctiously rebuked.

"Oh no, that's not true, you little rascal!"

Stephanie and her father tried to outdo each other in their declarations of affection.

"I love you a spoonful."

"I love you a cupful."

"I love you a bucketful."

"I love you a wagon-full."

"I love you a freight-train-full."

Kent and his mother also competed in the amount of love each felt for the other.

"How much do you love me?"

"I love you way up to here." Kent held his arms up straight.

"Well, I love you way up to the top of the room."

"I love you up to the roof of the house."

"Hey, I love you up to the top of the trees."
"That's nothing. I love you up to the top of the Empire State Building."
"I love you way up to the clouds."
"I love you way up to the sky."
"I love you to the stars, planets, and outer space."
"I love you to infinity."
That was usually considered enough.

Tina, the youngest child in a big happy family, wrapped up what she'd been hearing around the house in the following words, which she repeated in a singsong voice:

> I love you
> And you love me
> And everybody
> Loves their "chothers."

The last line was her effort to say everybody "loves each other." The family liked her chant, and it became a family motto cherished by the older children as well.

PEACEFUL LULLABIES

♦ ACTIVITY

Singing lullabies to establish an atmosphere of serenity and, hopefully, to *lull* your child to sleep.

♦ ACTIONS

As a new parent, you may have had to research at the library or buy a children's songbook to refresh your mind with the words and tunes of traditional lullabies. As your child gets older, you might like to expand your repertoire. Favorite hymns and spirituals make excellent lullabies for three- and four-year-olds. Folk songs such as "Michael, Row the Boat Ashore" and old summer-camp songs such as "Peace, I ask of thee, O river," impart the desired mood of tranquillity.

Remember, one song may not always do the trick. A child who is fearful, troubled, overtired, angry, or not feeling well could easily enjoy five or ten gentle melodies. If you have a rocking chair, you could rock your child as you sing. There's nothing wrong with humming if you don't know all the words to a song.

One mother made up songs about things her daughter had done

that day and about what she was going to do the next day. She sang the words to a familiar tune such as "Twinkle, Twinkle, Little Star."

Another mother made up songs using the names of relatives, friends, immediate family members, and pets. The words were sometimes as simple as singing a goodnight to each of them. Occasionally the parent sang about where they lived or the things they did.

"TALK 'BOUT LOVELY DAY"

◆ ACTIVITY

Talking over your child's day—a habit well worth initiating and preserving even into the teenage years.

◆ ACTIONS

The title of this activity came from the comment of a just-two-year-old named Shelley. Her mother, a confirmed optimist, was accustomed to reviewing the highlights of her toddler's day, accentuating the positive. After the grooming preliminaries were over and Shelley was under the covers, her mother would open with, "Shall we talk about your lovely day now?" When Shelley began speaking in full sentences, she issued an imperial command each night, "Talk 'bout lovely day." She relished a detailed account of significant happenings.

You have an ideal opportunity to communicate deeply with your child at day's end, when you are alone together in the semidarkness. You can review the pleasant events of the day and impart your own sage interpretation of those that were not pleasant. The mental climate is conducive to sharing your basic values.

You can start this nightly talk even at age eighteen months to two years. The child has a fast-developing memory at this stage, and even though she doesn't talk very much, she can understand a great deal.

To enhance a child's capacity to reflect back on her activities, you must be with her during part of the day and use words to describe her activities when she's engaged in them. She hears the vocabulary pertinent to the activities; then at night your words will evoke images in her mind of the day's experiences.

Suppose one day your child gives her doll a bath. Notice out loud what is happening. "You want to fill the dishpan with water. Not too hot. You're putting Dolly in so gently. She likes her bath. Wow, you're washing her all over. Is she splashing? Yes, she's getting you wet. Now wrap her in a towel. Hmmm, cozy, clean."

The same night at tuck-in time, you say, "Remember when you put your dolly in the bath? You washed her all over. How she splashed! Then you wrapped her in a towel." You can tell your two-year-old is recalling those moments with you by the alert look in her eyes and the animated expression on her face.

If your child is at a day-care center or in a family day-care situation, you want to find out how his day went. One working mother posed these questions regularly, but not all of them on one night:

"What made you happy today?"

"What made you sad today?"

"Who was your friend at school today?"

"Did you do anything today that you don't want to do again?"

"What do you want to do tomorrow?"

"What did you like most about your day?"

"What do you wish didn't happen today?"

◆ BENEFIT

Bedside chats help you keep track of your child's evolving feelings and boost morale when it's needed.

GETTING THE ROUTINE DOWN PAT

◆ ACTIVITY

Developing appropriate bedtime rituals for each age of your child.

◆ PROPS

Typing paper, felt-tip pen, gold stars or self-sticking shapes.

◆ ACTIONS

Two-year-olds can be very conservative. They prefer you to get them ready for bed according to a prescribed pattern that does not deviate from night to night. They get undressed, go to the bathroom one more time, hop into bed. Then you are to pull down the shades, put out the light, sit beside the bed, talk, say a prayer, and get the first drink of water. It's a tragedy if you turn off the light before you draw the shades or tuck in the blanket in a slightly different way from the usual. This precision and predictability in the series of events leading up to sleep helps children feel settled.

Part of one little girl's ritual was tucking in her doll every night, covering her up completely (with the blanket over the doll's face). Then the child leaned back in the rocking chair and sang to the doll. Any intrusion from other family members was extremely upsetting. Take your cues from your child and let her orchestrate the scenario to some extent.

For older kids, bedtime is not quite so sacrosanct. But they still enjoy an orderly routine. You could make a gold-star chart with drawings or words that show the sequence of events. This helps them become more independent, as at this age they can do some of the things listed alone, such as pick up toys, take off clothes, brush teeth.

Create the list together, so the child has some of his wishes, however whimsical, alongside yours. Throw in some things like "laugh a little," "hug a lot." Include on the chart the days of the week and let your child check a box beside each chore or paste in a gold star when done. (You could photocopy your chart so you have a fresh sheet for each new week.) This might be tedious if perpetuated over a period of months, but it's a fun way to start off a stage of increasing maturity when your child turns three and a half.

THE STORYTELLER'S ART

◆ Activity

Telling bedtime stories you make up as you go along or recounting anecdotes from your own childhood.

◆ ACTIONS

Making up a story is not as hard as you might think. Children are so eager to have you sit close and linger at their bedside that the simplest story will satisfy. Just plunge in courageously and you'll be surprised how ideas for a plot will develop as you go along. You don't have to know the ending when you begin. A character you talk about every night will acquire more and more dimensions. You'll end up thinking you've missed your career as a children's book writer.

You might start by inventing some adventures for your child's favorite stuffed animal or doll. Clyde had a teddy bear called Booper. His father told a new story about Booper every night. Sometimes he wandered around the neighborhood getting into mischief. Sometimes he went on business trips with Daddy and ate in posh restaurants. Sometimes he went fishing or tricycling with Clyde.

One dad made up a story about a family of Labrador retrievers. One was a naughty puppy, another a good puppy. Often this parent would describe his child's activities from the dogs' point of view.

A mother, who was intrigued with the life of the jet set, made up a series of stories about a little boy and his sister who lived on their parents' yacht.

Accounts of your own childhood can be a special treat: your first visit to the circus, a plane trip alone, a strange neighbor, the pet you cared for. Also stories about experiences you had when you were a teenager or in your twenties can be fascinating to a four-year-old. Think about your summer jobs, your time in the army, moving from one place to another, going off to college, traveling. Your child will be able to relate to some aspects of these experiences and comprehend the drama, excitement, fun, or happiness they gave you.

♦ BENEFIT

Stories with realistic details widen your child's horizons, build vocabulary, and perhaps help you get across your values.

TWO STORYTELLERS

♦ ACTIVITY

Letting your child tell part of a story so that you join forces in spinning a yarn.

♦ ACTIONS

After you've become an old hand at storytelling as described in the previous activity, give your child the idea that she can join in, too. The first time you narrate as usual, but then, at the climax, have your child guess the ending. "Yes," you could exclaim, "exactly what I was going to say." Or, "I like that ending. It's different from the one I had in mind."

As your child gets used to the idea of contributing, you can take turns throughout the whole story. Your child realizes that stories don't come ready-made but they can be worked on and shaped at will.

She may want to start a story one night. If she's searching for a subject, you might remind her of an unusual person you both saw recently, or an incident at the zoo, or a toy she admired in a toy-shop window. She could build her story around any of these observations and her feelings about them.

One little boy and his dad took turns being the storyteller at bedtime. Each evening it was to be the boy's turn, he looked forward to it so eagerly that he spent much of the day planning his tale.

♦ **BENEFIT**

The invitation to participate in storytelling stimulates imagination and exercises the ability to associate freely.

HEART TO HEART

♦ **ACTIVITY**

Getting close physically and mentally to your child in order to understand and help him with his innermost feelings.

♦ **ACTIONS**

Bedtime is the part of the day when children are most likely to reveal their private thoughts. Your proximity, your loving gentleness, and the darkened room make them feel comfortable about sharing their fears and desires.

Parents who had twins to tuck in at the same time made a habit of whispering their good-nights. The dad leaned over each one individually, nuzzled cheek to cheek, and carried on a whispered conversation. The mom did the same. So did the live-in caregiver. That way messages that each child had for either parent or caregiver were kept private. Neither the other twin nor the other parent could overhear the whispered words.

In another home a couple who had children close in age put them to bed a half-hour apart. The individual tuck-in gave each one a sense of the importance of his own identity.

One father was disappointed that at night his son didn't manage to tell him much about his day. The four-year-old couldn't seem to remember what he'd done. The dad realized that he had always been vague about his own day at the office, thinking his life was beyond the child's comprehension. He found ways to describe his work that were comprehensible to his son. "I talked on the telephone to someone in France. I wrote a letter to a man I never met. I took a taxi to a meeting at a bank." In addition, he began slipping into the child's bed for the relating of these daily events. The boy began to get the idea of sharing news and soon he followed his dad's example.

READ ME A STORY

♦ **ACTIVITY**

Sharing examples of the best in children's literature and reading them with enthusiasm.

♦ **ACTIONS**

Reading a bedtime story must be one of the most common of all parenting activities. But how many people take the trouble to make it a truly rewarding experience—to the parent as well as the child. Don't cheat yourself of the fun of sharing quality books because you don't take the time to track them down. Browse in your library every week. Thumb through volumes in the children's book section of local bookstores. Find books with fine artwork, good writing style, and thoughtful content.

Sometimes stories are humorous and bring a smile to your face as well as giving your child the giggles. Sometimes you find yourself shedding a sentimental tear. Together with your child, you're learning, laughing, and wondering about life. Shake your apathy and timidity and read with dramatic expression. In your effort to put across a story to your audience of one, you lose yourself and your cares a little, and that's therapeutic at the end of a busy day.

Getting into a children's book, you can get out of the adults' mind set. You enter a world of the artist and author's creating. These professionals are sensitive to what is appealing to children, so they help you tune in to your child's wave length. Sometimes they articulately convey attitudes and values that you would like very much to share with your child. Reading these books aloud puts the words in your mouth.

Stories about children and grown-ups or about animals who behave and talk like people sometimes tell kids how to be happy, good, kind, brave, tolerant, and considerate. You, too, may learn a new approach to parenting from seeing how the parent characters in a story treat the children characters.

Parents are often surprised at the urgent desire for a repeat reading. A child can enjoy a story over and over again. He takes pleasure in his familiarity with the characters and the plot, and perhaps he assimilates some details he didn't take in before. Parents can balance this penchant for the familiar by establishing a rule such as, "Every Wednesday evening we start a new book."

It is a good idea to start with books well before your child's second birthday. For a child of two, you are still "talking" a book rather than reading it word for word. You are pointing to pictures and labeling them. You're responding to your child's pointing and describing what she is noticing. You're asking questions, such as "Where is the fairy hiding now?" If she wriggles restlessly, perhaps you haven't adapted your presentation of the book to her level of comprehension. Or maybe the book itself is not appropriate. You may need practice at matching the book to the child. When the match is a perfect fit, storytime is magical.

Books help the older preschooler get to know his world. Don't miss the children's picture dictionaries, children's encyclopedias, and nonfiction knowledge books. Illustrations show what things are, what things are called, and how things work. (You often learn things you never knew before.) Your child is building a vocabulary of concepts as well as of words. While his actual experiences are still centered in the home, he can learn about life beyond those four walls through books.

Every once in a while you may censor stories as you read them, if you feel the material includes elements of cruelty, sadness, or references to loss or death that wouldn't be appropriate for your child at this time in her life. If you don't censor, the mischief or woes of a character might become the basis for a discussion in which you impart your philosophy of life in simple terms.

If your current bedtime reading to your child is putting *you* to sleep, do some active research! Discover the books that will make "read me a story" time a memorable experience for you and your little bookworm.

· 13 ·

COMMUNICATING FEELINGS

T his chapter may be good to turn to when negative feelings are spoiling your quality time.

The most important attitude to encourage in your child is self-esteem. One couple told me, "We tell our kids every day we love them. We all need so much love. None of us can ever get enough of it. We explain even when we punish them that it's because we care about them and care that they do the right thing."

Your face is a mirror in which your child sees how acceptable and lovable he is. Your facial expressions, gestures, words, and acts help establish a feeling of self-worth. The first three activities in this chapter suggest ways of showing affection. How openly a person expresses affection is usually a result of the family's style. Some families are very spontaneous and demonstrative in their expression of love; others are more reserved. Your child will probably adopt your style, whatever it is.

Often silence can speak as loudly as words. Your child lives, to some extent, in your mental atmosphere. If you are moody, she may be. If you are fearful, she may be. If you are uptight, she may be. A young child is very sensitive to your frame of mind. Masaru Ibuka, the author of *Kindergarten Is Too Late* (Fireside, Simon and Schuster, 1977), wrote, "The virus in a mother called 'anxiety' is far more contagious and powerful than a cold."

If you want your child to be happy, you must express joy. If you want your child to be fearless, you must express courage. Many parents strive to lift their own spirits and overcome character flaws in order to set a better example for their children. "I try extra hard to be upbeat in my thinking to keep my child from being cranky or sulky," one mother said.

Your child may be trying to convey certain feelings to you but not doing so clearly. Some activities that follow will help you figure out what's going on inside that little head.

One goal most parents have in common is to teach their children to be considerate of other people's feelings. Two of the activities are designed to help children become aware of the range of feelings experienced by others they encounter.

148

As kids reach the ages of two, three, or four, they may start to talk back and express turbulent emotions. Parents often find themselves at a loss as to how to respond. Some of the activities will give you ideas on how to listen to these feelings and respond in a constructive way. In a home in which there had been a lot of discord, a parent read a book about communication skills with kids. Her oldest child later complimented her: "Mommy, since you've read that book on how to be nice to children, you are so good!"

◆

THREE SQUEEZES

◆ ACTIVITY

Finding quiet ways to say "I love you."

◆ ACTIONS

Lots of parent-child games are handed down from one generation to the next. The fact that Mommy used to play a certain game when she was little may help a game take hold. In one family a mother walking down a street with her daughter remembered a special way *her* mother used to express affection. She introduced the game.

"Do you know, Katie, when I was a little girl, my mommy had a secret way of saying *I love you?* Nobody around us could tell she was saying it. Can you guess what she did? Well, we'd be holding hands like this as we walked along. Then she would squeeze my hand three times, like this—one, two, three. That would mean *I . . . love . . . you,* one squeeze for each of those three little words. So now, if *ever* you want to tell me that, just squeeze my hand three times and I'll know exactly what you mean. It'll be a secret signal just between us."

From that moment on Katie and her mother surprised each other often with the three squeezes. Each kept silent but smiled a knowing smile.

◆ BENEFIT

There are nonverbal ways to help a child feel lovable and loved.

AN "IGGABIGGABOO"

◆ ACTIVITY

Finding high-spirited ways to say "I love you."

♦ ACTIONS

The previous activity describes a silent and subtle way of expressing affection. There are also rambunctious ways to show kids you're nutty about them. Daddies seem to specialize in these.

Jonathan's father, when playing tag or hide-and-go-seek with his three-and-a-half-year-old, would cry out, "I'm going to catch you and give you an iggabiggaboo!" He then would capture his wriggling son and juicily kiss his tummy while snorting, growling, and enfolding him.

Humor often keeps the communication of affection from becoming maudlin. Susie's good-night kisses progressed from delicate pecks to vociferous smacks. Her mother protested at intervals, "You're kissing me so hard, you're pushing me off the bed." Mother finally fell off, accompanied by a trill of Susie's giggles.

♦ BENEFIT

Roughhousing is sometimes a means of communicating affection.

SEALED WITH A KISS

♦ ACTIVITY

Expressing feelings through written messages or drawings.

♦ PROPS

Large manila envelopes, pencils, pads.

♦ ACTIONS

We all love to get mail, even interfamily memos. Explain to your children that you can communicate with each other through the written word as well as the spoken word. Your children can decorate large envelopes and label them with each person's name. There should be individual envelopes for Mom and Dad on their door and separate envelopes on the door to a room children share. Tack up these "mailboxes" so the flap can be lifted to insert notes. Keep pencils and pads handy.

Help your child compose a brief letter to the spouse who may be coming home late tonight. Your child can dictate it to you if he doesn't write, and then you can read it back. Let him pop it into the right envelope. If a parent is leaving before a child gets up, he can leave a note in the child's envelope. This can later be read to the child after she pulls it out.

"Letters" don't have to be composed of words. A child who is learning to write his name can make a drawing and then sign his name underneath. This can be posted in an envelope. Or your child may draw wavy lines to represent script and then sign her name. When you unfold the note and "read" it, you can ask your child to tell you what it says. Explain that he can use an X to mean a kiss and a circle to mean a hug.

One year after February 14 had come and gone, a family began sending each other "anytime valentines." The dictionary defines a *valentine* as "a piece of writing . . . expressing praise or affection for something." To reinforce her child's good behavior, the mother would praise in print what the child did right.

In another family the older child sent letters of apology when he couldn't manage to say "I'm sorry" face to face. One day the four-year-old sister wrote several pages of little wavy lines after she'd been scolded for being naughty. She knew that her mother would understand that it was an eloquent apology.

Simple expressions of thanks can be dropped in these mailboxes, cultivating early the importance of appreciating the favors another family member does.

♦ BENEFIT

Deep feelings can sometimes find their way into the open more easily through the written rather than the spoken word.

PICTURES WORTH A THOUSAND WORDS

♦ ACTIVITY

Looking at sensitive illustrations or photographs of people and talking about the feelings revealed in their faces.

♦ PROPS

Children's storybooks illustrated by artists who try to convey the inner feelings of characters (perhaps the stories focus on relationships).

Books of beautiful photographs such as the Edward Steichen classic *The Family of Man* (Simon & Schuster, 1955; NAL paperback). Photography books portraying just children, just the elderly, or people from a particular country or region.

Books from the children's section of your library written purposely to teach children about feelings. Illustrations usually portray a variety of emotions quite clearly.

Book of reproductions of fine-art paintings that include portraits.

♦ ACTIONS

Sometimes children listening to you read a story, say, about Peter

Pan, will look at the accompanying drawing and ask, "Why is the Indian angry?" Rather than dodging the question and continuing the story, explore some reasons out loud. "Maybe he's afraid of Peter Pan. Maybe he's jealous that Wendy is looking after Peter Pan. Maybe he wants to scare Peter Pan." Finishing the chapter in one sitting is not nearly so important as exploring the feelings of characters if your child indicates some curiosity about them—or even if he doesn't. Perhaps an emotion a character is feeling is similar to a mood your child has been in lately. You might point out the similarity.

When you are browsing through a book of photographs taken by a professional photographer, you can ask questions that will get your child wondering and perhaps making up a story on her own. Photographs usually have no caption to tell you why the child or adult looks sad or happy. Ask, "Can you tell me a story about this little boy?" or "Why do you think such a big tear is rolling down her cheek?"

♦ BENEFIT

Through pondering the expression on people's faces, your child will begin to consider the feelings of others.

FEELINGS BELOW THE SURFACE

♦ ACTIVITY

Being interested in your child's feelings, listening when these are expressed, and accepting them in an understanding way.

♦ ACTIONS

That little children have deep feelings and are acutely aware of them was revealed to one mother in the following way. Her little girl, home with the chicken pox, wanted to dress up in her tutu. Her mother, realizing that the spots would show all the more in the brief outfit and disturb her youngster, explained why she wouldn't let her don the costume. The child was very disappointed but complied. Later this four-year-old's underlying respect for her mother surfaced. She told her, "Deep down, I knew you were right." Her mother realized her daughter must have heard her use this expression "deep down." She was pleased the little girl was learning that it was natural to have deep feelings and share them.

Of course, the deep feelings won't all be positive ones. Sometimes they will be negative reactions to what parents are saying and doing. When Harvard researchers were studying well-developing children, they noticed these preschoolers all were able and willing to tell their parents when they felt annoyed by them. They were not overawed by their elders. They were not too immature or too inarticulate to give voice to protests in a respectful way.

A child going on three told her mother, "I don't like when guests are here for you to say 'my high chair.'" The child was growing up enough to feel embarrassed about her raised chair. Another increasingly independent miss asked her mother, "Do you think a four-year-old does need help?"

"On some things," the mother responded.

"No. On no things!" the little girl adamantly retorted.

Parents have to be relaxed enough to let children express their negative feelings. If adults come down too hard on a childish expression of irritation, they will have kids who clam up and are afraid to express themselves.

A direct question to a child, without overtones of criticism, may help a child to describe what's going on inside. A loving father asked his daughter, "Why do you suck your thumb when you watch TV?" His simple question drew a simple answer. "If I don't suck my fumb, then I don't cozy up." It was such an honest answer, he couldn't bear to dissuade her from her habit.

ROLE SWITCH

♦ ACTIVITY

Acting out everyday events of life, your child role-playing you and you role-playing your child, in order to communicate feelings.

♦ ACTIONS

In this activity your child pretends to be you, and you pretend to be him. Let him suggest a situation for the two of you to act out. When your child starts imitating your voice and mannerisms, you may find it quite revealing. You will hear how you sound to your child in various situations. When you pretend to be your child, he can hear and see himself from a new perspective—yours. It may be his first lesson in learning the other person's point of view.

A child with a fertile imagination will be stage director for the pretend sequence. She might say, "I'm washing the dishes, and you're playing on the floor." One mother who kept the dialog going, talking as much like a child as she could, began to hear her child speaking in grown-up tones that were tense, cold, and negative. She wondered how often she sounded that way to her child. Her son said, "I'm busy. Go play with your toys," and later, "I'm in a hurry. Get going." Finally he wagged his finger at her and said, "When I tell you to do something, I expect you to do it." For the first time she felt what it must be like to be a little child with a big adult addressing you that way.

Of course, you also discover how nice you can sometimes sound! One mother was tucked into bed for a nap by her child. He spoke gently, hummed a tune, caressed her cheek until she felt quite moved by his tenderness.

If your child is enjoying these pretend scenarios, you might use such an occasion to get across a point regarding the difficulty a non-cooperative child is to a parent. For instance, a mother role-playing her child while her child pretended to be undressing her for bed acted stubborn. The mother pouted and kicked when her daughter tried to pull off her shoes. She jerked herself away when the little girl reached for her zipper. For a moment the child was nonplussed. Then the light dawned. She realized what a problem she had previously been to her mother by not holding still.

Sometimes a humorous approach helps and causes a problem to be self-seen. Two mothers vivaciously acted out the nuisance their children had been in the car on the way home from an outing. "I want to sit next to the window." "No, I want to." They exaggerated the squabble, pushing each other around. The children giggled at the two mothers behaving so childishly. During the next outing the kids were on their best behavior.

Sometimes a child introduces into a make-believe situation a real problem he is facing in his daily life. In Danny's case, he offered a solution at the same time. He tucked in his mother (who was lying on a couch pretending to be Danny). As he turned off the light he said, "I'm going out now. If you get scared of the dark, you can sleep in my bed." This was satisfactory solution number one. (Mother took note.) The next time they played the same scene, Danny offered solution number two: "I'm going out now. I have to get Daddy to stay with you because you're afraid of ghosts." If a child introduces a problem into a pretend game without offering a solution, it could still be a way of coping. He may be getting ready to solve it in real life. You could act out some solutions you would recommend.

Pretend dialogue can be not only charming but very informative, helping a parent discern a child's current concerns. A child, wanting to save face, might hesitate to bring up a fear in ordinary conversation. The child feels freer about airing a concern when she is in the guise of an adult or one of her playmates.

Jessica's mother found out she could practically reconstruct the scene in her daughter's nursery school on any given morning by playing pretend nursery school in the afternoon. Jessica played the role of one of her classmates, and her mother played Jessica. She found out the quality of that day's interactions and whether her daughter felt hurt or liked by classmates.

Sometimes this mother stayed as herself and Jessica played Miss Rose, the teacher. One day the mother pretended to call up Miss Rose. "My daughter, Jessica, seems upset this afternoon. Was everything okay at school?" Talking for Miss Rose, Jessica gave her mom an earful.

"USE YOUR WORDS"

♦ ACTIVITY

Encouraging your child to talk about a problem rather than pout, sob, sulk, or whine.

♦ ACTIONS

Two-, three-, and four-year-olds love the sound of their own voice. They relish their newfound capacity to talk. Will she ever stop talking? you sometimes ask yourself. However, when your child is upset she often reverts to nonverbal behavior—crying, looking sad or surly, kicking or hitting.

One parent, realizing how verbal his daughter usually was and how comfortable she was being verbal, began to say every time she entered the room crying, "Now, Caroline, use your words. Can you tell me what happened?" Caroline's efforts to describe the cause of the woe usually brought the crying to a halt.

With the younger brother, the father tried the same approach: "I cannot understand you when your thumb is in your mouth or when you're whining. And I want to understand. Use your words."

If you get the gist of the problem, you can paraphrase what you think your child has said. "You wish you had more bright shiny pennies."

If you state the problem correctly, that may bring your child some relief. She's gotten her message across. If you've misinterpreted her blubbering, her further efforts to explain may help calm her down. Finally you see. "Oh, so you've dropped those new pennies and they've rolled out of sight. You must be afraid you've lost them for good." When you've articulated the problem and her reaction to it, your child feels comforted. She has an advocate in you.

♦ **BENEFIT**

When problems get described in words, they're half licked.

SOMEONE UNDERSTANDS

♦ **ACTIVITY**

Listening sympathetically to your child when he's expressing negative emotions and acknowledging his feelings.

♦ **ACTIONS**

In recent years there have been a number of books for parents on communication skills. One of the skills often described is how to respond effectively when kids indicate they are feeling angry, scared, glum, or resentful. Most parents feel very uncomfortable when their kids are not being positive, and they hasten to talk them out of those feelings. They start lecturing their kids, or advising, warning, pitying, or reassuring them; in short, denying or deploring the feelings they've just expressed. This causes friction to build.

A parent's denial of a child's feeling tends to turn a conversation into an argument. But a sympathetic acknowledgment helps a child off-load the negative feeling and move into a problem-solving mode of thought. Yes, even at three and four years of age.

For instance, "I hate mashed potatoes," a four-year-old said, plonking her fork on the table loudly.

The father wanted to respond, "No, you don't. You're just not hungry today."

The child then would have felt annoyed at this disregard of her statement and might have said, "I am too hungry, and these potatoes are yukky!"

Instead this father tried to paraphrase his child's feeling: "To you the taste of mashed potatoes is not good." The child felt her views were heard and accepted. This acknowledgment softened the negativity. The little girl, calmed by her father's paraphrase of her feeling, noticed, "The mashed potatoes are cold." He offered to warm them up, and the problem was solved.

The parenting books urge an empathetic response to distressed kids. *Empathy,* according to Webster's dictionary, is "the capacity for participating in another's feelings." If you make even a one-word remark or show by a nod or a pat on the arm that you understand how your kid is feeling, your child will be relieved.

"Meg keeps pushing over my tower," said Steve.

"Oh," said Dad, looking right at Steve.

"Every time I build one up, she starts crawling toward it."

"Hmmm," said Dad, looking again at Steve and walking over to the fallen blocks. "You've got a problem."

When Steve felt his dad understood, he stopped focusing on his resentment toward his baby sister. A brighter attitude helped him think clearly. "I'm going to take all my blocks into my bedroom and build my towers there."

If that dad had tried to talk his child out of his resentment by preaching, "You should share your blocks," or "You shouldn't feel mad; your sister doesn't know any better," he would have thrown up roadblocks to communication. What a kid wants most is someone who looks at him thoughtfully, listens to his problem, recognizes what he is experiencing, and acknowledges his discomfort by a few words, a gesture, or an act.

Try practicing empathetic responses to your child when she moans and groans over a problem. For more enlightenment on how to do this, you might read *Parent Effectiveness Training* by Thomas Gordon (McKay, 1970) and *How to Talk So Kids Will Listen and Listen So Kids Will Talk* by Adele Faber and Elaine Mazlish (Rawson Wade, 1980; Avon Books, 1980).

EMOTIONS DESCRIBED

♦ ACTIVITY

Figuring out the feeling behind a child's emotional outpouring and describing it in a few words that show you understand.

♦ ACTIONS

Naturally kids have negative feelings some of the time, and parents naturally want to help dissolve them. They try distracting little kids from a concern by diverting their attention or jollying them up. They try covering up an unhappy feeling by describing an opposite happy feeling. Or they give logical reasons for why a child shouldn't feel the way she does.

These normal reactions seem to aggravate the woe. Popular books on parent-child communications (see previous activity for titles) suggest identifying out loud the feeling underlying your child's distress.

When Melissa sobbed, "I don't want to go to Jeffrey's party," her mother discerned the feeling that prompted her remark. She reflected it back to her. "Sounds like you're feeling a little shy about being with a big group of kids."

A parent's instinct might be to say, "That's silly, he's your best friend," or "Nonsense, you'll have a great time." But there's a more constructive type of response: decoding the child's anguished comment by detecting the feeling behind it and giving it a name.

Melissa got the idea that her mother understood it was okay to feel shy about a party. Instead of a power struggle developing, with the mother coaxing and Melissa resisting, Melissa calmed down. She was able to see her own specific concern more clearly. "Maybe I'll be the only girl there." Her mother again clarified the feeling. "You might feel left out."

The mother, having drawn out the child with empathetic remarks, made an intelligent move. "I'll call Jeffrey's mother and find out who's invited." The episode ended when Melissa found out two other girls were coming.

Parenting books dealing with communication skills give many examples of the harmonizing results that occur when a parent puts into words for a child the very feeling churning around inside him. The adult isn't necessarily agreeing with the concern, but she is teaching the child about human emotions and indicating that they are understandable and can be coped with.

Give yourself some practice at responding to your child's whines and pouts with a simple labeling of the probable emotion within. If you guess wrong, guess again. Your interest and effort to understand will go a long way toward assuaging your child's worry. You will also free her to engage in some problem-solving of her own.

· 14 ·

SHARING SOCIAL, MORAL, AND SPIRITUAL VALUES

P arents sense in their young child a need to form social, moral, and spiritual values. Little ones want to know how to get along with others. They want to do the right thing. Feeling part of a larger whole, feeling a spiritual oneness, can help them overcome loneliness, insecurity, and irrational fears.

When children look to parents for guidance in these areas, parents often realize they must first clarify their own views on the fundamental issues of life. What do they believe? What ideals do they want to transmit to their offspring? Then how do they go about transmitting them? The deep search our children cause us to conduct often benefits our own inner psyche.

A family therapist, Virginia Satir, says in her book *Peoplemaking* (Science & Behavior, 1972; paper 1975) that "the essential learnings" of every child fall into several categories: what parents teach a child about herself, others, the world, and God. Now, when your child is two, three, and four, is the time to start thinking actively about your input on these subjects.

Children seem to welcome rules and a system of beliefs. However, any strictness on your part should be interwoven with warmth. If you adhere to a strong code of ethics, share it with your child, translating it into simple terms he can understand. Your rewards for a strong stand may come later. One teenager said to her mother, "When I get confused and troubled about what I'm doing, I get back on the track—what you taught me, Mom. But you know, some of my friends have no track to get back on."

Value sharing is something you can't help but do all the time. What you consider important in attitudes and relationships shows up in the minutiae of daily life. Children absorb a sense of your priorities even if you don't verbalize them.

You may want to become more conscious of how you are conducting your daily transactions during this most formative period of your child's life. You may want to make sure you are acting in accord with your deepest convictions. You and your spouse can consciously decide on some values you agree have high priority and strive to impart these to your child.

No matter how busy you are, try to set a time for talking about deep and serious subjects with your child. You can create a climate for this by scheduling time for an after-dinner walk on a summer evening or during a rocking-chair cuddle. Celebrating religious holidays may ease you into a discussion. You can try to relate the great mystical teachings—whichever ones you adhere to—to your child's everyday life. Attendance at church or synagogue can lead to opportunities to clarify values after the service or religious education class. But in these days of overscheduled family lives, earnest effort will have to be made to set aside brief quiet times for nourishing innate spiritual hunger.

At night, with an older preschooler, you might think back on the day together. Did some problems arise that you could talk about? Did one of you lose your temper, shout, hit, or use a harsh word? Talking about it in retrospect, not during the heated moment, is quite constructive. When emotions have subsided, you can agree on alternative ways of handling the situation and resolve to do better tomorrow. A Bible verse or inspirational poem could be introduced to show your child that there are principles to which we try to conform our everyday words and acts.

If you think, I'm not sure I like the values I was brought up on, I'm going to let my child make up her own mind about spiritual things when she grows up, you are actually imparting a strong value. It is probably a value of noncommitment, treading water, a wait-and-see attitude.

If you avoid talking about values either because you haven't made up your own minds as to what you believe or because you find it hard to express your thoughts in words, you are still communicating a position. You are saying, "Moral standards or spiritual qualities are not subjects to bring out in the open, examine, and establish a consensus of thought on."

The following activities may spur you to give some special thought to your child's moral and spiritual education. Views on such a subject vary widely, of course, so the content of these activities may not be in accord with your principles. However, they may serve to get you started on a plan of your own whereby you can nourish the inmost self of your child.

In order to simplify a complex subject, a variety of values have been divided into three categories: social, moral, and spiritual. Such lines of demarcation are blurry, as some social values might be considered moral ones, and some moral values might be considered a direct outcome of your commitment to spiritual things. The division is just to help you focus on one cluster of similar values at a time.

♦

TOP TEN SOCIAL VALUES

◆ ACTIVITY

Thinking over what social values you prize and imparting them to your child.

◆ SHARING

Have you consciously focused on some traits you would like to see underlie your child's interactions with others? Many parents I interviewed were striving to cultivate certain attitudes in their kids. Here are the qualities of character mentioned most often as their objectives; you can use them as a checklist. Perhaps there are certain ones you haven't thought of trying to bring out in your child.

> Be kind.
> Share and take turns.
> Sympathize with others.
> Be gentle and patient with younger children, in particular, one's siblings.
> Talk it out, work it out, if there's a squabble.
> Understand how others feel.
> Be considerate of Mom and Dad.
> Get along with others.
> Stick up for yourself.
> Be a good host or hostess when playmates visit.

Pick just one of these to work on at a time. Perhaps for a week you could give little morning and evening pep talks explaining one of the qualities and how your child can exercise it in his daily round.

Most parents seem to realize the necessity of modeling these qualities themselves. They recognize that a good example is the best teacher. New parents often start working on some long-neglected character flaws of their own in order to demonstrate the behavior they are expecting of their child.

They verbalize often about right attitudes as their children are mingling with others. They try to head off disagreements during play. But if one occurs, they find their children more receptive to talks about conduct a little time after the incident has taken place than in the middle of it. With two-year-olds who have short memories, correcting, comforting, or mood changing has to be done on the spot.

THE MORAL TOP TEN

♦ ACTIVITY

Pondering the moral values you wish to implant in your child's character and starting to instill them.

♦ SHARING

A lot of earnest parents realize the early years are extremely formative ones. Some research shows that personality is largely established even by age three. Parents I interviewed indicated that they felt their role was largely one of character building. During all the minor trials and tribulations of their children's lives, they cheered them on with both praise and admonition. Here are some of the moral qualities they sought to inculcate:

> Be good.
> Do unto others as you would have them do unto you.
> Be brave.
> Be honest; keep your word.
> Try.
> Keep trying.
> Help make your home a happy place.
> Be fair.
> Help others who are upset.
> Be cheerful; be positive.

Don't feel your child is too young to comprehend such attitudes to some degree. Or don't abdicate your present responsibility to shape character because you hope that after he gets through a particular stage of development he'll be more tractable. It's important not to underestimate the receptivity of the preschooler. Even at the age of two and three your child can glimpse the meaning of these virtuous qualities and reflect them in rudimentary ways. His innocence even predisposes him to find the expression of these qualities natural.

On the other hand, your expectations shouldn't be so high as to make you react harshly when your child doesn't exhibit these qualities in the rough-and-tumble of everyday life. A primary caregiver can always gently remind a child, if necessary, of the behavior expected in each situation. But that gentle reminding may sometimes turn into persistent nagging or stern exasperation. Somehow you have to find fresh reserves for continuing the shaping of character in an upbeat way.

Most parents philosophize about Rome not being built in a day. They realize child rearing is hard work, only sometimes blessed with moments of inspiration wherein they find themselves saying just the right thing and the children responding in an utterly delightful way.

COACHING FROM THE SIDELINES

♦ **ACTIVITY**

Identifying a particular social or moral standard and getting it across to your child in words.

♦ **SHARING**

Behavioral scientists write long treatises about the egocentrism of little children. Perhaps it's just as well that new parents seldom read these works or they might be discouraged from socializing their young offspring. While there may be a very powerful tendency in preschoolers not to take the perspective of others, this tendency diminishes as consideration of others is nurtured. Caring parents (whether or not they're well read in the field of child development) seem to march resolutely forward, constantly coaching their kids to put themselves in the place of others and think what others must be feeling.

The following paragraphs indicate a range of wishes parents have regarding their child's behavior. Extensive quotations from interviews with them show how they try to communicate these wishes.

Parent's wish   That a child be tolerant when faced with difficult behavior in peers.

Parent's words   One parent said, "I tell my child there are lots of different kinds of people in the world. You have to understand other people's feelings as well as your own." Other parents echoed this view with such comments as: "You're a member of a world community, and people have different characteristics," or "I encourage not judging other people; everybody does the best they can."

One mother said, "Kids are so quick to say someone is awful. I teach my kids not to judge, condemn, whenever a problem comes up. If other kids are rude or rowdy, I say, 'Maybe they don't know any better yet. I'm sure they didn't mean it. When they get older, they will play more considerately with your toys.' I teach them to become more understanding."

Another mother said, "If there is a difference of opinion between two playmates, I encourage them to work it out together, to talk about it. 'I know you can,' I tell them. I remind them to be kind. I bring out laughter whenever I can."

Parent's wish   That a child conform his actions to the golden rule of doing unto others as he would others do unto him.

Parent's words One father said, "I ask my daughter, 'How would it be if I sat down with a neighbor and said that I didn't like her cookies? Would she ever ask me over again? If you are nice to others, they'll be nice to you.' Kids can see that rule in operation every day of their lives."

Other parents echoed this view. They urged, "If you want to have friends, you have to share and take turns." "You have to offer the first choice of a toy to a guest."

Parent's wish That a four-year-old be gentle and patient with a younger sibling.

Parent's words A mother said, "I explained to my son, Keith, how patient we were with him when he was Amy's age. I told him that I taught him step by step everything he knows. I said, 'So now you have to be patient with Amy and her friends and teach them. You are big and strong, but you don't have to be rough and rowdy. You can be very gentle around little children and protect them.' He understood and became more patient with his little sister."

Parent's wish That a child be brave.

Parent's words "Life is full of hard knocks, and a child needs to react with courage. If another child hurts my daughter, I often say 'Bad luck!' This impersonalizes the problem somewhat and diverts her attention from blaming the playmate. With a visible sore knee, I say, 'Now be brave. Try not to make a fuss. Don't look at it. Try not to think about it or talk about it.' When a crisis is over, I praise her and say, 'My, you were brave! You were wonderful!' "

Parent's wish That a child be thoughtful of his parents.

Parent's words One mother encourages consideration of her spouse. "Daddy's taking a nap now. Let's tiptoe around the house." Another mother brings out a maternal quality in her daughter. "When I'm feeling sick or worried, I ask my child to take care of me. I lie down and she rubs my feet, strokes my forehead, brings me my slippers and a glass of water, and sings a gentle song. My daughter likes acting like an adult. It makes her feel good if she can be of help."

Another parent said her child likes to feel himself a working part of the family. She makes known simple needs and shows her child how he can meet those needs. "I keep talking to my child about how he can help us."

Parent's wish That a child persevere.

Parent's words A father said, "I see my child getting frustrated at playing catch. I explain, 'When you're learning new things you have to work at them. Think of your baby-sitter, playing her pieces on the piano again and again before she gets them right. To be good at a skill, you have to practice it over and over. When you're not doing well, you don't stop. You keep trying.' We played with a ball daily for a while. He saw himself getting better because he kept trying.''

Parent's wish   That a child be a problem solver.

Parent's words   "There are big problems in the world that need solving. Daddy's trying to help solve them. That's his job. That's why he goes abroad so much. When you grow up, you can help solve those big problems, too.''

Another father demonstrated problem solving in the home. "I show Mark that I have trouble with things, too. I point out, 'Look, I'm having trouble with this light fixture. The glass won't fit back into the lantern. I'm frustrated, but I'm going to try to figure it out.' Then I mention things that his mother has trouble with and how she reaches a solution step by step.''

Parent's wish   That a child be cheerful and positive.

Parent's words   Several couples spoke of boosting a child's morale yet urging the child to take responsibility for her own happiness.

"We're born cheerleaders,'' spoke one parent of her and her spouse's efforts to build into their child a positive attitude toward life. "We won't accept a 'nothing's right' approach. We try to pep him up when he's discouraged.''

Another set of parents wanted to give their child the feeling that he had control over his own experience. "If he's not happy about a situation, he doesn't have to accept it or be resigned to it. He can work to change it by talking it over with us, a teacher, or a peer. He can try acting differently, more positively, and watching to see if the someone he's interacting with then changes for the better, too. We teach him he has the power to make choices regarding how he is going to feel, think, and act.''

A third couple worked on building the concept of home as a "happy place.'' They urged, "It's the responsibility of all of us to make it that way. We can all be cheerful, wear a smile on our face, and not be crabby. We can all help with the chores and keep our rooms neat. Cooperation is a two-way street. You can do what you are told right away, and lovingly. We can answer your requests right away, and lovingly.''

When your child is two, three, and four, you have thousands of opportunities to mold character. You could try picking one of the qualities mentioned in the "parent's wish" paragraphs, say, tolerance. Work on bringing that out in your child for a couple of weeks at a time. Whenever an opportunity arises to reinforce that quality in everyday interactions, do so. Then pick another quality, perhaps persistence, and work on teaching that for a two-week period.

One earnest mother of three-year-old twins didn't expect miracles overnight. "The process is gradual and continuous. I'm polishing, refining, fine tuning all the time." The home is a classroom; the lessons concern character development, and you are the teacher with a highly influential role.

LET BOOKS SAY IT FOR YOU

♦ ACTIVITY
Reading stories in which the characters hold the attitudes you want your child to value.

♦ PROPS
Storybooks.

♦ SHARING
Books are not just for amusement and information, however important both those functions are. They can also educate a child about social, moral, and spiritual values. They can be your dearest allies in inclining your child's thoughts in the direction you deem best.

You must first spend time finding books of real merit. Browse in libraries and bookstores. Church bookstores, Christian school libraries, and retail outlets for religious or metaphysical publishers may be good sources. There is a "Values to Live By" series of books for young children you might send for (distributed by Children's Press, 1224 West Van Buren Street, Chicago, Ill. 60607).

When selecting books at a store or library, read through them. The text is usually brief, so you can tell by scanning whether the contents are in line with an outlook you desire to share with your child. See if the author portrays the characters (animal or human) expressing some of the mental qualities you want to bring out in your child. For instance, does a lonely child express more friendliness and then gain a friend? Does a frightened child discover there's nothing in the dark to be afraid of? Does a bully learn to be gentle?

The stories can talk for you. They make points subtly. They can save you from sounding too preachy. Clever words and appealing pictures illuminate an approach to a life situation in an entertaining way. Yet your child learns from listening to the story and looking at the illustrations.

Whatever book you choose, if it's a good one, you'll probably be reading it over and over again. You needn't strive to get the full meaning across to your child upon the first reading. Talk about the story. At first your conversations after each reading may just be establishing some of the outward facts. You may be answering your child's questions or simply explaining the events of the plot. Later you may touch on deeper meanings in the story. You may want to clarify the motives or the qualities of thought that the characters manifest.

What enabled the child in the book to find the lost object—persistence? Why did the grumpy old man become cheery when the child in the book came to his home—because the child wasn't impressed with his grumpiness?

As your child matures, successive rereadings will unfold new levels of meaning. When you own a book you can bring it out after a six-month rest. Or if you liked a particular library book, take it out again when your child is a little older.

As you talk over a story you have just read, perhaps you can relate it to a current experience your child is having. Is he being teased by kids down the block? A storybook character may have demonstrated a lot of courage when faced with an adversary. Is your child shy about meeting strangers? Perhaps a storybook character has a wonderful time exploring new places and encountering new individuals of all types.

In books your child finds gentle introductions to what the world out there—beyond the cozy confines of her home—is like. She prepares for it by experiencing vicariously the adventures of young literary characters. She finds out how she should behave when she gets out there. She assimilates information on how the characters deal with the problems and people they encounter. She learns how they succeed and build solid relationships. These characters can in some cases become role models for your child.

Sometimes a book portrays characters with negative values. You can use the story then to teach a lesson in reverse. Discussing what happened, you might bring out the consequences of the character's impatience. Perhaps rash impulses got him into trouble. Wouldn't he have been much better off if he had waited patiently and considered alternative actions, you might wonder aloud. With you at his side interpreting, your child can examine negative traits and reject them as unworthy of imitation.

You needn't avoid altogether stories that portray evil and wickedness in various forms. But some books may present a sad event in too maudlin a manner or dramatize the forces of evil too boldly. Other books may raise an issue such as divorce, death, or disease that is too delicate a topic at this particular time in your child's life. You will want to select carefully. Knowing your own child's temperament and sensitivity will help you steer clear, if these books will hinder rather than help her state of mind. But if the author has shown the triumph over evil by innocence, unselfishness, or trust in the forces of good, the story's moral may dissolve irrational timidity and strengthen moral courage in your child.

ON THE WALL

♦ **ACTIVITY**

Posting a sign that briefly expresses a philosophical attitude; reading it and discussing it from time to time.

♦ **PROPS**

Plaques, greeting cards with inspirational lines printed on them, homemade signs.

♦ **SHARING**

The beautiful needlepoint samplers of yesteryear have been replaced these days by tiles with a magnetic back that stick to refrigerator doors. Never mind; a lofty sentiment still has power to inspire.

Gift stores have plaques that decoratively present proverb-type statements. These often embody principles that can guide a child in getting along with others or in acquiring new skills. An old saying, such as "If at first you don't succeed, try, try again," may seem trite to us, but it is fresh and new to a child. In one kitchen a mother posted "Friendship starts in loving hearts." A nursery school teacher kept this benediction on the wall:

> *May we live in peace*
> *And be kind to one another always.*

One parent recalled a mystery slogan taught him as a child: Myself third. "What do you suppose that stands for?" he asked his child. After puzzling over the possibilities, the dad explained that those two words were the end of a motto: God first. Fellow man second. Myself third.

A child who needed a lot of encouragement was urged to remind herself frequently, "I'm loving, lovable, and lovely." Eloquent phrases such as these can be printed on 3-by-5-inch index cards and tacked in the corner of a bulletin board. They could be glanced at occasionally and read aloud by a parent who might add, "I needed that thought today."

THE FIVE Gs

♦ **ACTIVITY**

Explaining to a very young child his relationship to God.

♦ SHARING

A Sunday-school teacher of two- and three-year-old pupils uses one simple sentence to describe how God helps His little children, "God, good, guides, guards, and governs me." She calls her sentence "the five Gs."

She makes use of the five fingers of a child's hand to trigger the memory of the five main words. As her pupils slowly say the words along with her, each child touches his own fingers one by one. When they get to the word *me,* each points his thumb at himself. The tiny pupils soon memorize the statement, using their fingers to help them remember every word. The teacher tells them that wherever they are, whatever they are doing, whomever they are with, they can think about that sentence if they need comfort. Just looking at their hand and touching each finger will help them remember it. Then they will not be afraid or do the wrong thing.

She carefully explains the meaning of each word. *God* she describes as "the power of good, an invisible Father-and-Mother Who is always with you. You can't see Him, but you can feel His nearness. He makes you feel happy and peaceful inside. He helps your work and play go smoothly." To help clarify the sentence, she has her pupils act out the meanings of the verbs.

She demonstrates the word *guides* by closing her eyes and saying, "I can't see. *Guide* me to the door of this room. Take my hand. Don't let me bump into the chairs or table." A pupil guides her. "Now I feel the door. Put my hand on the knob. Okay, I've got it." Then she compares this experience to God directing a child. "He guides your thinking and your footsteps."

Next she demonstrates the word *guard.* She says, "Suppose there's a little baby in this room and a wolf is lurking nearby. Let's act this out. I'm the baby and you are going to *guard* me from the wolf. There it is! Stretch out your arms to protect me. I'm all right. Oh, now it's coming from that direction. Guard me!" Then the Sunday-school teacher explains, "That's the way God stands guard over you. He won't let anything bad hurt you."

To teach the concept of governing, the teacher uses a marionette. She shows her pupils that when she pulls a string, the puppet's arm or leg moves. She controls all its actions. "In a similar way," she explains, "God *governs* all your movements."

Parents who feel comfortable with this line of reasoning might like to share these images as a way to illustrate the relationship between God and humans.

PRAYER: "A 'THINK' IN MY MIND"

♦ ACTIVITY

Defining prayer or meditation, teaching specific prayers, and praying with your child.

♦ SHARING

Age two, three, or four is not too soon to be concerned about your child's spiritual development. Some parents have found that children possess a natural spiritual intuition that can be nurtured. Also, they have seen their children gain equanimity through a feeling that they can rely on divine love to meet their needs.

You may want to set aside a few moments every day to seek together an understanding of spiritual things. This search might take the form of praying with your child, either silently or aloud. You may be open to a broad definition of *prayer,* not confining it to formal petitions or grace said at the dining table.

Prayer can be a time of quiet contemplation of the love and beauty and goodness of God. It can be a talk about the good child of His creating, who is cared for, protected, and helped by a gentle spiritual presence. It can be the recitation of verses designed for meditation, influenced either by the Judeo-Christian tradition or by Eastern tradition. *Prayer* can be explained as thinking about God or as talking to God or perhaps as listening to God.

Prayer time might be a few minutes of counting the child's blessings with her, rehearsing what she's grateful for, or asking for God's protection for each beloved friend, pet, and family member. The title for this section came from a four-year-old praying for her brother as she was about to fall asleep. She said, "I have a 'think' in my mind. I'm going to think *God* for Peter all night and then he won't cough anymore."

Prayer can come to mean simply a moment in which children are consciously expecting good to happen. It's natural for children to trust that there is a beneficent power working in their behalf when they are so familiar with the constant care of devoted parents. Even though children seem to understand best the world of the concrete, they are surprisingly sensitive to abstract concepts if your own mind and communication are clear on such subjects. If in your heart you yourself feel a reverence for spiritual things, children catch the spirit of your conviction.

Little children are good at memorizing, and they enjoy it. You may want to teach them some brief, simple prayers to say out loud with you at night or when they wake up in the morning. At first they can chime in at the beginning or the end. Soon they will learn a whole verse by heart. Of course, they can repeat prayers without understanding them at all. Try to impart a sense of the spirit behind the words—trust, love, serenity, harmony, security, goodness, gentleness.

You may find a book with some prayers you like, or you may remember a favorite prayer from your childhood. Sometimes poetry books have inspirational verses that can serve as prayers. Following are two comforting poems that show the omnipresence of God, a mothering-fathering spiritual presence caring for children and adults all the time.

> *God is in*
> *God is out*
> *God is always*
> *All about.*
>
> *Good is up*
> *Good is down*
> *Good is always*
> *All around.*

Three longer prayers that help strengthen a child to face the minor challenges of the day with poise are as follows:

> *I am the window God shines through.*
> *I shine with light that's clear and true.*
> *He helps me want what's good and right.*
> *He helps me play without a fight.*
> *Afraid? I won't be any day,*
> *Because I trust Him all the way.*
> *When things seem hard, I'll say "I can."*
> *And I'll be happy with His plan.*
>
> *Dear God I pray,*
> *Show me the way*
> *Good thoughts direct,*
> *Angels protect*
> *My path today.*
>
> *When my mom and dad are out*
> *My Friend, God, is all about.*
> *He keeps me calm*
> *As well as Mom.*
> *He makes me glad*
> *As well as Dad.*
> *So, safe and busy I will be*
> *Until they come back home to me.*

The verses of hymns or spiritual songs make good prayers, too. The following one is well known.

Day by day,
Oh, dear Lord, three things I pray:
To see Thee more clearly,
To love Thee more dearly,
To follow Thee more nearly,
Day by day.

GETTING TO KNOW THE BIBLE

♦ ACTIVITY

Reading Bible stories that are rewritten for children and sharing well-known Bible verses to comfort, strengthen, and guide your child.

♦ PROPS

A Bible and a children's book of Bible stories.

♦ SHARING

Often a grandparent likes to give a grandchild a Bible. In one case a grandmother wrote some of her favorite texts on the flyleaf, thus personalizing the gift.

There are quite a few Bible verses simple enough for a young child to appreciate. You could quote one now and then as an evening or a morning prayer. You could write one out on a three-by-five-inch card and tack it to the bulletin board in your child's room for a few weeks, referring to it occasionally. When your child is troubled about something, you could remind him of an appropriate Bible verse and assure him that it has comforted others in similar circumstances.

Here are some easy-to-understand verses that can reach the heart of a child.

On overcoming fear with courage
"Fear nothing, for I am with you; be not afraid, for I am your God. I strengthen you, I help you, I support you . . ." (Isaiah 41:10).
"Be strong, be resolute; do not be fearful or dismayed, for the Lord your God is with you wherever you go" (Joshua 1:9).

On feeling a sense of security
"The eternal God is your refuge, and underneath are the everlasting arms" (Deuteronomy 33:27).
"He has charged His angels to guard you from all evil wherever you go" (Psalms 91:11).

On knowing the right thing to do
"Put all your trust in the Lord and do not rely on your own under-

standing. Think of Him in all your ways, and He will smooth your path"
(Proverbs 3:5).

"Treat others as you would like them to treat you" (Luke 6:31).

On the goodness of God
"God saw all that He had made, and it was very good" (Genesis 1:31).

"Goodness and love unfailing, these will follow me all the days of
my life" (Psalms 23:6).

On the power of positive thinking
"You shall know the truth, and the truth will set you free" (John 8:32).

"For God has not given us a spirit of fear, but a spirit of power and
love and a sound mind" (II Timothy 1:7).

On loving
"Love one another" (John 13:34).

"Love your enemies and pray for your persecutors; only so can you
be children of your heavenly Father . . ." (Matthew 5:44, 45).

On God within
"The kingdom of God is inside you" (Luke 17:21).

If you'd like your child to be aware of the Bible as a treasurehouse
of wise and noble perspectives on life, you might acquaint her with some
of the stories and characters from the Old and New Testaments. These
have been retold in simple language with colorful illustrations in various
books. Look for a title such as "Bible Stories for Young Children." In the
retelling the author may put his or her own interpretations on each story.
Therefore you may want to look over editions by various publishers to
find the one most in accord with your religious views.

Two stories from the Old Testament that are apt to appeal to children, perhaps because they are about both people and animals, are the
accounts of Noah and his ark and Daniel with the lions. Noah was guided
by God's voice (an inner urging) to build an ark that would protect his
family and two animals of every species from a flood. Daniel, plotted
against by rivals and thrown into a den of lions, finds they don't harm
him. If they are told gently, these stories can give a child a feeling of
protection from adverse circumstances. The flood and the lions become
symbols for the big or mean things he is afraid of.

Two stories from the New Testament that can be made clear to little
children are the parables of the prodigal son and the good Samaritan.
The prodigal son is like a naughty boy who runs away from home and
gets into trouble. When he realizes his mistake and returns home, his
father doesn't punish him but gives evidence of his unconditional love.
The good Samaritan tale describes an unselfish person who goes out of
his way to help a total stranger who has been robbed and hurt. The

morals of the stories are obvious. You can easily relate the practical lessons they teach to your child's everyday life.

SPIRITUAL EXPERIENCES REMEMBERED

♦ ACTIVITY

Sharing with your child a spiritual experience you personally have had.

♦ SHARING

Describe a moment in your childhood when you felt the presence of God. If, as an adult, entering a certain church put you in a lofty mood, you might embellish on that. Perhaps some spiritual insights you have entertained were caused by the striking beauty of nature in a particular spot. Music might have been a source of inspiration to you. Perhaps a person you once talked with seemed to have a deep understanding of life; tell your child about that person. Perhaps the birth of your baby or the care you've seen parents give their little ones has given you hints of the sublime.

Can you recall a time when prayer changed something for you? You may have had a sense of protection from imminent danger. Or perhaps you "pulled through" at a time when you were very ill. You could share with your child an account of these changes. You may have a friend who has had a dramatic spiritual experience that you can relate to your child.

Some consider it natural that innocent children have moments of spiritual insight. Your child may have them but not know how to identify them as such. You may want to help her talk about these.

EXPLAINING GOD

♦ ACTIVITY

Deciding on your own views and offering your child some simple explanations of the nature of God.

♦ SHARING

Young children do ask questions about God. They usually accept without argument what you tell them. They have more receptivity to things of the spirit than adults. They regard spiritual phenomena as natural rather than mystical.

However, you may not want to wait till your child asks questions. Often if parents put off discussing the subject of God, they are forced to deal with it at the time of the death of a pet, a relative, or a friend of the family. If the first mention of God occurs then, this isn't as constructive as introducing the subject gradually at moments when there is no stress.

As a couple, you may want to start talking over what you wish to tell your child about God. Some people find this time a threshold at which they assess what views they've previously held about religion and God and decide to reaffirm them or search in new directions. Their desire to pass on to their children the most helpful philosophy of life possible is very strong.

In an effort to clarify your own views, you may visit various churches or synagogues and inquire about their instruction for children. You may also find some books that help you decide what your own position is.

If you say nothing to your child about God, this is almost the same as a statement of the nonexistence of God. You may want to embark on some form of spiritual education, even though you cannot chart the whole course at this time.

Parents I interviewed shared some of their efforts at explaining God to their tiny kids. Their descriptions included:

"He's a force for good that makes you want to be a good person."

"Sometimes you're wrong. Sometimes I'm wrong. The only person who is always right is God."

"God is a feeling. He is omnipotent and mysterious. He can do anything. He is even stronger than Daddy."

"God is the Creator who made everything, including you. He loves you very much and sees that all goes well for you."

"God is an infinite mind."

"God is everybody's Father."

"He made the world. He looks out for us. He watches over us."

"You can't *see* my love for you, but you can *feel* it. It's the same with God. You can't see Him, but you can feel the joy and love He sends you."

"God is everywhere." When the child asked, "Is He in the tree, is He in the dirt?" the parent answered, "He's in your mind."

"God is a spiritual guide. He speaks to your inner self."

"God comes as a strong feeling that you should do something or that it wouldn't be right to do something else."

"He comes as a good idea or as a mood of peace or contentment. He appears as a desire to express love to some person or animal."

If you are wishing to offer some spiritual enlightenment to your child, some of these phrases may help you get started. Two other books that discuss the sharing of spiritual values are *Whole Child/Whole Parent,* by Polly Berrien Berends (Harper Colophon Books, 1983), and *How to Help Your Child Have a Spiritual Life,* by Annette Hollander, M.D. (A & W Publishers, 1980).

· 15 ·

DEMOCRACY ON THE
HOME FRONT

P arents worry about their child-rearing styles. Are they too permissive? Are they too authoritarian? When parents are permissive, little kids sometimes seem inconsiderate, demanding, and self-willed. When parents are authoritarian, children sometimes seem to lack spunk, initiative, and courage.

Some parent educators and psychologists who have worked with families suggest striving for a middle-of-the-road style that reflects the democratic spirit that is so alive and well in our society. After all, if children are one day going to be active citizens in a participatory democracy, it makes sense for them to grow up in a social unit—the family—that functions in a democratic way.

This doesn't mean government by the children and for the children. Parents' needs are as important as children's. And it doesn't mean the parents dictate all decisions. The needs and wishes of both are weighed in the balance. Rather than thinking of adults as superior and children as inferior, dare to think *equality*. The current development of the children is just as important as the current development of the parents.

At the core of successful democratic functioning is the self-esteem of every individual. A child gains self-esteem when she feels herself highly valued by those around her. A child gains self-confidence when she is helped to be competent at her endeavors. She gains self-importance when her feelings count, her opinions are listened to, and her wishes sometimes influence the direction of events. She learns to trust her own judgments when others trust them.

The quality of the relationship with the primary parent strongly affects the child's relationship with others throughout the growing-up period. Democratic elements that would contribute to a healthy relationship might be some of the following: cooperating with a reasonable adult rather than blindly obeying a demanding one; expressing regret for an inconsiderate act to a forgiving adult rather than submitting to a punishing one; and talking things over with a patient adult rather than feeling humiliated by an angry one.

If adults consider their child capable of understanding the point of view of others, they will share their opinions with their child, even when these opinions are a little over the child's head. This child begins to realize that each family member has her or his own point of view, own concerns and wishes. The child learns that agreements get forged; they don't come ready-made. Decisions aren't handed down from on high; they are shaped by the views of several. A child thus gets a feel for the blending, compromising, and adapting that has to go on if individuals are going to live and work together as a harmonious group.

The following activities will help create an atmosphere of democracy in your home.

DECLARATIONS OF INDEPENDENCE

♦ ACTIVITY

Providing more opportunities for your child to do things alone.

♦ ACTIONS

Your child has a tremendous drive to dress himself, eat by himself, do small jobs without assistance, and get organized for play without a hovering adult. He wants to demonstrate mastery over his own small world.

On the other hand, you have an equally tremendous drive to protect, care for, and direct this child. The two drives are often at cross-purposes.

Were it not for the fact that you are so busy, you might baby your child a lot longer. But nowadays the necessity for your child to do more on his own fits with your child's wishes for independence. But necessity shouldn't be your only reason. Helping your child take progressive steps of responsibility for little daily acts is proof that the spirit of democracy is alive and well in your family unit.

Each step of increasing independence may require initial instruction by you and a period of preparation. Start to think of things your toddler can do on her own in the next few months. Then think of how you might change current circumstances or modify the physical environment to help her accomplish these things on her own. For example, could you give her a box or stool that she can climb on to turn out her room light herself at night? Think also of the verbal instruction you can give in new skills.

Why not begin at dawn and run through your average daily schedule. You might introduce some new little step of independence once a week. Talk to your child about your plan, even though it's unlikely that future weeks or months have meaning for him. He'll begin to notice his increasing minor freedoms and responsibilities as "part of our plan." When he's not ready for autonomy in some area, you can promise it as part of "our plan"—for later on "when you're three" or "when you're three and a half."

Try sketching some possible steps toward independence along the following lines:

WAKE-UP TIME

getting out of bed by self
going to bathroom by self
playing in a room for 15 minutes by self

To facilitate these changes: switch from a crib to a child bed; arrange the toilet for his use the night before; lay out toys he's especially fond of for alone play. Then talk about these new steps one at a time.

BREAKFAST TIME

obtaining some food by self before Mom or Dad go to the kitchen
helping self to milk and sugar under supervision, buttering toast
clearing own dishes

To facilitate these changes: lay out dried fruit or cereal the night before. Teach pouring of milk and sprinkling of sugar. (You could ration it by providing child's own sugar bowl.) Leave butter pat out so it's soft for easy spreading. Leave dishwasher rack out so she can load her dishes into it. Talk about each of these changes one at a time.

DRESSING TIME

get out clothes
put some clothes on by self

To facilitate these changes: arrange clothes in lower drawers, on lower hooks, or hanging from low pole in closet. Buy clothes that are easy to put on. Introduce practice sessions for getting into pullover shirts or putting legs into two different pant legs.

Continue charting your daily routine, looking for areas in which your child's ever-increasing abilities can be exercised. Of course, often the solo act may be only like the tip of the iceberg. You will have done most of the work that enabled him to take that solo flight.

◆ BENEFITS

Growing self-reliance will be particularly helpful if you are expecting a second child.

CHANCES TO CHOOSE

♦ ACTIVITY

Showing kids how to make choices or reach decisions and then giving them lots of practice at it.

♦ ACTIONS

One aspect of democracy is freedom of choice. We need to help our little ones early on to be wise choosers.

As always, a good example is the best teacher. Let your child see you making sensible choices. Let her hear how you arrive at decisions. This means occasionally thinking out loud, so that she can hear you go through a thought process. As you stand in front of the coat closet, you can say, "It's rainy today, so I could wear my raincoat. But it's also cold. Since I don't have a sweater handy to wear under my raincoat, I'll take my parka instead."

Our children see us take action countless times a day, but they don't realize how many of those actions are the result of a decision-making process. We need to let them in on this undercover secret.

Sometimes we use the trial-and-error method. "Look, Sam, I want to pry open the lid of this paint can. I'm trying a spoon. It's too lightweight. I'm trying this knife. It won't fit under the rim. I guess I'll have to get the screwdriver off the workbench. Ah, that works."

You can use the words *choose* and *decide* more often in conversation. You'll be surprised how our days are made up of minor decisions. "Before I go shopping, I'm going to decide what we will have for dinner tonight." Then indicate the reasons for your choices.

As you begin this habit of sharing your internal dialogue, you can also start supplying your child with situations in which he can make a choice. At first start with areas in which any choice he makes will be fine with you. "Which doll do you want to take in the car with us today? Which paper plate do you want your sandwich on?" Then later move into areas that have more significance. "Either of these shirts goes with navy shorts. Which do you prefer? You could put your bookshelf under the window or beside the closet. Where would you like it?"

You can help with the pros and cons when decisions get more complicated. Suppose a friend wants your child to bring a toy when she visits. Help her think through her choices. Does the puzzle have too many parts? Is the dollhouse too heavy? "If Susie has never seen your new marble game, maybe that's the best choice." It's exciting to watch your child learn to reason with and, soon, without you.

Whenever possible, allow your child a choice even though it may prove to be a mistake. Let her know we all learn from our mistakes.

Then next time we remember our experiences and make better choices. Of course, if safety is an issue, step in quickly to prevent a bad choice.

More ideas on teaching decision making are found in *Open Connections: The Other Basics,* by Susan D. Shillock and Peter A. Bergson, a husband-and-wife team who run a nursery school. (For a copy at $12.50 plus $1.25 for postage and handling write Open Connections, Inc., 312 Bryn Mawr Avenue, Bryn Mawr, Penn. 19010.)

PROBLEMS ARE FOR SOLVING

♦ ACTIVITY

Teaching your child problem-solving techniques and supporting early efforts to solve simple problems independently.

♦ ACTIONS

Engage your child's mind as early as possible in the business of solving problems. In a democracy each person strives to be resourceful, competent, self-reliant, not overly dependent on a caretaking authority. This training should begin in the home.

A relaxed attitude toward everyday problems helps. Don't view them as calamities or distasteful burdens in overcrowded days, or as justification for loss of temper and a sour mood. Let your children see you encounter problems with *equanimity,* which Webster's dictionary beautifully defines as "coolness under strain."

Talk out loud when you're considering domestic problems that are understandable to children, such as a door that doesn't shut properly, a garbage can that is raided by the neighbor's dog, a closet that is too dark to find things in. Give your child a running commentary as your mind considers solutions. "I might tighten the screws on that doorknob or I might adjust the weather stripping."

A next step is to give the child a chance to offer solutions. "Gary, how can we keep Tasha away from the garbage?" A child who sees his idea implemented gets confidence in approaching the next problem.

If your child isn't used to the opportunity for input on family problems, her mind may be a blank the first few times you try this. But soon she'll catch on to solution-searching. If her idea seems impractical, it still may trigger a closely related solution in your own mind. You can credit your child for the spark that ignited your thought and thus reinforce her brainstorming efforts.

Use the words *problem-solve* or *debug* or *figure out a solution* often as you talk together. Tell your child that each time you consider a solution, you have to evaluate it. "I see you need light in that deep dark toy closet. An electrician could install a ceiling bulb, but that would be expensive. We could move your standing lamp to the doorway, but somebody might trip over the cord. We could give you a flashlight and leave it just inside the closet door—yes, that would be a cheap and safe solution."

As you get used to the idea of teaching your preschooler that problems are for solving, give him opportunities to solve little problems on his own. Don't rush in too fast with solutions. Hold back and let the wheels of his mind turn. When you see him take a misguided course of action, if not much is at stake, let him experience the consequences. "Never mind," you can encourage, "you'll think of another solution tomorrow." Let him know you expect his intelligence to work for him. It's more important to show respect for his efforts to think up solutions than to come up with a better idea yourself. For more ideas on problem solving, read *Open Connections: The Other Basics* (see previous activity for the address to obtain copy).

FAMILY POWWOWS

♦ ACTIVITY

Holding regular home meetings at which your child has a chance to contribute, however simply, to the discussion of family affairs.

♦ ACTIONS

One specific way to bring a democratic style of child rearing into the home is to hold family business meetings, in which everyone gathers for the purpose of discussing issues of mutual interest. The goal is to enable you all to live together as a harmonious group. A somewhat formal setting for hashing out the nitty-gritty concerns has worked for lots of families.

Dr. Rudolf Dreikurs, author of *Children, The Challenge,* called this kind of gathering a "family council." The approach is effective only if the meeting is held regularly. This means setting aside a particular time each week and keeping the date with each other. This may not seem significant when your child is two, three, or four. But as she grows and the family grows, parents will find the system a great help. The sooner the system starts operating, the more skillful at group interactions the family members will become. A child is ready when she is able to communicate verbally.

The agenda can include a variety of items. Only a few of the following would be appropriate for a single meeting:

good happenings of the past week
things that show improvement
things that need improvement
calendar for the next week
chores that need to be divided
plans for the weekend
individual wishes
new solutions for old problems
complaints
summarizing the strengths of each person

Often there are no ready-made answers for complaints. They have to be searched for. Mom might complain about winter boot clutter in an outside vestibule, Dad about not being able to sleep in on Sunday morning, your child about no room to build with blocks. Problems won't get ironed out at once. But in searching together for solutions, your child and you will learn a group-dynamics process that will help you over bigger humps in the future.

Start believing in the budding wisdom of your child. When a problem is brought forward, let your child try to think up a solution. Maybe it'll be a little unconventional, but sometimes the craziest ideas work. Certainly if the child offers an idea and it's accepted, he's going to be more willing to implement it. A cardinal rule should be that everyone's suggestion is taken seriously. There is no laughing at a proposition. In every comment there may be a valuable kernel of truth. When little kids are shown that their voice counts, they naturally become more mature.

When weekend excursions are being considered, the council meeting can be used to plan thoroughly for an outing, say, a picnic. Even a two-year-old can give input: she can express a wish for a favorite food and agree to put some of the item in the picnic basket during preparation time.

Occasionally discussion can focus on creating rules for smoother family interaction. In one large family each of the older children enjoyed playing alone with the cute toddler. They decided to hang a "one-on-one time" sign on the outside of the closed bedroom door during these sessions so no one could enter and distract the toddler from the cozy time the older child was enjoying with her.

Another family forged a rule to operate when two brothers both wanted the same set of toys. One child divided the cars into two equal groups; the other child chose which half he wanted. This worked for food, too.

The family forum is an opportunity for a child to learn to express herself and get experience at being listened to. At first she may say only a few words about a subject and attend for only a few minutes. That's enough. If there are older children in the family, preschoolers may catch on sooner.

THE NEGOTIATING TABLE

♦ **ACTIVITY**

Settling parent-child conflicts by negotiating an agreement.

♦ **ACTIONS**

You're bigger, wiser, and more experienced. True, but does this entitle you to win all conflicts by pulling rank, exerting pressure, and forcing obedience? If so, does your child get used to feeling like a loser, a person who must yield blindly to authority at all times?

A mother picked up her daughter at a birthday party. The mother wanted her to wear her cardigan home. The little girl refused. The mother, becoming more childish than her child, threatened, "I'll burst your balloon if you don't put on your sweater." The child still refused. The mother poked the balloon. The child burst into tears and meekly allowed the cardigan to be put on. Generally that mother and daughter had a good relationship. For days after the four-year-old seemed to sense the inconsistency of her mother's act with her generally loving attitude. She kept asking wistfully, "Aren't you sorry you burst my balloon?"

How often do we seem to burst the balloon of joy when little conflicts arise suddenly? We are usually sorry after we have become angry and autocratically brought about our child's compliance with our wishes. We long to settle differences with sweet reasonableness.

This is possible. Even big adults and little kids can reach agreement through conferring rather than fighting. Negotiation is a form of resolving conflicts used by parties who are considered fairly equal: labor and management representatives, for instance, or husbands and wives. While children are not equal in knowledge to their parents, they are equally important as human beings. The development of their personalities is just as important as the ongoing development of their parents'.

In the past two decades parenting experts have recommended new, more democratic ways of resolving conflicts to replace the old-fashioned Father-knows-best rule. One of the most prominent methods proposed was the no-lose method of Ira Gordon, the clinical psychologist who started the classes called Parent Effectiveness Training and who wrote a book by the same name. Many other parent educators have been influenced by his thinking.

His no-lose method is composed of six steps:

1. Identify the conflict.
2. Search together for solutions.
3. Evaluate the solutions.
4. Accept a solution.
5. Work out ways of implementing the solution.
6. Later evaluate the solution.

Although this method was first applied by parents with older children, parents with younger children found they could adapt it to interchange with their four- and five-year-olds. A father and son wanted a dog. The mother didn't. "Son," the father said, "we have to figure out ways to care for that dog so it won't be a nuisance for your mom." They approached the problem like a puzzle that had to be solved. They talked about a doghouse, a fenced-in area, feeding and walking routines. Mother saw their willingness to spare her. After the purchase some solutions weren't working, so Father and four-year-old went back to the drawing board. Impositions on Mom were kept to a minimum, and she felt her wishes had been regarded considerately. The no-lose method means neither side loses in a conflict.

If this step-by-step method seems too complex for your very young family, consider it a goal you'll be working toward when your child becomes five, six, or seven. In the meantime keep discussions short and keep giving reasons for your requests, showing that they are not arbitrary whims but logical preferences. "Turn down your record player because I can't hear the man on the telephone." Build up reserves of patience, often pausing before reacting so you can endure long minutes of negotiating with an immature mind. You are building a relationship that's going to last a lifetime, so you don't want to burst too many balloons at the beginning.

♦ BENEFIT

Children who learn to settle differences reasonably within the family apply the approach to relationship problems outside the home.

III

LEARNING GAMES
FOR SMART TIMES

· 16 ·

KNOWING COLORS

One of the intellectual skills surfacing in every well-developing child at age two and three is the ability to notice similarities and differences. Parents who help children observe details by verbalizing about look-alikes and discrepancies forward intelligence. Burton L. White, Ph.D., head of the Harvard Preschool Project, wrote in *The First Three Years of Life,* "The number of subjects that can serve as a basis for pointing out similarities and differences is infinite!" Color is one of these subjects. It is one of the first concepts to pass along to your child in a cognitively oriented home curriculum. And most parents hasten to teach it.

Children learn the concept of color at any age from eighteen months on. Most learn between the age of two and a half to three. Those who learn close to two may not label colors verbally, but they will be able to look at something blue and find other blue items out of a bunch of diversely colored objects.

Many children learn to recognize colors, shapes, letters of the alphabet, and numbers from "Sesame Street" without their parents trying to teach them. Others pick up these concepts both from TV and from parents who are frequently mentioning the names of colors, shapes, letters, and numbers in relation to concrete objects that their children are looking at.

Colors are fun to teach. En route parents naturally teach transferable skills such as making comparisons, discriminating among similar objects, making selections, matching, sorting, and seeing and forming patterns. When their kids have learned their colors, parents feel they have crossed the first hurdle of the academic world.

Remember, when teaching such things as colors to your child, that learning is not arduous for her. The capacity of a preschooler's mind to absorb new information is far greater than yours. For her, learning new things is a form of play. So a lighthearted approach to the color games that follow is appropriate.

In any learning situation the three key ingredients, according to one nursery school director, are interest, pleasure, and success. Having attractive materials for teaching concepts heightens your child's interest. Having your company enhances her pleasure. Arranging materials cleverly and talking about them appropriately increases the likelihood of her successful grasp of new concepts.

◆

PRIMARY COLOR SAVVY

◆ ACTIVITY
Teaching your two-year-old to distinguish the basic colors.

◆ PROPS
Color sample cards from your local paint store. Obtain two cards exactly alike from each manufacturer for use in matching games. (If your child is two or under, you only need charts showing the strong primary colors. Later on get the cards of several different manufacturers so you have plenty of hues.)

Alternative objects with which to teach color: colored blocks, poker chips, spools of thread, balls of play dough, pack of construction paper of many shades.

◆ ACTIONS
Start with objects (blocks or spools) that are exactly alike in shape, only different in color. Begin with red, yellow, and blue; then go on to white and black. Present only two colors at first, during several brief sessions.

If you are using paint sample cards, cut the rectangles of color out of one of the cards. Lay the red paint chip on the table. Point to it and say, "This is red." Then lay down a blue chip. Point and say, "This is not red. This is blue." Next tell your child, "I'd like you to point to the red," or "Show me the blue." Finally you can point to either chip and ask, "What is this color?"

This system includes a method common to nursery school teachers:

> naming the item to be learned
> having the child locate it by pointing or some other nonverbal action, such as matching it with a look-alike
> having the child name the thing being learned

A softer way to teach is to play matching games with the colors. This gets you away from a testing kind of situation in which you are asking the child to point to or name out loud a certain color. Here are some little games:

Match 'Em Up   Take your sample paint cards and lay a cutout yellow chip next to the yellow on each chart. At first you can do the observing. "Here's a yellow! Oh, look! I found another yellow." Teach each new color in a similar way.

Look Around   If you are teaching red, take your red paint chip and hunt around the house for other things that are red. Hold your chip next to a book and notice out loud, "Here, we've found a red." Perhaps a picture on your wall has some red in it. "Hey, look up there. Red again." A light signaling that your oven is on may be red. "Oh, goody! Another red."

Singin' the Blues   Comb through the toys in your child's collection together. Find the toys or toy parts that are blue and gather them into a pile. Do this with each color you're teaching.

As your child catches on, he'll naturally start labeling things red as well as spotting red things. When he makes a mistake, avoid saying, "That's wrong." Instead you can say, "I see orange there," and continue playing games that involve placing two objects of similar color side by side.

AN EYE FOR COLOR

♦ ACTIVITY

Exercising through matching games the newfound ability to distinguish many colors.

♦ PROPS

As in the previous activity, two duplicate color sample cards from each paint company whose products are carried at your local paint store.

Yogurt cups, scissors, construction paper.

♦ ACTIONS

Cut one of the duplicate cards so each rectangle or square of paint color is a separate little chip. Put these in a pile for your child. Ask him to pick up any color chip and scan the duplicate card (which is whole) looking for that same color. When he finds it, he can lay his chip on its match. The younger your child, the fewer the chips you should use.

◆ **VARIATION**

Another color game can be played with a dozen lidded yogurt cups and construction paper. Cut little squares from each color in a pack of construction paper. Cut several squares of each shade. Cut slits in the lids of the yogurt cups. Place the lids on the cups. Your child can glue one different colored square to each lid. Have your child drop each of your many squares through the slot of the appropriate cup.

If you would rather not make your own games, many commercial board games such as Winnie-the-Pooh or CandyLand exercise an ability to distinguish color.

HUE REVIEW

◆ **ACTIVITY**

Challenging your child to retain a color in her mind's eye and find the match from memory.

◆ **PROPS**

Wide range of color chips of some kind, including two of each color. Use your paint charts or construction paper cutouts from the previous two activities, or make a new batch of pairs with crayons and paper.

◆ **ACTIONS**

Have one pile of color chips, one of each color, in one room, and a pile of identical color chips in another room. Start with just a few. Pick up one shade and show it to your child. Ask, "Can you find another one like this?" or "Can you find another gray?" She should take a good look at your choice, trying to remember it, and then trot off to the next room. There she should look through the chips, pick up the matching one, and run back to you with it.

◆ **BENEFIT**

This game tests visual memory and strengthens color recognition by removing the extra help of the concrete model when matching.

A SEQUENCE SNAKE

◆ **ACTIVITY**

Grasping the concept of a pattern by repeating a sequence of colors.

♦ **PROPS**

Many squares of each color of construction paper; or colored blocks, tiles, pegs, or beads from one of your child's games.

♦ **ACTIONS**

Start with a pile of chips, cubes, or paper squares of many colors. Start picking out some of the blues and reds and alternate them in a straight or curvy line. Leave some reds and blues in the original pile. Now ask your child to copy your line with a parallel line. If this seems too hard, work together on one long snake. You can talk about your work: "Now the red, now the blue . . . let's see, what's next? A red. Will you hand me the red?"

If your child catches on easily, create a more complicated sequence, perhaps two reds, a blue, two reds, a blue. Let him reproduce your pattern. Watch his progress with interest.

Next introduce a third color, such as yellow, and line up the objects in a blue-yellow-red order. Your copycat's job is to pick out the right color and place it in the right order.

♦ **BENEFIT**

Children enjoy the sense of mastery that comes from sorting miscellaneous items and assembling them in a required order.

WHAT'S MISSING IN THE MATRIX?

♦ **ACTIVITY**

Cultivating an early ability to solve problems while reinforcing your child's knowledge of color.

♦ **PROPS**

Stiff paper or posterboard.

A collection of little colored cubes, counters, or tiles—all the same shape, but in several different colors.

Felt-tip pen.

♦ **ACTIONS**

Make a matrix board for playing this game. Cut out a 9-inch square of paper or posterboard. Draw straight lines as you would for a ticktack-toe design. Draw the lines neatly with a ruler so they form nine 3-inch-square boxes.

A matrix board displays a pattern of objects vertically and horizontally, each of which is related to the others. In this game you set up a color pattern. Then, when your child isn't looking, you remove a cube of a particular color. Your child then guesses what is missing and replaces the missing cube.

Start with a red cube in each box of the lefthand column, a green cube in each box in the middle column, and a yellow cube in each box in the righthand column. Run your finger from the top to the bottom and say to your child, "Look, you have a column of red cubes, a column of green cubes, and a column of yellow." Then run your finger horizontally and say, "Here you have a row of different colors: red, green, and yellow; another row of red, green, and yellow; and a third just the same."

Now, while your child closes her eyes, remove a cube—perhaps the center one, which is green. Put it in your collection of cubes in a pile beside the matrix. Now tell your child, "Open your eyes. This center box is empty. What belongs there? I want you to problem solve and replace the missing cube."

To help her at the beginning, point and say, "Here the boxes all have red cubes. Over here they all have yellow. Which color do you need to make the middle row like the patterns in the other row?"

Next time she closes her eyes, remove the top righthand cube: a yellow. Try showing her the sequence of colors across the rows—red, green, yellow. By getting information about their patterns, your child will reach a conclusion about the missing one. It's fun to watch her think this through. A child can get quite excited when learning about patterning. When she picks up the yellow and places it correctly, compliment her. "Wow, you completed the matrix again! That's good."

When your child has mastered this game, playing it with different colors and patterns increases its complexity. Make a matrix board with four boxes across and four down; sixteen in all. You can remove two cubes at a time as a further challenge.

It is a little more difficult if you cover a cube with an upside-down measuring cup and then ask your child to name the color of the hidden cube.

♦ BENEFIT

A precision matrix calls for a "right answer," and your child has to put on her thinking cap to arrive at it—a healthy contrast to less structured activities.

SUBTLE SHADES OF DIFFERENCE

♦ ACTIVITY

Arranging various shades of one color in order, from the lightest to the darkest.

♦ PROPS

Paint store sample cards that show various gradations of a color. Get two identical cards of perhaps a half-dozen quite different colors. (Sometimes interior decorators have decks of cards or fabric swatches with increasingly deeper tints attached to a key-ring device or bound in a little book. You might obtain one that is no longer in use. Each card or swatch can be cut in half to create pairs.)

♦ ACTIONS

Cut up one of the paint sample cards, showing perhaps a range of pinks. Mix up the shades. Lay the matching intact card with its correct order of shades on the table. Indicate that your child is expected to line up the loose chips in the same order, palest to deepest. Try the game with another set of hues, perhaps those from light gray to dark gray. The appropriate age for playing this game will depend on your child's previous experience at recognizing colors and sequencing objects.

When your child has the hang of this, remove the model card and challenge him to arrange them correctly by his own sharp eye. Gradually you can set up one pile of all the pinks, grays, blues, greens, and more perhaps, and your child will be able to pick out of the collection each subtle shade he needs to build graduated columns of each basic color. In a Montessori classroom the pupils work up to arranging over sixty color tablets.

♦ BENEFIT

Color sequencing sharpens visual discrimination and reinforces a sense of pattern and logical order.

CRAYON FLASH

♦ ACTIVITY

Naming colors for your child from a large stack of homemade flash cards.

◆ **PROPS**

Several dozen 3-by-5-inch index cards, a large box of crayons with several dozen shades.

◆ **ACTIONS**

Crayon each card a different color together with your child. Write the name of the color on the back. Then go through a half-dozen or more, flashing the cards at your child and naming the color.

When you've flashed the first dozen colors periodically over a week or two, add another dozen to the repertoire. Keep adding till you've included all the shades in the crayon box.

One mother I interviewed had studied techniques for developing intelligence at the Better Baby Institute in Philadelphia. She did a lot of flash-card work with her daughter, imparting all sorts of information on them. But she never quizzed her child. She just cheerfully and quickly told her the name of whatever was shown, in this case colors. She could read the name from the back of the card as she held it up to her daughter, who sat facing her. The mother didn't worry about whether the little girl remembered the name or not. She just felt she was exposing her to the glories of all the colors in the rainbow and that that was bound to enrich her store of knowledge.

A boy who enjoyed associating names with his crayons began to see everything around him in terms of those colors. He wouldn't let his mother say, "That's a nice green tree." He'd correct his mother and say, "That's a pea green tree" or "that's an apple green tree."

IF YOU HAVE A COMPUTER

◆ **ACTIVITY**

Matching colors in designs on the computer screen.

◆ **PROPS**

A personal computer; software designed for preschoolers' learning of colors, such as a disk called "Juggles' Rainbow" made by The Learning Company, for Apple, Commodore 64, and Radio Shack Color computers. For IBM the same disk is called "Juggles' Butterfly."

◆ **ACTIONS**

If you have a personal computer, you may be thinking about introducing your preschooler to it. For a parent accustomed to sitting at the computer, taking a child on your lap to view some colorful graphics on the terminal can rank as just as cozy an experience as curling up together with a good old-fashioned storybook. It is natural to want to share the fun you're having with the new technology.

In educational circles the comparative value of learning on computers versus learning with manipulative concrete materials is still being debated. It is certainly not necessary to buy a computer for the purpose of teaching your child the concepts generally included in an early-learning curriculum. But if you have one already, you may want to collect diskettes that are cognitively oriented. For the purpose of teaching colors, the disk "Juggles' Rainbow" is of good quality. It works as follows.

Pressing a key on your computer keyboard produces a beautiful rainbow of six colors on the screen. Next time your child presses a key, colored raindrops fall from each band of the rainbow. But the colors of the raindrops don't match the bands on the rainbow. Your child has to keep pressing until each line of raindrops matches the band of color from which it falls. A certain number of key-presses guarantees the match.

The next game on the same disk is called Juggles' Butterfly. The colorful graphics will delight your child. Through punching keys, your child makes the colors of the wings on the left of the butterfly match the colors of the wings on the right.

A third game, Juggles' Windmill, also reinforces the color-matching skill. Your child works until the hues on all four broad arms of a windmill match each other.

· 17 ·
PICTURES, PATTERNS, AND SHAPES

After learning colors, a common next step in conceptual learning is to understand and match pictures, recognize and label geometric shapes, and discern patterns in the arrangement of objects. This early visual acuity often leads a child to all kinds of remarkable feats of recognition. One preschooler may distinguish among several dozen cars, another may know forty different flags, a third may name the states when presented with their outlines. These achievements may not be common, but children's abilities have been underestimated in the past.

In recent decades various educators have proved that children, before school age, can learn far more than they have been given the opportunity to do. A look at trends tells us cognitive learning is "in" for the eighties, assuming a stature equal in importance to creativity, social adjustment, and physical coordination. Today's parent is called upon to perform quite a balancing act, forwarding all these areas of growth at once.

Why should parents provide opportunities to learn concepts that were once reserved for the kindergarten or primary-grade classroom? For several reasons.

1. Some learning is easier for the younger child. The preschooler mind (called "the absorbent mind" by Maria Montessori, founder of the Montessori method of education) grasps information intuitively and therefore effortlessly. Older children and adults grasp information through the more laborious process of reasoning. Preschoolers retain concepts easily, perhaps because they are not sophisticated enough to fear they won't.
2. Learning side by side with an adult who's crazy about you—your parent—can have an edge over learning with a schoolteacher, however kind. The parent's exuberant delight over each new concept grasped imparts to the child an eagerness to learn that nothing else can. The child gets a good feeling about the process of learning and becomes hooked on it for life.

3. The case for early learning is further supported by the fact that the preschooler can do it. Like Mt. Everest, you climb it because it's there. So you present abstract concepts like colors, geometric shapes, letters, and numbers because it's now known that children have the ability to comprehend abstractions. They understand them better, though, with the help of concrete materials. Pictures are abstractions because they are representations of the concrete thing. Numbers are abstractions because they are symbols of quantities. Words are abstractions because they describe actual things. The ability to work with the abstract (illustrated by the concrete) begins after the age of two.

4. Early knowledge enhances self-esteem. A little girl who begged her mother to do hard puzzles with her every day was asked, "Why do you like to do puzzles so much?" She answered, "Because it makes me be a four-year-old." There's no greater aspiration for a three-and-a-half-year-old. Expanding knowledge and refining abilities at home make children feel good about themselves. And this bright self-image helps performance later on in school.

As you initiate the following games with your child, joyfully begin each one with a nothing-ventured, nothing-gained air. Be like a charming hostess organizing a party game who invites her guests to join but doesn't coax or insist. Offer your materials and present your game as enticingly as possible. Don't force-feed and be sure to stop before your child is bored. Your efforts will be rewarded by the chance to observe how your child's mind ticks.

◆

MATCHING MANIA

◆ ACTIVITY

Helping your child notice similarities and differences through matching games.

◆ PROPS

A dozen or more picture postcards—two of each picture.
Two identical copies of a magazine.
Fabric swatches and two little boxes.
Matchbook covers—two from each restaurant or hotel.

♦ **ACTIONS**

Most kids usually stun their parents with their sharpness in observing details. Here are several games that reinforce a child's natural powers of observation.

Unmailed Postcards Start with three pairs or more, depending on your child's stage of development. Lay one from each pair in a vertical straight line. Hand your child the identical card from one of the pairs and tell her, "Find the matching picture and lay this postcard beside it." Then hand her another card. Say, "Put this next to the picture that's just the same." When the third pair is side by side, you have two columns of look-alike pictures.

This basic game can be played with many more pairs, if your child enjoys it. To increase the difficulty, gradually find pictures that are more and more alike. For example, at first you might have one picture of a cow, another of Niagara Falls, the third of the Empire State Building. Later on you might challenge your child with three slightly different aerial views of Manhattan. Then judgment will depend on her reading of minor visual clues.

Magazine Fun From two current copies of a magazine, cut out pictures of the same cake, dress, piece of furniture, and houseplant (or any familiar object). For a two-year-old, choose things that are very different. For a three-year-old, you might select things that are very similar, such as four or five cakes or four or five houseplants.

Line up one of each pair in your series of pictures in a vertical column. Mix all the twin pictures and place them in a pile. Point to any picture and ask your child, "Hunt in the pile for a look-alike." Have him place it to the right of its mate. Point to another picture. Again, when he's found the mate, place it to the right. This aspect of the game—placing matches to the right of the model—encourages left-to-right movement that is necessary later for reading.

Soon you won't have to make a beginning column. Your child will be able to sort through a half-dozen or a dozen and a half pairs of cards, find the matches, and build the left and right columns by herself. Your presence, though, is still vital. You are appreciating her skill, either by paying attention to the process or by your occasional approving comment. This fosters her continuing interest in the game.

Scrap Basket Sort-Out If you have scraps in your sewing basket, cut small squares of up to twenty different colors and patterns. Have two squares of each fabric. To make this game a little different from the previous one, introduce an empty box with a divider, such as a box for two decks of cards. Or use two small shallow boxes side by side. Lay one of the fabric swatches in the lefthand box. Let your child hunt for the mate and drop it in the righthand box. Then put a swatch with a different design in the lefthand box. And your child's search is on again.

Matchbook Covers   Matchbooks are lots of fun. Their covers come in a variety of colors, widths, and typefaces. Some have pictures or smart logo designs that can be very eye-catching. Even if there are only words and your child doesn't read, she will differentiate among the restaurant names by the configuration of the words as a whole, the color combinations, and the style of type.

Cut the cover off the matches, disposing of the matches carefully. When you have collected over a half-dozen pairs, start playing a matching game such as those just described.

TRADEMARK LOTTO

♦ ACTIVITY

Identifying various symbols, as in company trademarks or logos, and finding each one's match.

♦ PROPS

Any of the following: manufacturers' glossy brochures (car dealers are a good source)—two of each; magazines—two of each issue; company annual reports—two of each; cereal boxes or labels from bottles or cans—two of each brand. 3-by-5-inch index cards.

♦ ACTIONS

Cut four trademarks or logos from brochures or magazine ads and paste them on blank index cards. For example, a jaguar from a Jaguar ad, a rampant lion from a Peugeot ad, a big *H* for a Honda. If you're working with cereal boxes, cut out things like a sun from a Raisin Bran box and a tiger from Sugar Frosted Flakes. From identical brochures or cereal boxes, cut out four matching trademarks. Glue this second set of trademarks on a shirt cardboard that has been divided by lines into four rectangles. This becomes your lotto game board.

A lotto game is usually played by one player picking an individual card from a pile and showing it to the other players. The one who first fills his board with matching pictures wins. With a very young child, lotto doesn't have to be played as a competitive game but rather as a solitaire game with your helping. You can simply see that your child is laying cards correctly on each board picture. Gradually he can learn to name each trademark verbally as he makes his match. This gets him in the habit of linking a visual symbol with a spoken word.

Gradually add to your collection more individual cards with their twins glued to lotto boards. Your future boards could have six or eight trademarks to make matching more difficult.

♦ VARIATION

You can also use logos that have a word in a decorative typeface rather than a picture or geometric design. The lettering of a product or company name has a distinct configuration that a child can identify even without reading.

♦ BENEFIT

As your child progresses from matching pictures to matching words in distinctive lettering, perceptual abilities are sharpened in a way that is preparing him or her to read.

GEOMETRY BINGO

♦ ACTIVITY

Distinguishing geometric shapes on a bingo card and covering three in a row to win.

♦ PROPS

Five-by-8-inch blank index cards, felt-tip pen, pennies.

♦ ACTIONS

Make a large bingo card for your child and one for yourself. Then make the caller's little individual cards. On your index cards, draw a box 4½ inches by 4½ inches. Cut it out. Draw lines dividing the now-square card into nine equal boxes. Keep the center box blank, but draw with felt-tip pen a geometric figure in each of the others. Start with circles, squares, and triangles, drawing one or two of these in each row (all the same color). Each card should be a different combination.

For the caller's cards, cut out about thirty squares, each 1½ inches by 1½ inches, from your index cards. With felt-tip pen, draw a shape on each. There should be several of each shape you are teaching your child.

Describe each shape to your child. "The circle is round and smooth, with no points. The triangle is flat on the bottom and has a sharp point at the top. The square has four just-alike sides and four corners." (You can also point out these shapes in commonplace objects around the house—jar lids, cushions, drawer handles, etc.)

Play this game much like an ordinary game of bingo. You start by being the caller. Draw a card from a pile of the caller's little cards. Hold it up and say, "A triangle. Do you have a shape like this? Okay, put a penny on it. I'll put a penny on my triangle too." The first of you to have three pennies in a row wins. Make a rule that each of you must say the name of the figure before covering it with a penny. Soon your child will not need the visual clue. Then do not show the caller's card. When you draw it, simply announce the name of the shape.

◆ VARIATION

You'll be surprised how many shapes your child will be able to identify if you keep at this game. When she learns the basic shapes, make new bingo cards with a rectangle, pentagon, and quatrefoil. Continue with still more sophisticated geometric figures—rhombus, trapezoid, hexagon, octagon, dodecagon, star, oval, isosceles and equilateral triangles. Once your child has digested these, trace drawings of solid geometric figures. After the sphere, cone cylinder, pyramid, and cube, you can extend the game to include various other polyhedrons.

◆ BENEFIT

Detecting differences in outlines of geometric shapes prepares the way for detecting differences in letters of the alphabet.

MATRIX COVER-UPS

◆ ACTIVITY

Recognizing an overall pattern or sequence and thereby guessing the missing link.

◆ PROPS

Posterboard or paper, felt-tip pens, self-sticking shapes (or construction paper).

◆ ACTIONS

Follow the instructions for making a matrix board in What's Missing in the Matrix? on page 194. Instead of the colored cubes in that game, use self-sticking geometric shapes or shapes cut out of construction paper. Or you can draw the shapes on a piece of paper.

The pattern suggested here draws on the child's perception of both colors and shapes. Vertically he sees rows of things the same shape. Horizontally he sees rows of things the same color.

Left column: place a blue circle in the top box, a red circle in the middle box, and a purple circle in the bottom box.

Middle column: place a blue pentagon in the top box, a red pentagon in the middle box, and a purple pentagon in the bottom box.

Right column: place a blue triangle in the top box, a red triangle in the middle, and a purple triangle in the bottom box.

Now cut out one piece of posterboard 3 inches square, the size of one of your boxes. This blank piece is used to hide one of the shapes.

When your child's eyes are closed, cover a geometric shape with the blank piece—perhaps the lower righthand triangle. When he opens his eyes, talk to your child about what shapes are still visible and how he can figure out what's under the blank piece from the orderly patterns.

"Scott, we see a row of blue shapes across the top, then a row of red shapes, and the bottom has two purple shapes. So what color is likely to be in the third box under the blank piece? Yes, purple. But what shape?

"Now we look from top to bottom to guess the shape. We see circles on the left, pentagons in the middle, and, running a finger down the right column, we see two triangles above the covered box. So what shape is likely to be in that bottom box? Another triangle. Right. Which color did we say? Purple. Now pick up the card and there you have a purple triangle. You solved the problem.

"Close your eyes again. I'll cover another shape for some more problem solving together."

You can introduce any number of shapes and reinforce proper labeling of them by playing this game. You can increase the complexity by making a grid of sixteen squares instead of nine. You can challenge your child further by covering two or three boxes with blank pieces.

♦ BENEFIT

Your child learns to scan the patterns and, on the basis of available information, draw a conclusion about the identity of the hidden element. Good training in thinking!

ANIMAL AND FISH CONCENTRATION

♦ ACTIVITY

By means of the time-honored card game called Concentration, teaching your child to recognize and name numerous animals and fish and, if you wish, birds, shells, trees, and flowers, too.

♦ **PROPS**

Two identical paperback nature books (such as those published by Golden Press). Three-by-five-inch cards.

♦ **ACTIONS**

Your child can help you make the materials for this game. You must have two identical cards of various species, as Concentration consists of pairing look-alike cards. If you've chosen African animal books, cut out the zebra, rhino, giraffe, and others from each book until you have twenty pairs. Paste each picture on an index card.

Start your first game with half of the pairs or less, depending on the age of your child. Lay them facedown in four rows of five cards each. At each turn you and your child pick up any two cards and lay them faceup in the same position. After taking a look, flip them over again. Your job is to remember their positions. The next time you pick up your first card, you may remember where its mate was positioned, if it has been turned up before. If you do, pick up the mate as your second card. You will then keep the pair. As your child gets used to the game, each of you names the species as you take the pair.

A preschooler has an uncanny memory for the position of sought-after cards and may easily beat you. Meanwhile you will both build a knowledge of flora and fauna.

You can make the game harder through the use of tropical fish or butterflies that differ only slightly from each other.

♦ **BENEFIT**

Perceptual skills, the ability to label objects with words, and memory are all exercised.

SHAPE OF THE STATES

♦ **ACTIVITY**

Learning the shapes and names of many of the United States and of various countries in the world.

♦ **PROPS**

Maps and puzzles of the United States, Latin America, Europe, or Africa.

♦ **ACTIONS**

Preschoolers who are keen at shape recognition can, with a little encouragement, discriminate the outline of one state from that of another. One couple kept a huge world map on the wall near the kitchen table. They pointed to places mentioned in the evening news and places to which some member of the family was traveling to. Another family worked with a map of the United States to show where friends and various members of the extended family lived. Other parents bought a puzzle of the United States soon after their child had mastered simpler puzzles of twenty-five pieces or so.

A mother of a four-year-old pasted a cutout of each state on a flash card and introduced several of these each week in regular sessions. (She'd learned the technique of presenting "bits of intelligence" on flash cards at The Better Baby Institute in Philadelphia.) One day her little girl who was eating a slice of bologna suddenly held up her slice and said, "Look, Mommy, Arkansas!" She had eaten around her slice in such a manner that it now had the contours of that state. For the next few months biting out a special shape from her slices of bread or cheese became commonplace.

Any parent-child duo fond of baking cookies can have some fun trimming slices of refrigerated cookie dough until they form shapes that simulate familiar states or countries.

♦ VARIATION

If your child enjoys learning about the states, you might introduce foreign countries, too, with a little information about each that would be of interest to a very young child. A children's encyclopedia will help you relay some colorful facts to make the country's shape and name come alive in the mind's eye.

PUZZLE PARTNERS

♦ ACTIVITY

Fitting together pieces of a homemade puzzle to form a picture, and working with commercial puzzles.

♦ PROPS

Picture postcards, wooden jigsaw puzzles, and cardboard puzzles.

♦ ACTIONS

Cut each postcard into three or four pieces. At first make the lines straight but vary the angles at which you cut into the picture. A few zigs and zags will do. Later you can separate the parts of the picture with more curvy lines, cutting out the bulges and indentations typical of a jigsaw puzzle.

Place the pieces that belong together in an envelope. Each night put a different envelope beside your preschooler's bed. Put it together before you tuck your child in, and leave it for her to do by herself in the morning.

♦ VARIATIONS

Assembling commercial puzzles together can be a lot of fun. You will love watching your child's mind at work. Looking for pieces that interlock certainly enhances your child's visual discrimination. Some towns have toy libraries from which expensive puzzles can be borrowed free. Use wooden jigsaw puzzles for a two- to three-year-old and cardboard puzzles for a three- to four-year-old. If you work at puzzles from toddlerhood up, your child may be able to handle a hundred-piece puzzle by the time she's four or five.

IF YOU HAVE A COMPUTER

♦ ACTIVITY

Classifying geometric designs according to their shapes and colors.

♦ PROPS

Personal computer; software that familiarizes young children with geometric shapes, such as "Gertrude's Secrets," a Learning Company disk for Apple computers and soon available for other computers.

♦ ACTIONS

Working with two-dimensional or three-dimensional shapes that a child can pick up and finger may be a more effective way to learn basic geometric shapes at first, but this knowledge can be reinforced while you and your child play with your computer keyboard (perhaps *your* new toy) and move these shapes around the screen.

This disk invites your child to solve puzzles involving diamonds, hexagons, squares, and triangles, each of which appear in four different colors. Gertrude is a goose who has made up some rules about the way these colored shapes are to be classified. Your child has to figure out the secret rule in order to solve the puzzle. When two frames on the screen are connected by a *single* line, your child must put a different geometric shape in each frame or the same shape but of different colors in each frame. "One line, one difference" turns out to be Gertrude's rule. When two frames are connected by two parallel lines, the rule is "Two lines, two differences." Then each frame must have a geometric design that is different both in shape and color from the other.

In another game on the same disk, your child solves an array puzzle. The shapes in the vertical columns must match each other in contour. The shapes running in horizontal rows are to match colorwise.

In still another game, the child punches keys to put various shapes inside a box on the screen. If a shape "belongs" in a box according to Gertrude's wishes, the computer lets it stay in the box. If it doesn't belong, the computer makes it drop out. Through this electronic sorting, all the similar shapes end up inside a box.

♦ BENEFIT

Problem-solving skills are developed while shape and color recognition is reinforced.

ALPHABET MASTERY

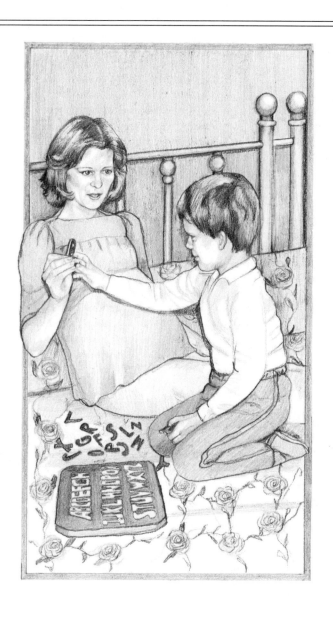

I n recent years many parents have been teaching their preschoolers how to read. This trend was launched by educators and researchers working in nursery schools and other child care centers. Professionals were experimenting with early reading in the sixties and seventies; in the eighties parents are doing it.

One mother's journal records this story about her child's momentous discovery of the meaning of those wiggly lines we call words:

Melissa at two years four months knows seventeen words. She has been learning them since her second birthday. When I lay out all her big-print word cards, she makes mistakes on only three or four.

After she learned about a dozen words, something clicked inside her head. Those letters she saw everywhere (not just those on the cards in Mommy's game) meant something. Here's how the revelation took place. She was walking on a little wall near the bank drive-in window. She suddenly started studying the very large letters mounted on the brick facade: Union Trust. She ran over and pointed to them, wanting to know what they said. I told her.

On the way home I got the idea of pointing out the stop sign: "That says *stop.*" She gave me an incredulous look and asked, "Dat say *stop?*" She seemed to think about the sign a long time. I pointed out each stop sign en route.

Later she was sauntering around the kitchen. Suddenly under the sink she saw words. She touched the bumpy metal sign. She looked up at me and queried, "Dat say?" I answered, "General Electric."

Then a few minutes later she was confronted with words on the dishwasher. They seemed to startle her, as if she wondered why she'd never noticed them before. *"Dat* say?" It was as if she were thinking, Do you mean to tell me there's a message embedded in all those squiggles? To her actual question I simply responded, "Kitchenaid Automatic Dishwasher." She was delighted. You'd think she'd just unwrapped a giant box from the toy store.

The next day she asked me what every road sign said. A month later she called out "Mobil" every time we passed the large gas station sign.

This mother's diary, recording in such detail her daughter's first steps in literacy, reflects the pleasure the mother had in the child's progress.

There's no longer any doubt that two-, three-, four-, and five-year-olds can learn to read. In fact, some theories say that before age six is the easiest time to learn. Theories also suggest that the close parent-child duo facilitates the grasp of reading skills in a way the school setting, however artful the teacher, never can.

The process of learning to read can be very interesting, even thrilling, for both child and parent, as countless families testify. But there are also many families for whom the adventurous effort isn't a success. By studying the pros and cons of early reading and by investigating some of the methods, you will make up your own mind whether you wish to pursue it. If so, research at the library or in a bookstore and perhaps conversation with some knowledgeable early childhood teachers in your area will lead you to a system with which you feel comfortable. One book with a complete series of lesson plans is *Teach Your Child to Read in 100 Easy Lessons,* by Siegfried Engelmann, Phyllis Haddox, and Elaine Bruner.

This chapter on the alphabet and the next chapter, Games for the Eager-to-Read, are filled with activities regularly used by several nursery school teachers who teach reading to their small pupils with enthusiasm and success. You should probably follow the activities in the order given, as each one builds on previously attained skills.

◆

TOOLS OF THE TRADE

◆ ACTIVITY
Buying or making movable individual letters of the alphabet.

◆ PROPS
Three-dimensional commercial letters or textured two-dimensional ones to be made with posterboard, glue, and either sandpaper, felt, or yarn.

◆ ACTIONS
If you shop for three-dimensional letters, you may have a choice of wood (natural or painted), plastic, foam rubber, or plastic with magnetic backing. Magnetic letters can be kept on the refrigerator door, where you and your child can form words during dinner preparation. Wooden let-

ters sometimes come packaged with a tray with grooves into which the letters fit like puzzle pieces. You can try your local toy store or ask a nursery school teacher for the name and address of a school supply store. Invest in the most attractive set you can afford. Children are drawn naturally to handsomely constructed materials. Buy upper case letters first, or buy both upper and lower case. Two-year-olds may enjoy free play with a set of letters before they are ready to learn letter names.

To make your own letter cards, cut out 5-by-5-inch squares from posterboard. Then cut out capital letters about two inches high from sandpaper or felt. Glue one letter to each square. If you use yarn, dribble glue onto the posterboard in the shape of a letter and lay a length of yarn on your sticky pattern. One mother cut letters from the stiff pages of a dimestore book about the alphabet and glued these onto contrasting-colored cards. Your child can watch or help.

Hold your child's finger and glide it over the textured letter shape in the same direction you would go (from left to right) if you were drawing it with a pencil. Say the sound the letter makes when it's in a word. (More about pronunciation in The Sounds Letters Make on p. 216.) In Montessori schools, pupils are helped to learn a letter sound not only by seeing the letter, hearing it pronounced, and saying it themselves but also by feeling its shape with their fingertips.

You don't have to begin teaching with A, B, C, D, but start with any letters that look quite different from each other as S, T, O, M. Or start with the letters of your child's name.

Some teachers prefer to start with upper-case letters. (For their reasons, see the next activity.) Then they proceed to lower case. Others prefer to start right out with lower case, since most primers are printed in lower case. Reading teachers often prefer to present letters in a particular order. For instance, Montessori teachers, using lower case, begin with m, b, t, and h.

All agree that preschoolers need large letters in contrast to the tiny print of letters in a book, plus tangible materials in contrast to the flat typeface on a book page.

♦ **BENEFIT**

Tactile experiences with letters foster visual discrimination.

SUCCESS WITH CAPITALS

♦ **ACTIVITY**

Teaching your child to recognize and name out loud various letters of the alphabet, using upper-case letters only at the start.

♦ PROPS

Three-dimensional letters or letter cards made in the previous activity.

Any objects in the home with letters on them. Open your eyes to how many you have: for example, kitchen appliances with brand names on them or labels such as WASH, DRY, RINSE, NORMAL, SHORT, ON, OFF, MEDIUM, BLEND, etc. Also the labels on food boxes, cans, bottles, jars, and plastic bags. Paint cans, lawn seed bags, cleaning products. Newspapers, magazines, books with colorful paper jackets.

♦ ACTIONS

There are good reasons for teaching your child capital letters before lower-case letters. It is much easier to distinguish visually between the various shapes of the capitals. Many of the lower-case letters are so similar—for example, p, d, b, and q—that a child becomes frustrated trying to remember them. A second reason is that capitals are everywhere, not only on objects in the home but also on traffic signs, street names, store names, billboards, and ads in store windows. Learning of new letters is constantly reinforced by seeing those shapes during everyday routines.

A third reason for teaching capitals is children's evident partiality toward them. Even after they learn to recognize lower case, novice letter writers always write to Grandma in all caps.

Since upper-case letters are easier to learn than lower case, the child experiences success sooner with them. And nothing succeeds like success. The good experience a child has with capital letters ignites his interest in learning more about reading.

One nursery school staff redesigned the beginning reader books in their library by pasting blank paper over the text and rewriting it in all capital letters. Then school parents created homemade picture books with picture captions lettered in all caps and found three- and four-year-olds learned more easily with these materials.

As you go about your daily routine, point out letters and take notice when your child points them out to you. Hold the identical three-dimensional letter next to the one you are noticing. Listed under Props are the many commercial products in your home bearing capital letters printed in many bright colors. You might tour the house with one of your textured letter cards and look for special letters. "Today we hunt for Ws." When you repeat the name of the letter, use the sound it makes rather than its formal name. In other words, purse your lips and blow out air— "w." Don't say "double-u." Also try not to say wih or wah because such pronunciations really include the sound of the vowel that follows w.

THE SOUNDS LETTERS MAKE

♦ ACTIVITY

Starting off right by teaching your child not the names of the letters but the sounds they make.

♦ PROPS

Letter cards or three-dimensional letters.

♦ ACTIONS

If children are going to learn to read by the phonics method, they must be taught the sounds letters make. Don't bother teaching the names of the letters as they are pronounced in a memorized recitation of the alphabet or in a singing of the alphabet song.

When you help a child learn to sound out a three-letter word such as *pot,* you want her to think and say a breathy *p* by pressing her lips together and producing a little burst of air. You don't want her to think and say *pea,* which is the letter name. The letter sound is clipped. It's not *pah,* as you might say when looking at the word *pot;* neither is it *puh,* which you might say if you were looking at the word *put.* When you pronounce a consonant, keep the enunciation as pure as possible. Notice the position of your lips. Say it crisply and don't follow with a drawled vowel sound.

If your child is picking up the formal names of letters from TV or other children, you can easily make clear the difference between the letter name and the letter sound. Compare letters to animals. When your child sees a picture of an owl, she knows that the name of the creature is *owl* and the sound it makes is *hoot.* When she sees a cat, she knows that the name of that furry creature is *cat* and that the sound it makes is *meow.* Tell her it's the same with letters. The name of this squiggle *S* is *ess.* The sound it makes is *ssss* (hiss like a snake).

The squiggles we know as letters are symbols for sounds. This is the basic concept to get across. It is not strange to a child to hand her a wooden letter and say, "What sound does this shape make?" Children love to learn these important grown-up symbols they see everywhere. You will need patience and a knack for making the learning times fun times. But it is very exciting to observe your own child gradually piecing together the information that turns her into a full-fledged reader.

There are lots of game-oriented ways to get familiar with these various shapes symbolizing various sounds. Start with consonants. Then teach vowels, referring to the short-vowel sounds only at first. Many simple games are included in the activity Getting to Know You, on page 218. You'll invent some of your own, too.

Try to proceed at just the right pace, not introducing too many letters at once, yet not letting your child get bored. Pressure or wrinkling your brow at a wrong answer will spoil the gamelike atmosphere. Don't react in a judgmental manner if your child doesn't know something. Avoid testing with "what's this" questions. Just give information cheerfully: "There's our old friend *M.*" Keep at-home alphabet sessions short and sweet, laughing and loving your way through them.

♦ **BENEFIT**

Mastery of letter-sound correspondence is a big leap toward the goal of linking the sounds in a sequence and thereby reading a word.

CLEVER CLUES

♦ **ACTIVITY**

Making and working with cards that show one letter of the alphabet plus a picture of a familiar (even loved) object that begins with the letter shown.

♦ **PROPS**

Twenty-six 3-by-5-inch cards, felt-tip pens, magazines or catalogs, your own photographs, and scissors.

♦ **ACTIONS**

This activity is a way to help your child remember the sound name of each letter of the alphabet. The easiest way to do this is to see a picture of something familiar and pronounce its name. Then he can train himself to hear the initial letter sound. If he sees a picture of a cat and says *cat,* he can clue himself on what a *c* sounds like. These picture cards, perhaps made together with your child, can be used by your child at times for self-teaching.

Make a set of twenty-six cards. Write each letter of the alphabet on one side and draw or paste a cutout picture on the other. Write either the upper case or the lower case, whichever you are teaching, or write both. Have fun selecting pictures (or your own photos) of objects your child is especially fond of.

As you go through a few cards on any given day, see if your child pronounces the letter sound after just seeing the letter. If not, turn the card over and show him the picture. He should name the object and repeat the name, listening for the first sound in the word.

GETTING TO KNOW YOU

◆ ACTIVITY

Becoming familiar with the letters of the alphabet—their shapes, sounds, and sound names—through lots of little games.

◆ PROPS

Three-dimensional letters and/or letter cards and/or Scrabble tiles.

Flash cards (commercial or 3-by-5-inch cards with hand-drawn letters).

Alphabet puzzle game.

For Gone Fishin'—glass fishbowl, construction paper, staples, magnet, yarn.

Newspapers and magazines.

Toys from your child's collection.

◆ ACTIONS

These games can be played with either upper-case or lower-case letters. After playing the games many weeks with one type, play the games again with the other type. Use sound names preferably.

Launch forth with consonants. When there is a consonant that could be pronounced the hard or soft way, stick to just the hard form. *G* as in *get,* not the soft *G* as in *gym.* With vowels, stick to the short vowel sounds: *A* as in *hat, E* as in *pet, O* as in *pot, I* as in *pin, U* as in *tub.* You could play the first few games with some two-year olds.

Hide a Squiggle   Hide a three-dimensional letter such as *B* under a chair cushion with some of it peeking out. "Kathy, go find the *B.*" When your toddler runs back with the letter, reinforce her learning of the letter's sound by repeating it. "Great, you found the *B!* Now *you* hide the *B* this time, and let's see if *I* can find it." (Don't say *bee.* Pronounce it in a clipped way, as for the very beginning of the word *bit.* Almost whisper it. The result is a breathy sound. Don't say *bih,* elongating the sound with a vowel.)

In the Groove   Toy stores or school supply stores carry alphabet puzzles. Each letter fits into a groove carved in the frame. You can start with most of the letters in place and just ask your child to find the right letters for the last few openings. Or you can lay the letters near their correct slots and let your child insert them. Talk about their shapes, the similarities and differences among them. Work together till your child can do the puzzle on her own. Mention the sounds of each letter often, but don't be too laborious about it. Smile a lot. Perhaps talk for a letter as though it were a doll. "You know the sound I make. It's a growly one: *mrrr.* I scared you, so put me in my proper slot in the frame."

Alphabet Athletics   You or your child can bend your body to form the shape of some letters. For instance, if your child stands with her feet together and her arms held out to the side, she's a *T*. If she raises her arms, she's a *Y*. If Mom and Dad stand straight facing each other and then bend their arms at the elbow, touching fingertips, they form an *H*.

Your child can also dramatize the sounds of some letters. He might slither across the floor like a snake, repeating *sss* over and over. He might fly like a bee, saying *zzzz*.

Invent a Game   One parent reported that there were letters on her child's bedsheet. When asked to sit on an *M*, his daughter eagerly slid over and covered the *M* with her bottom. Any silly ways of playing with letters can be not only amusing but educational.

Match from a Batch   If you have more than one of each letter in your set of cards or three-dimensional letters, you can play this game. Make a little pile of any three to five different letters. Then hand your child a duplicate of one of the letters in the pile. Let her pick the matching letter from the pile. At first start with letters that are quite different so finding a pair will be easy. Work up to the challenge of picking an *E* out of a pile with such similar-looking letters as *Z, F, H,* and *T* in it. Don't ask your child to name the letters at this point. You're interested mainly in her choosing the look-alike.

Letter Lotto   Make a lefthand column of letters. Suggest your child place a matching one to the right of each letter. If you have several of each letter, let her make a row of *T*s or *P*s.

Gone Fishin'   A Montessori schoolteacher has a glass fishbowl filled with fish shapes cut out of construction paper. Letters, also cut out of paper, are stapled to each fish. The fishing pole is a slotted spoon with a horseshoe magnet dangling from a twelve-inch piece of yarn. You might construct this learning tool with your child. As your child dangles the fishing line into the bowl, the magnet attracts the staple. Your child can pick up the fish, draw it out of the bowl, and pronounce the letter sound on it.

Flash It   Flash cards can be fun, not tedium, because kids love to learn. Set a regular time, just after meals or while in the bath, to show your child a letter. When you hold it up, he could give the letter sound. If he gets it right, he can keep the card, lining up the cards on his eating table or the bathtub rim. If not, you keep and review the ones he doesn't know.

Search and Circle   Ask your child to take a crayon and circle all the *R*s in today's newspaper headlines. Or ask her to decide on a letter and look for it among the blurbs on a magazine cover.

ALPHABET BINGO

♦ ACTIVITY

Playing bingo with letters instead of numbers on your bingo cards.

♦ PROPS

Typing paper, pen, three-dimensional letters or letter cards or Scrabble tiles; poker chips, pennies, or M&M's.

♦ ACTIONS

Draw horizontal and vertical lines to make a grid of sixteen squares on several sheets of typing paper. Fill in the squares randomly with various letters of the alphabet. Make sure each card is fairly different, with no single row exactly like a row on another card.

To play, gather a grandma as well as a pa, a ma, and a child. The caller pulls a letter out of a box of letters, shows it and announces it, or just announces it without showing it (more difficult). He calls it by its sound name, not its letter name—that is, *v* not *vee*. Grandma may have to be reminded not to use the formal name of the letter. Any player who hears a letter called that is on his card covers it with a poker chip, penny, or M & M. The first to cover a row of letters wins and eats his M & M's.

♦ BENEFIT

This game reinforces sound-letter correspondence.

TAPPING WITH A TYPEWRITER

♦ ACTIVITY

Teaching a three- or four-year-old a few simple rules about how a typewriter works and giving her time to experiment with it.

♦ PROPS

Old manual typewriter (although the keys may be hard to push) or electric typewriter (under supervision if you're uneasy about its survival).
Books or boxes with brand names on the lids.

♦ ACTIONS

From early toddlerhood on children love simple mechanisms. Age four is considered by some to mark a peak interest in letters, words, and reading. Typing combines these two interests—working mechanisms and reading words. So if you put a four-year-old in front of a keyboard, sparks of excitement may fly. Mothers have reported total concentration while a child has typed line after line of a single letter. A whole page of *L*s typed by a Lisa or a Laurie can be a treasured document.

Notice the size of the typewritten letter—a teeny *L*. Have your child compare it with the *L* on the keyboard, an *L* on the telephone pushbutton, an *L* on the cover of a book, and an *L* on a cereal box. Interesting size and style variations on a theme!

Press the shift-lock key to enable your child to type all capital letters. You can load and unload the paper. At first let her explore, hitting any key at random. Later you can play little games. One boy wanted his mother to call out a letter, any letter. He proudly located it on the keyboard and produced it on paper. Instant satisfaction! Here the manual labor—easy and quick—can keep up with the bright mind. The arduous task of forming a letter with a pencil in the hand is inconsistent with the four-year-old's quickness of mind.

Your child may be eager to type her name; then your name, Dad's name, his cousins' and friends' names. At some point he might like to copy book titles or the brand names on the top of his boxes of games or on cereal boxes. Prop the box close to the typewriter, and let him copy the words.

Any combination of letters, whether they form real words or not, can constitute a letter to Grandma. He might like you to spell *Dear Grandma* for him to type in at the top of the page of jumbled graphics.

Later when he asks you to spell lots of words for him, you might choose a time when you are doing some mindless work, such as cleaning up the kitchen. Then you will be free to spell out patiently word after word. Why not offer correction fluid if your child is upset with a mistake.

IF YOU HAVE A COMPUTER

♦ ACTIVITY

Learning to master some tricky letters of the alphabet with the help of a computer.

♦ PROPS

Personal computer; software designed to aid alphabet recognition, such as "Juggles' Rainbow" (see p. 222 for computer details).

♦ ACTIONS

Parents who have recently purchased a computer for themselves may enjoy introducing their offspring to the keyboard. While computers are by no means necessary for teaching the cognitive concepts in the

Learning Games section of this book, disks put across these concepts in a lively way. Not only will your child enjoy the animated graphics, but what's more important, you may get a special kick out of time spent with your child in front of the terminal. Prolonged time together may be the principal boon of the home computer for some young families.

One of several games on the "Juggles' Rainbow" disk teaches in a clever way the four hardest letters of the alphabet. Most children have difficulty telling apart lower-case *p, q, b,* and *d.* They keep mixing them up because each is composed of one straight line and a bubble. Notice that in *p* and *q,* the straight line goes below the bubble, but *p* has the straight line on the left and *q* has the straight line on the right. Take a deep breath and analyze *b* and *d.* With these the straight line is above the bubble, but *b* has the line on the left and *d* has it on the right. Do you despair of a four-year-old figuring out these difficulties? "Juggles' Rainbow" comes to the rescue.

The game starts by working on the concepts of *above* and *below.* The child hits any keys of the keyboard to place bars of color either above a horizontal line on the screen or below it. Later the screen displays a dotted bar above the line. The child then learns to hit only the keys that are above a corresponding strip placed along the middle of the keyboard. The screen presents new variations of the game until the concepts are thoroughly comprehended.

The next series of activities invites your child to place colored bars either to the left or the right of a vertical line running down the middle of the screen. There is a corresponding strip down the middle of the keyboard.

With the concepts of both *above/below* and *left/right* established, the disk introduces the letters *p, q, b,* and *d.* Then their configurations are not such a mystery. For instance, the letter *p* is now seen more clearly as composed of a line below a bubble and to the left of the bubble. *Below* and *left* are concepts your child has been playing games with.

"Juggles' Rainbow" doesn't present any other letters of the alphabet, but there are other diskettes that do. Just try your local computer store.

ZOOMING IN ON INITIAL SOUNDS

♦ ACTIVITY

As you work around the house, pointing out objects or asking for things that begin with a letter sound you are currently teaching your child.

◆ **ACTIONS**

This game involves auditory rather than visual discrimination. Your child listens to the sound of a beginning consonant in a word without seeing the letter. You might say, "Let's find some toys in your closet that begin with *b*. How about this—your ball? Here's another one: boat. But the car won't belong. It doesn't begin with *b*." Emphasize the *b* as you say *ball* and *boat*. Collect in a pile toys beginning with *b* and lay your three-dimensional capital *B* beside them. Eventually set out several letters and collect various toys or toy parts around each one that begin with the appropriate consonant.

As you sit at your desk paying bills with a little helper, notice out loud, "Wow, there are several things here that begin with, *p:* pen, pencil, paperweight, paper clip." As you cook dinner, say, perhaps, "I'm using utensils tonight that begin with *s:* spatula, spoon, scissors, spreader for butter." When changing a baby sister's diaper, you could ask, "Would you please hand me one at a time those things that begin with *p:* powder, Pamper, pin."

You could also tell a little guessing game story about things your child has done during the day. "It was cold out so you put on your c. . . . We went to the garage and got in the c. . . . With a long list of food to buy we went into the s. . . . Then we returned some books to the l. . . ."

You can also make up silly sentences in which all the words begin with one letter sound. "Let's make mud pies in the morning" or "Sophie sits on the sofa sipping soda."

◆ **BENEFIT**

Detecting the initial sound in each word is the first step in "sounding out," the phonics way of learning to read.

LETTER BOOKLETS

◆ **ACTIVITY**

Binding together cards portraying things that all begin with a particular letter.

◆ **PROPS**

Five-by-8-inch cards, hole puncher, brass paper fasteners or individual metal rings like those in a looseleaf notebook or yarn, magazines or catalogs.

♦ ACTIONS

As your child is learning a certain letter, flip through magazines together to discover pictures of objects or people that begin with that letter. You can identify the object or suggest that your child name things. Listen for the initial sound and help your child recognize it. If you are working on c, you may cut out pictures of a cake, a cook, a can, a cup, and a crab. Paste them onto 5-by-8-inch cards. Punch holes in the corners and thread them onto a metal ring or thread yarn through the holes. Or use a brass paper fastener.

Make books also for all the short vowel sounds. Draw pictures if you can't find appropriate ones. It will be easier to find objects for which the vowel is the middle sound rather than the initial sound. Your e book might have pictures of a pet, a net, and a jet. Another book might have pictures of a hat, a bat, and a man who is fat.

Go over these books together till your child readily names the objects in the pictures and hears the first or middle sound. You might then go on to think together of other objects or people in your child's experience that begin with the letter of the booklet you've just gone through.

If you still have the twenty-six 3-by-5-inch cards you made for Clever Clues, the activity on page 217, you can use each of those as the first card on each ring.

While making booklets may seem like a lot of work as you read about it, the interest your child has in mastering the art of reading will keep you going.

· 19 ·

GAMES FOR THE
EAGER-TO-READ

T his chapter is for those parents who are interested in having their children read early or for those eager children who won't wait till first grade to try. Whether your child masters reading before the age of six depends more on your attitude than on your child's native intelligence.

If you're indifferent to the matter and deep down would rather leave the teaching of reading up to schoolteachers, your first few tentative efforts to teach reading to your child probably won't blossom into an all-out campaign. If you're uptight about your child's level of achievement, your tension may spoil her carefree approach to learning. But if you love words and books and are excited about the possibility of your child enjoying them too, then your enthusiasm will enable you to take advantage of the games in this chapter.

While controversies continue to rage over the instruction of reading, during recent years many preschoolers have been happily learning to read both at home and in nursery schools. But it's not for everyone.

A purer motive is needed than your Johnny not lagging behind the Johnny down the block. Not every parent is a born teacher. Working with preschoolers demands patience, persistence, and a calm, cheerful nature that shines through every second of the brief teaching session.

Your reading habits will influence your decision on teaching reading. A love for books, an interest in words, a curiosity about ideas, a fascination with fantasy may fill the hearts of parents who want to help their children learn to read. These attitudes naturally facilitate the process.

Most parents I interviewed mentioned that reading aloud to their children was among their own favorite activities as well as one of their children's particular preferences. Here are some of their experiences:

One family always lingered after dinner, the parents reading at the table from the time their children, Leslie and Meghan, were tots. When the girls were older, they took turns reading to the group.

Some mothers became engrossed in the tales. A mother confessed that she and her son, Christopher, cried together over *Charlotte's Web.*

Another mother said, "Sometimes I could barely finish a touching story such as *The Dolls' House,* I'd be sniffling so."

Rules developed in some homes over library books. To avoid a literary rut, Rob's mom said they had to first read each library book once before they reread any of them. Clancy's mom let him pick out his own books at the library, but she always introduced one or two each week to correspond with a new life experience he had just had. One parent and child drove home with twenty books at a time from a suburban library. A city parent wheeled even more home in a supermarket cart.

Habits about reading evolved. "Whenever Sarah comes to me with a book, I sit down and read it," said a mother keen on early education. A more relaxed mother said, "I take my own book to bed and invite Dougie to bring his stack of picture books and climb in beside me. He lets me read in peace, happy to be doing exactly what I'm doing." One couple said, "In family attics we discovered our own old-fashioned, rather dogeared books dating from our childhood. These seem to have a special attraction for our kids." Tina's parents kept one of her books beside her bed, another on the back porch, a third in the bathroom, and a fourth in Mom's handbag to use when waiting in lines or reception rooms.

These parents are providing an ideal atmosphere for teaching reading. In these kinds of homes, some children have taught themselves to read with the parents helping only in an unsystematic way. But most storybooks are too advanced to be a teaching tool in the instruction of reading. More primary teaching tools are needed. This chapter offers ideas for such tools. It also gives parents who are rank amateurs rather than teaching pros some how-to-do-it tips.

First, though, should you or shouldn't you teach reading at home? In the past many parents have thought it not right to teach reading before first grade. They feared they might do it badly, or they believed preschoolers couldn't learn unless they were geniuses. They worried that it might be damaging to their child's eyesight or take the fun out of childhood. They wondered if their child might be bored later on in school if she was ahead of her peers. Now a new trend is developing.

Montessori and other nursery school teachers have proved that children can read before the age of six. Parents who are aware of early-childhood teaching methods have proved that they can teach reading at home without professional training. A little knowledge and a lot of love can accomplish wonders. Public opinion is leaning to the position that eyesight is not damaged by early reading. Early readers are showing they have a great time in first grade with the more advanced books their teachers are wise enough to offer them.

Advocates of teaching reading at a young age give the following reasons in favor of it:

1. Little kids can do it. Why not teaching reading to preschoolers, since many have the ability to master it!
2. Kids have an intense interest in the words they see all around them and in what they mean.
3. Proper development from birth seems to depend on two basics: exercising innate abilities and satisfying interests. By trying to read, a child does both—he exercises a latent ability and he satisfies an interest.
4. Kids' morale gets a big boost when they learn to read. Unlocking the code, deciphering those squiggles, seems to enhance self-esteem like nothing else. If they can experience this solid self-worth before they enter formal school situations, all the better.
5. Some educators believe children's interest in words and reading peaks at four or five and that therefore this is the easiest age at which to learn to read.
6. New worlds are opened up to beginning readers. They can always occupy themselves. They need never be bored again.

It will be up to you to decide if you are the kind of parent who enjoys teaching a child to read. Once you embark on this project, your attitude has to be one of gentle lightheartedness. You have to feel as relaxed and loving during this interaction as during other types of interchanges. If you feel tension about your child's performance, forget the whole thing. Your child has to feel that you feel that learning to read is a lark. It's got to be fun for you both. Scowling, sighing, losing your temper, and other signs of irritation are out. Your child won't be attracted to the reading games. You need to be detached enough not to show disappointment over wrong answers. Your comments should be nonjudgmental.

There is more complexity here than in teaching skills for riding a tricycle. So you'll need time to familiarize yourself with the games in this chapter and make the materials for them. The game time itself won't be too long. Two to ten minutes a day are plenty to spend on teaching reading.

You will have to be the judge of whether this month is the time in your child's life to begin teaching reading. You can make a start with some of the following games and see if she likes them. If your first few sessions are a flop, go back to other recognition games (of colors, shapes, and the alphabet). Try again in a few months. You may be more hopeful if you follow Joan Beck's reasoning in *How to Raise a Brighter Child* (Trident, 1967; Pocket Books, 1975). She writes that if little kids can learn to speak and understand words they hear (the oral symbol), they should just as easily recognize and understand words they see (the printed symbol). The mind is what understands, not the ear or the eye.

The following activities are sample games that reading teachers play with preschoolers. They represent more than one method of teaching children to read. Don't rush through them. Play one of them off and on for several weeks before going on to another. Progress will depend on your child's current interest and aptitude.

One last hint: always quit when you're winning rather than dragging on a teaching session. Don't feel you should reward your child for being a "pupil." He should enjoy being with you and have such fun learning that the activity is its own reward. Keep the game so involving and exciting that your child relishes the sessions as experiences that boost his feeling of success and satisfy his innate desire to learn his way in the adult world. Working on reading will bring you closer together.

◆

ON THE VERGE OF READING

◆ ACTIVITY

Encouraging your child's involvement with both the pictures and the text in storybooks.

◆ PROPS

Books you buy or borrow from the library.
Tape recorder, blank tapes (both optional).

◆ ACTIONS

As you read your child a story, pause to "read" the pictures, too. Label everything in the illustration, or point to things and ask your child to identify them. Let him describe some of the pictures as you go along.

Your child will easily memorize the text of a short book he loves after you have read it, at his request, over and over. Let him "read" it to you, repeating the text by heart as he turns each page. "This is Dougie's favorite thing in life," gushed one mother.

If your child hasn't memorized the text, she may know the gist of the story. Encourage her to ad-lib her way through the book. It's also okay to have her make up a new story, basing her tale on what the pictures tell her.

Act as though you are highly entertained by her rendition—which you will be. If you read with colorful expression, your child will probably vary her inflection and phrasing. Encourage a dramatic reading.

As your child is pretending to read, you might suggest she run her finger under each line of words. Make sure she is moving from left to right and from the top line to the bottom.

If you have a tape recorder, record yourself reading storybooks to your child. Let your child be with you at the mike. Giggle together at the funny parts. Let him ask questions about the story or pictures. You ask him questions, too. Your child can play back this tape when you are out or busy and follow along in the book as the tape is running.

Another time you can record his pretend reading of a book. Then play it back later in the week.

Libraries lend tape cassettes with storybooks. Your child can follow the narrator, looking at the pictures and perhaps reading some of the text. Sit with your child while you play these recordings the first few times to be sure she knows when to turn the page. Also your presence verifies your focus on enjoying literature, not just on keeping her occupied.

♦ BENEFIT

Your avid interest in the written word—the delight you show in funny, scary, or touching stories—ignites your child's desire to read.

CATCH A WORD

♦ ACTIVITY

Tossing a word written on a piece of paper and "tossing" a spoken word to a child—two games invented by playful fathers.

♦ PROPS

Typing paper, red or black pen.

♦ ACTIONS

Many a father teaches his toddler the game of catch. At first he may roll a ball to his child, who rolls it back. Later he throws it. The child may let it bounce and roll before retrieving it. Finally the child learns to catch it in mid-air and throw it back.

Here are two games of verbal catch invented by fathers from New York City. "Catching" the word involves the child reading it in the first game and trying to pronounce it after hearing it in the second.

The first dad set up an indoor slide made of a stained plank. He propped one end against the sofa seat. The other end rested on the floor. He sat on the sofa beside the top of the slide. Amanda sat on the floor at the foot of the slide.

This dad printed one word per sheet of typing paper. ("I forced myself to learn how to print.") He released one sheet at a time from the top of the slide. It slithered down to Amanda. She caught it. Then her dad said, "Do you want to try or shall I tell you?" Amanda would guess at the word or furrow a brow and let her father read it. They had a good time. The game was a treat for her.

The second dad played around with long, hard-to-pronounce words in a mischievous way. He would toss a long word at his daughter as someone might throw a ball. She listened hard and tried to repeat it, just as another child might scramble to catch a ball. He said, "I give her the hardest words I know. 'Jolan, say *Euripedes!*'" Jolan would throw back her head and then nod emphatically as she pronounced it. "Now, Jolan, try this monster—*Mephistopheles!*" He varied his voice tone—high, low, gruff, smooth—partly to give character to the words. *"Sacré bleu! Sayonara."* She repeated them pretty accurately.

Sometimes he explained the meaning and sometimes he didn't. He never corrected her pronunciation or said, "No, that's not right," but sometimes he repeated the same word. The smiles never disappeared from their faces during this verbal game of catch.

SOUND-OUT SENSE

♦ ACTIVITY

Teaching your child to read by the phonics method—sounding out words.

♦ PROPS

Three-dimensional letters or letter cards, 3-by-5-inch cards.

♦ ACTIONS

While reading the previous chapter, Alphabet Mastery, you may have begun explaining to your child the sounds for various letters. Perhaps you got used to saying the letter sound rather than the letter name, for example, a clipped *b* rather than *bee*. As soon as your child is familiar with several consonants and one or two vowels, you can help him decipher his first words.

To read a simple three-letter word by the phonics method, your child has to first separate the three sounds (which are printed together as one word, one unit) and then roll them back together again. Your child has to think and say aloud to himself *c . . . a . . . t. . . .* If he repeats the individual sounds more and more quickly, he blends them into an understandable word. Using your three-dimensional letters, spell a few words composed of the letters he knows. Practice sounding them out. Then write them on index cards and let him become familiar with the look of the word on paper.

You can tell your child that reading a word is like a take-apart, put-together plastic toy. First you see a whole toy car; then you pull it apart, perhaps into three odd sections; then you fit these back together in the form of the car. And so it is with a word. You see a whole word, you pull it apart into separate letter sounds, then you fit them back together, listening for the word the sounds make when linked together.

♦ BENEFIT

Common sense plus the majority of experts favor phonetic methods over sight reading.

PROVOCATIVE WORDS

♦ ACTIVITY

Collecting words that are names of things that are important to your child.

♦ PROPS

Three-dimensional letters or letter cards.
Five-by-8-inch index cards.
Felt-tip pen.
Self-sticking address labels.

♦ ACTIONS

Take some three-dimensional letters or letter cards and compose a word or two that would be especially meaningful to your child, perhaps *fun, mom, dad.* If your child is interested, make word cards of these special terms. Deposit them in a word bank (a file card box) for safekeeping.

Jolan's mother found her daughter was very excited about the names of her friends printed in large letters underneath their snapshots which were tacked to a bulletin board in her room. These were very important words because to her her friends were VIPs.

A pioneer in early reading achieved success by using words such as *kiss* that describe something touching a child's emotional life. Try to think of some simple words—nouns or verbs—that describe something currently vital to your child; perhaps *sand, snow, slide, jump.*

You may not want to use long words, even if they are meaningful, or words that are hard to sound out by phonetic rules. Here are some simple three-letter words that are provocative. *Cut,* if your child has a scrape on his finger. *Bug,* if you've recently examined an insect on your patio. *Big,* if you've noticed a large truck. Confine your choice of words to those that have a short-vowel sound.

You can also label furniture and objects around the house. Use self-sticking address labels if they won't damage your furniture. Print the name of the piece of furniture or objects. Let your child peel off the backing and slap it on. You can write a name for anything your child wants labeled, but here are some possibilities for domestic objects that can be labeled with three-letter words having a short-vowel sound. Start out with only a few. Use upper- or lower-case letters, whichever you've chosen to teach.

hat	bed	rug	pot	pin
cat	pet	hut	hot	bin
can	net	jug	top	gin
pan	set	mug	cot	tin
fan	wet	tub	mop	kit
man	end	gum	box	bib
Tab	pen			lid
pad	peg			

When your child becomes familiar with some of these, try removing several signs. Hand these to your child in a day or so and suggest he stick them back onto the objects they describe.

◆ BENEFIT

The words that are the most interesting to try to read are the ones that relate to everyday life.

WORDS DESCRIBE PICTURES

◆ ACTIVITY

Looking at a picture and then scanning word cards to pick the one that describes the picture.

♦ PROPS

Three-by-5-inch index cards (unlined).
Five-by-8-inch index cards (unlined).
Magazines or catalogs.

♦ ACTIONS

Cut out a dozen or more pictures of objects that can be labeled with a three- or four-letter word that has a short-vowel sound. Paste the pictures on the larger index cards. Draw objects if you can't find pictures. Cartoonlike sketches are fine.

You should write out the name of each object on a smaller card. Use caps or lower case, whichever you are teaching. Some suggestions: egg, cap, pad, hubcap, lug nut, lap, pal, pet, lab, hen, yen, keg, gas, bag, cob (of corn), sun, gal, pit, cop, ump, rag, fan, sod, rod, job, bat, kit. You can also use some words where the last two letters are the same: hill, dill, sill, mitt, butt.

Locate or draw pictures that depict an action: sit, beg, cut, run, ask, sip, jab, dig, rub, hum, pat, jog, win, hit, rip, hug. If you're still looking for more ideas, find pictures that suggest an adjective: sad, bad, tan, red.

Lay out a picture card of a paper bag for your child and lay nearby about three of the word cards. "Let's see now—which word shall we lay under this picture? Yes, it's a bag. *B . . . a . . . g.* Does this word say *bag?* (Point to the wrong word.) No, it starts with *c.* We need one that starts with *b.*" (Remember, always pronounce letter *sounds,* not letter names.) Continue working with your child, helping her sound out each possible word till she hears the right one.

As a variation, start with one word and three pictures and help your child read the word and pick the picture that fits the word.

If you are currently working only with capital letters, keep the picture cards and later use them with word cards that are printed in lower-case letters.

♦ BENEFIT

Pictures with labels establish connections between familiar objects and written symbols representing those objects.

LINEUP FOR CONSONANTS

♦ ACTIVITY

Making a row of pictures of objects that begin with a certain consonant.

♦ **PROPS**

Three-dimensional consonants or letter cards, upper or lower case.

A collection of dollhouse accessories, small toys, toy parts, or household objects that begin with consonants you are teaching. (You can also use nature finds—leaves, stones, pinecones.)

Picture cards you made for Clever Clues (p. 217), Letter Booklets (p. 223), Words Describe Pictures (p. 233), Your Vowel, My Vowel (p. 236).

Any new pictures of objects with names longer than three letters.

♦ **ACTIONS**

From your collection of three-dimensional letters or letter cards, choose a few consonants that your child has become familiar with and perhaps one that is new. Put these letters, one underneath the others, in a column at your left.

The first game is played by lining up actual small objects next to the letters. The second game is played by lining up pictures of objects.

Game I   Gather miniature toys or toy parts whose names begin with letters you've laid out. You could also use household objects or nature finds for your lineup. If the letter at the top of the column is *c,* help your child pick out objects that begin with *c:* cup, cone, cap, calculator. Line them up in a horizontal row to the right of the letter. Do the same for the other letters in the column.

Game II   From your collection of pictures choose those whose names begin with consonants in your column. Suppose the top one is *b.* Your child may pick up a card at random and name the object shown— *man.* You might say, "I don't hear a *b* sound at the beginning. How about this picture? What is it?"

Your child says, "Basket." You then might ask, "Does that begin with a *b* sound—*basket?*" Work to build a horizontal row of pictures of things that begin with the *b* sound: bath, bed, basket, bumper (if you have pictures of things other than those described by three-letter words.) This may be all your child can do in one session.

If this is done quickly, you can go on to the next letter, which might be *m.* Choose pictures of meat, muffin, merry-go-round, and line them up in a horizontal row to the right of the letter. Working from top to bottom and from left to right reinforces a skill that is important for reading.

♦ **BENEFIT**

Thoughtfully pronouncing object names out loud reinforces the ability to hear similarities and detect differences in sounds.

YOUR VOWEL, MY VOWEL

♦ ACTIVITY

Identifying the vowel sound in short words and matching the vowel you hear to the vowel you see.

♦ PROPS

Pictures of objects with one short vowel in their names.

The five vowels as three-dimensional letters, letter cards, or Scrabble tiles.

♦ ACTIONS

This game was played at the Connecticut nursery school called The Early Learning Center, where a teacher and four pupils each held a vowel. At home, one parent can hold one vowel, a second parent or sibling another, and the preschooler a third vowel. Then two dolls or stuffed animals can join the circle, each with a vowel at its toes.

The picture cards are turned facedown in a pile. Dad can hold up the picture cards one at a time. Each player identifies the picture to himself. If the word describing the picture has the vowel you hold, you claim the picture. Suppose it is a sketch of a dock. The person who is holding *o* should claim the picture.

Mom could think for the dolls. If the picture is of a dish, and one of the dolls has the *i* letter, then she could say in a high-pitched doll voice, "That's mine." Then she places the card in the doll's lap. If your child is advanced enough to listen for more than one vowel sound at a time, he can think for one of the dolls as well as himself. He has to sound out the word to himself, then look at his vowel and the doll's vowel and decide if the word has either of those vowels in it.

If your child is only a beginner at this game, start with only two or three vowels and sound out the word for your child. Then give him the card, if it's his, till he catches on.

FINALLY THE FINAL SOUND

♦ ACTIVITY

After working on initial sounds and the vowel sound in the middle of a word, pressing on to teach the final consonant.

♦ PROPS

Three-dimensional letters (upper or lower case), miniature objects, pictures.

◆ **ACTIONS**

Re-sort your miniature objects and/or the picture you've been using in the two previous activities to teach initial sounds and mid-word vowels. This time keep together those that end with the same letter.

If you have word cards to identify each object or picture, reorganize them so that all the ones that end the same are together.

Now you are ready. Start with just three items. Have your child make a column of objects or pictures, and then with the three-dimensional letters spell the appropriate word. A column of final *g*s would be:

> pig
> bug
> rag

A column of final *t*s would be:

> hat
> pet
> dot

◆ **BENEFIT**

Your child discovers the final sound, somewhat hidden by the first two sounds, by playing games that sharpen auditory discrimination.

FLIP AND SAY

◆ **ACTIVITY**

Creating and working with booklets similar to materials made commercially for early-reading teachers.

◆ **PROPS**

A stack of scrap paper (perhaps sliced at the office by a paper cutter) about the size of a 3-by-5 card.

A stack of paper exactly half that size.

Stapler, pen.

◆ **ACTIONS**

First make a booklet. On the bottom page of your booklet, write the core of a word—for example, *at, en, ug*—on the righthand side. On the lefthand side of the bottom page, staple a stack of pages half the size.

The core of the word on the bottom page (the only full-size page) should show.

Each of these smaller pages should have a different consonant near the edge of the paper, so that this initial consonant is next to the core of the word.

Together with your child flip through the top half-pages. Each flip creates a new word. When r shows up beside *at*, you and your child read "rat." A flip to the next half-page might bring *m* next to *at*, and you read "mat." Another flip to the next half-page, which has *c* on it, and you both say "cat." The top page may have *b*. As you are saying the word, you may be sounding it out gradually. Saying it will consist of rolling together the three sounds—*b . . . a . . . t*.

You can have nineteen scrap-paper booklets. Following is a list of the core sounds that produce a lot of words preschoolers know. Write any one of these sounds on the bottom page of a booklet, the larger page. Then on the half-size pages, write any consonant that will make a real word when combined with the two letters of the core sound. A few nonsense words are okay, too. Remember to write the consonant near the edge so that it looks like one whole word as you flip.

an	id	op	un	en
ap	ig	ot	um	eg
at	ip	ox	ut	et
ag	it		ug	
			ub	

Nursery school, kindergarten, and first-grade teachers have various teaching tools, such as the vowel wheel, which accomplish the same purpose as these flip-and-say booklets. If you have access to such a tool, you might be easily able to copy the idea and make it out of materials found in the house. Check with a teacher friend or a school supply outlet.

READER'S LOTTO

♦ **ACTIVITY**
Pairing matching word cards.

♦ **PROPS**
Three-by-5-inch cards, colored felt-tip pen.

♦ **ACTIONS**

Write the same words on two cards so that you have five to ten matching pairs of cards. Play this like the games in Matching Mania on page 201. The format reinforces the left-to-right direction necessary for reading.

Make a column on your left of one word from each of the pairs. Mix up their mates in a pile. Find the mate to the top card yourself. Then invite your child to find the mate to the next card. Instead of asking "Can you find it," which could be disturbing if she can't, say "I'd like you to find the mate for this word *pit.*" Avoid can/can't language and situations whenever possible.

CONCENTRATION ON WORDS

♦ **ACTIVITY**

Playing the time-honored game of Concentration with word cards instead of picture cards.

♦ **PROPS**

Sixteen to forty 3-by-5 cards.

♦ **ACTIONS**

You are going to play the game of Concentration with words instead of pictures. See Animal and Fish Concentration, page 206, for the rules. It is probably better if your child has played with picture cards first.

Print the same word on two cards. Start with eight pairs of words, either words you are reviewing or new ones you are introducing.

Of course, with words only this becomes a real reading game as well as a memorizing game. On one turn your daughter may turn up *tot* and *tan.* She reads them out loud. Then she puts them facedown. Then you turn up *jet* and *tot.* You read them and turn them back down. Your child now knows exactly where the second *tot* is. She can probably remember where the first *tot* is, which she herself turned up on her earlier turn. She now turns up both *tot* cards and takes the pair.

♦ **VARIATION**

You might soon play with harder words that are not so easy to sound out phonetically but that your child can pair by sight reading—that is, by recognizing the configuration of the letters composing each word.

PRESCHOOLER SPELLING BEE

♦ ACTIVITY

Sounding out a word, listening to the component sounds, and then choosing the letters needed to spell it out.

♦ PROPS

Three-dimensional letters (upper or lower case) or Scrabble tiles.

Miniature objects such as from a dollhouse or from a glass, china, or plastic animal collection; or Crackerjack box surprises and party favors. The trick is to find objects with names that are only three-letter words.

Picture cards if you don't have enough objects.

♦ ACTIONS

In Montessori classrooms a child lays out a felt mat or square on which he does his work. On the left he makes a column of objects. At the right of each object, he spells out its name.

When you and your child set up your materials for these games, you might choose to place them on a brightly colored silk scarf (plain, not patterned) or on a polished glass coffee table. You might perch each little object on a little stand such as a box lid and lay the letters to the right. The prettier and brighter the objects or picture cards are, the more interested your child may be. Aesthetics plays a selling role in word games as in any area of life.

Line up some cute miniature objects (or pictures of objects) in a column. In a nearby pile of letters you might place only those necessary for the names of these objects. Include a few extra letters if your child needs a challenge. Beside each object, your child places the letters needed to label the object.

Spelling requires thinking of the name of the object, saying it out loud, breaking up the name into its component sound parts, then translating each sound back into the corollary letter that makes that sound, picking out the letter from the pile, and building the word. It seems a complex procedure, and it is, but it's not beyond the ability of some four-year-olds. For success, the parent must be interested enough in the goal to assemble the materials, proceed patiently step by step, and put in time one on one with her child. But to be there as your child makes the breakthrough to reading is surely one of the biggest thrills of parenthood.

♦ BENEFIT

Spelling a spoken word provides practice at transforming information heard into information to be seen.

HOMEMADE STORYBOOKS

♦ ACTIVITY

Making and reading together books that are especially easy to read.

♦ PROPS

Paper, magic marker, magazines (optional).

♦ ACTIONS

A book for teaching a child to read is called a primer. The average primer published for beginning readers actually seems too hard for the real beginner. Parents can bridge the gap between word cards and first reading books by making delightful preprimers.

If you're halfway decent at sketching, even stick figures, you can draw and subtitle your drawings. Otherwise go through old magazines for pictures that suggest three-letter words with which you can build a skeletal story.

Print your letters about ⅜ inch high. Write only one line per page.

Some examples of text for such books follow. In the effort to confine the text to two- or three-letter words, the prose will be a little truncated. But never mind; it will be thrilling to your child to be able to sound out every word in a "real" storybook.

Use the following stories and illustrate appropriately, or make up your own equally simple stories about subjects meaningful to your child.

cat sat on mat
cat has rat
cat is fat
pat cat

Bud in tub   *(show boy in bath)*
sub in tub   *(show toy submarine in bath)*
cub in tub   *(show lion cub in bath)*
Rub dub dub   *(show towel being rubbed on boy)*

mug is hot   *(show steaming mug)*
sip mug   *(show mug at someone's mouth)*
lip hot   *(show scowling face)*
fan mug   *(show a fan blowing on mug)*
not hot   *(show a person with a happy face holding mug)*

pig is big
pig is fat

pig is sad
pig is fed
pig did a jig

tin can
jab top
cut it
dig in
wet jam
yum yum

man fix bug   *(show Volkswagen beetle)*
top up   *(show hood up)*
hit it
rub it
tap it
it can run   *(show man driving away)*

IF YOU HAVE A COMPUTER

♦ ACTIVITY

Using a diskette to help the prereader indentify letters, recognize their associated sounds, and begin to spell simple words.

♦ PROPS

Personal computer, diskettes such as "Word Picture" from the Micro School Programs of Bertamax, Inc. (TRS-80), "Letters and First Words" from the Kids' Corner Line of C & C Software, and "Word Families" by Hartley (the latter two are available for Apple-compatible computers).

♦ ACTIONS

A children's librarian I interviewed said that her library's new computer in the children's room is riveting parents' attention, especially that of fathers. Involvement with the computer seems to give dads a way to play with sons that intrigues them. The librarian hopes to see mothers and daughters interact together with the computer just as enthusiastically.

As computers become more commonplace in the primary grades at school, it may well be an advantage to your child to have had experience with one at home. But the principal benefit may be the fun *you* have learning to work the computer and helping your child become acquainted with the new technology. The decade may witness many parent-and-kid partners both starting as beginners in front of the terminal, learning computerese with and from each other. This can't help but make for quality time.

"Letters and First Words" includes three programs: ABC, Letter Sounds, and Building Words. ABC presents a letter and asks your child to match it to one of a group of upper- and lower-case letters. An animated graphic display rewards each correct answer. Letter Sounds presents a letter and a group of objects. Your child has to pick the word that corresponds with the letter (which might be an initial, a final consonant, or a middle short vowel). Building Words requires your child to type the single letter that completes a word. A clown waves approval.

"Word Picture" reinforces the basic concept that letters form words and words name things. As you help your child type the name of a noun the computer knows, its picture is displayed on the terminal.

In "Word Families," your child practices substituting beginning and final consonants or middle vowels in closely related words. For instance, when the word *bag* appears on the screen, a group of consonants appears also—*s, w, k, r.* Your child chooses one of these to substitute for the *b* in *bag.* If he chooses *w,* the screen shows he's made a good new word, and the *w* disappears from the group. He finds out sooner or later that *k* will not work as a substitute.

· 20 ·

SKILLS FOR
WRITERS-TO-BE

To hold a pencil firmly and guide it deftly across paper in those dancing lines we call letters require fine-motor skills. These skills can be developed long before your child gets that primeval urge to write her own name. And they can be gained by manipulating objects other than a pencil.

This chapter is full of playful pastimes that will give little hands practice at small-muscle movements. If you introduced your child to activities in Chapter 1, Kitchen Companions, and Chapter 2, Art Start, she is already making the transition from actions that are cute but clumsy to actions that are well coordinated. Manipulating cooking utensils and artists' tools provides a workout for the fingers.

Perhaps you are observing your child and thinking, Oh, dear! She isn't attracted to finicky games such as fitting puzzle pieces together. She likes action on a big scale—running, climbing, and sliding. To provide a balance you may need to enhance the appeal of fine-motor activities.

Using colorful, pleasantly tactile material will help your cause. Making sure the play tasks are easy enough so your child experiences success at them almost right away is a trick of the parenting trade. Sometimes this involves preparation behind the scenes or setting materials up in a special way to facilitate manual actions. Then you can increase the difficulty level gradually. As an example, read ahead on how to make cutting with scissors a do-able feat even for a toddler. Then engage your superactive kid in some sit-still moments with an eyedropper, a socket wrench, a shoelace, yarn, or chalk. As mastery of manipulative tasks increases, your child's interest in these will grow. Later on, writing her name and other first words will be the frosting on the cake.

♦

SCISSOR-HAPPY AT TWO

♦ ACTIVITY

Helping a two-year-old manage a pair of scissors.

♦ PROPS

Short, sharp scissors with blunt ends. (Good-quality scissors are necessary. Cheap ones are so dull they frustrate a small child.)

♦ ACTIONS

A two-year-old who is yearning to cut scrap paper may find using a pair of scissors a difficult operation. His fingers are little and clumsy. But there is an unconventional way to hold scissors that enables an ex-toddler to have the satisfaction of snipping away to his heart's content.

Have your son hold the scissors the way you would hold pruning shears. Put one handle in your child's left hand and the other in his right. The scissors should be kept on the horizontal. Hold a piece of paper vertically between the blades and tell your child to cut. "Open. Close." He pulls apart the handles, then pushes them together.

You can keep moving the paper so your child keeps snipping it in different spots until he's snipped off a shape. It doesn't matter how it's contoured. A child likes to be the cause of an interesting effect. Here he transforms a whole piece of paper into a pile of asymmetrical scraps.

♦ BENEFIT

Keeping the scissors horizontal and opening and closing the handles again and again develops manual coordination.

MANIPULATING À LA MONTESSORI

♦ ACTIVITY

Manipulating small objects in amusing ways that exercise the small muscles of the hands.

♦ PROPS

Clothespins, coffee can or basket, spools, shoelace, ribbons, walnuts, scooper to make small ice cream balls, melon baller, marbles, pitcher, rice, doll dishes, dish towel, shoe polish, silver polish, polishing cloth, eyedropper, nutcracker, almonds.

♦ ACTIONS

To develop finger dexterity and hand-eye coodination, let your child practice handling some of the simple mechanisms, safe tools, and interesting objects in your house. The following exercises are similar to those practiced in Montessori classrooms.

Pinching Clothespins   Find some weak ones that open easily. Let your child squeeze the two ends till the clamping end opens enough to clamp onto the rim of a bread basket or coffee can. Let your child arrange a circle of clothespins all around the rim, perhaps alternating colors.

Stringing Spools   Take a shoelace and wrap transparent tape near one end to make the stiff point longer. Have your child string your spools of thread together. If you don't have empty spools, perhaps you'd permit the stringing of full spools as long as hands are clean. (Tape the thread end to keep the thread from unwinding.) Commercial beads are fine, too, of course.

Braiding Ribbons   Give your child three ribbons or lengths of fat yarn. Knot them all together at one end. Lay them on a table, anchored at the knot, if possible. Show her how to braid, perhaps taking charge of one or two ribbons yourself.

Transferring Walnuts   Turn out a bag of walnuts into a pretty bowl or basket. Have a similar empty bowl or basket next to the full one. Give your child a scooper that makes small ice cream balls. Suggest that he scoop one walnut at a time and transfer it to the second bowl. After he's mastered this feat, you might introduce a pair of wooden tongs to move the nuts with as the next challenge. The same operation is fun to do with marbles and a melon baller. Slightly finer motor skills are needed.

Pouring Rice   To help your child learn to pour milk, juice, or cream from a pitcher without spilling a drop, let her try this exercise. Fill a two-cup measuring cup full of rice. The cup should have a beak like a pitcher. Show your child how to grasp the handle in her right hand and support the bottom of the cup in her left so it won't seem so heavy. Practice at pouring dry ingredients protects your child from having to "cry over spilled milk."

Spic 'n' Span   A set of doll's tea dishes plus a colorful absorbent dish towel can provide experience at careful washing and drying. After the tea party is over and the doll guests have gone home, let your child slosh the dishes in sudsy water, rinse them, and wipe each one dry. Watching every droplet disappear with a finger rub is a peaceful pastime.

Quick Shine   You can show your child your respect for beautiful things by the care you give them. Provide him with a polishing cloth, too, and access to appropriate wax, polish, or cleanser. Rub up a few silver serving utensils or earrings. A brass planter, knocker, or drawer handles may need spit and polish.

Also work on a setup whereby your child can polish his own or your shoes without making a mess. Have a basket or tray in which is a newspaper for protecting surfaces, polish, cloth, and paper towel for fingers.

Coating the dining room table with sprayed-on polish or paste wax or rubbing wood furniture with oil is especially enjoyable when you apply the elbow grease together. Close, hard looks before and after reveal the improvement.

Drop by Drop Fingers get a workout if your child learns to pinch the rubber bag of an eyedropper and squeeze out the water in the glass tube. Give her two tiny dishes, one with water in it. Show her how to suck the water into the eyedropper; then how to squeeze it out. Color the water with food coloring. Borrow a thimble from your sewing basket and ask your child to delicately prepare a minidrink of juice for a nearby elf.

Nutcracker "Sweet" Find an easy-to-work nutcracker and present your child with a dish of almonds. They have soft shells for cracking.

♦ **BENEFIT**

Increasing dexterity enhances self-esteem.

APRIL FOOL'S LACE-UPS

♦ **ACTIVITY**

Threading shoelaces into the wrong pair of shoes.

♦ **PROPS**

Closetful of shoes with laces.

♦ **ACTIONS**

If Daddy is a good-natured soul, he may not mind this scheme that kept one child who loved learning to lace very busy. David drew the brown laces out of Dad's business shoes and threaded them into his dad's sneakers. Then he took the sneaker laces and threaded them through the business shoes. "That will make Daddy nuts!" he gleefully announced.

It's only fair if Mom, an April Fool's conspirator, helps repair the damage. Don't miss a hole now! Let your child point to the next hole for the end of the lace to enter each time.

♦ **VARIATIONS**

Here's a kinder in-the-lap game for tired fathers and energetic kids. Seat your child in your lap facing you. Teach her to unbutton your shirt buttons. Show her how to hold the shirt edge with her left hand and pinch the button with the fingers of her right hand. Then help her guide the button through the buttonhole.

For comic relief, close your eyes and pretend you don't realize all the buttons on your shirt are being unbuttoned. Then open your eyes and fake shock. "Who did that?" Snooze again while the elf buttons the shirt front.

Look for zippers, snaps, hooks and eyes, and toggle buttons on your own clothes that work fairly easily. Let your child practice on these. Then the situation is more of a just-for-fun exercise, rather than the serious business of dressing or undressing oneself.

◆ BENEFIT

Seemingly mundane finger movements prepare a child for future accomplishments with pen and paper.

CARPENTER FINGERS

◆ ACTIVITY

Wielding a screwdriver and socket wrench to develop the manual dexterity later needed to control a pencil.

◆ PROPS

Three 2-by-4 fir blocks about 6 inches long.
Molly bolt for large screw.
Molly bolt for medium-size screw.
Drill, screwdriver.
Two hex-head nuts of different sizes and two matching bolts (about a half-inch in diameter is a good size).

◆ ACTIONS

For this activity you first have to make, through your own carpentry efforts, two devices that enable your child to practice using a screwdriver and a wrench. These devices are copies of learning materials used in Montessori classrooms.

Screwdriver Practice Saw a 2-by-4 into two 6-inch lengths. Nail one block on top of the other. Now, toward one end, drill a hole and drop a molly bolt into it until the neck is flush with the surface. Keep turning the screw till the molly bolt expands and is secure in the wood.

Sink another molly bolt, made for a smaller screw, toward the other end of the block. Now your child can practice twisting the screwdriver to make the screw go in or come out.

Socket Wrench Practice Saw just one 6-inch length off a 2-by-4. Drill a hole $7/16$ inch in diameter. Insert the bolt and hammer it down so the head of the bolt is flush with the surface of the wood. Turn the block over. The bolt will protrude through the 2-by-4 block. Place the hexhead nut on the end of the bolt. Sink another bolt if you want two sizes to practice on. Now show your child how to turn the nut on the end of the bolt with the wrench.

"SEWING" FOR DEXTERITY

♦ ACTIVITY

Poking yarn through holes to complete a design on homemade sewing cards.

♦ PROPS

Cardboard rectangles (back of legal pads or shirt cardboards).
Crayon.
Bright colored yarn.
Tape or nontoxic glue.
Hole-puncher.
Pictures from old magazines (optional).

♦ ACTIONS

Sewing at this age is really lacing. It's a snap to make your own sewing cards like the ones in the toy store. Draw a big smiling face on a rectangle of cardboard. With a hole puncher, make holes all along the circumference of the face.

Create a lace by wrapping tape around the end of a length of yarn. Or dip the end into glue, make a point, and let it dry. Make a knot at the other end bigger than the hole in the cardboard.

Your child can do a running stitch, guiding the yarn in and out of each hole. Let her start at the chin of the smiling face and work around the circle.

Paste pictures of houses, people, or toys onto cardboard. Punch holes around each shape for outlining them with yarn stitchery.

You can reinforce knowledge of numbers or letters through sewing card designs. Write two rows of numbers, each 2 inches high, on your cardboard rectangle. Print the numbers 1 to 5 on the top row and 6 to

10 on the bottom row. Then punch holes at the upper lefthand corner and lower righthand corner of each number. Your child will make the yarn cross each number in a simple diagonal line from top to bottom. (She will not follow the difficult line of the numeral.)

Starting at number 1, have her poke her yarn into the hole at the upper left of the numeral 1. Then she crosses the yarn over the numeral and pokes it down the hole to the lower right of the 1. Next she brings her yarn out of the hole at the upper left of the numeral 2. She crosses the yarn over the digit and threads it through the hole at the lower right of the number. This pattern reinforces left to right and top to bottom directions that are so important in writing letters.

You can think up other designs for your child to crisscross with yarn.

PENCIL OUTLINES

♦ ACTIVITY

Mastering holding and guiding a pencil.

♦ PROPS

Geometric shapes (plastic toy parts or cardboard cutouts), animal or bird cutouts, puzzle pieces.

Box of objects with simple outlines such as a shell-shaped ashtray, a memo-paper holder, a perfume bottle, a paperweight, a margarine tub, a pencil sharpener, a leaf, a flat rock, a ruler, a magnifying glass, a trivet, jar lids.

Pencil or felt-tip pen.

Scrap paper or colorful construction paper.

Masking tape, paper clips, or clipboard (all optional).

♦ ACTIONS

Place an object with a simple outline on a piece of paper. Hold the object stationary while your child guides a pencil around it. Remove the object and observe its penciled outline. Have your child try another object.

Watch how your child holds the pencil and teach him from the beginning to grasp it correctly. If you yourself have a quirky way of holding a pencil, make note of the conventional way.

It is frustrating to try to complete an outline accurately if the paper moves. So fasten the sheet of paper to the tabletop with tape or clips. A clipboard works well.

Turn certain objects upside down, such as the ashtray or margarine tub. The perfume bottles should stand upright for the bottom to be traced.

CHALKBOARD FREEDOM

♦ **ACTIVITY**

Scribbling with chalk held in the correct position for writing.

♦ **PROPS**

Large chalkboard (blackboard), about 12 by 20 inches, that is not an easel. Before buying, test to make sure it accepts chalk marks easily. Colored chalk, chalk eraser.

♦ **ACTIONS**

The purpose of this activity is to get ready for writing. Lay the chalkboard on a low table. If your child is standing at an upright blackboard or easel-type board, her posture for writing won't be correct.

Teach your child to hold the chalk as she should a pencil. Enjoy your child's experimental scribbles. Gradually phase her into making nice healthy circles. Later show her how to make xs or plus signs. Have her make rows of round os and rows of straight-lined crosses. Any design your child makes, holding the chalk as she would a pencil, is good practice for writing.

Erasing and doing the same thing umpteen times gives your child a free feeling, partly because you're not worried about the consumption of costly paper and partly because she can quickly erase what doesn't satisfy her.

Later you can use the board to demonstrate how to form letters and words, and your child can practice copying samples.

WIGGLY GROOVES

♦ **ACTIVITY**

Making a pencil follow grooves etched to form the letters in a child's name.

♦ **PROPS**

Thick cardboard rectangles, ice pick or other sharply pointed tool, pencil.

♦ **ACTIONS**

Scratch the letters of your child's name into a piece of cardboard with a sharp tool. Invite your child to hold a pencil properly and guide it along the grooves you've carved. You can draw some arrows along the letters to indicate where he should start and the direction in which he should go if he were forming the letters himself.

PEANUT BUTTER LETTERS

♦ **ACTIVITY**

Forming letters with an index finger.

♦ **PROPS**

Shallow baking pan.
Jar of peanut butter.

♦ **ACTIONS**

With your child's help, spread peanut butter a half-inch thick across the bottom of a pan. Your child can begin by drawing designs in it with her index finger. Later you can show her her initials on a piece of paper. Let her copy them in the peanut butter. Use cornmeal if you prefer something dry.

♦ **BENEFIT**

It's easier to learn to form letters directly with the finger than by incorporating a pencil into the act.

· 21 ·

BREAKING INTO PRINT

M any a child at age four can be more interested in writing and more patient with his early crude efforts than he'll be at age six. By then writing may seem boring compared to reading. So even if your offspring isn't a gung-ho paper-and-pencil kid, it may be worth his while to try out, with your encouragement, the activities in this chapter.

The younger child may be especially willing to follow your guidance regarding how to hold a pen and where to start and finish a letter of the alphabet she's learning to form. Thus good penmanship habits will be established at the outset. Hand-eye coordination is developed without a sense of toil if your child is having fun with tracing as described in V.I.P. Nameplates and Dot-to-Dot Delights in the previous chapter. The pride a preschooler feels (and the praise he gets) when producing words in his own hand often make him hardly notice the intense effort he's making.

Often curiosity about writing leads to curiosity about reading. With some children this order is reversed. In either case, a three- or four-year-old can begin to comprehend that a word in a roadside sign or a book is a word that can be reproduced by a parent or by himself and thus, in a sense, made one's own. Also a word heard can be recorded. It need not evaporate into thin air but can be held on to. Those wonderful words written down and shelved for a while can be "miraculously" enjoyed again, as in Instant Recall.

When a child dictates a story or a real-life event and a parent takes it down word for word, a child may discern one reason we write—to preserve ideas and experiences. When a child writes a Welcome Home sign or even a Keep Out sign, he glimpses another reason—to communicate. When you show your child your list of things to do, notes from a meeting, or a calendar of appointments, he understands still another purpose—to remind. Appreciating these reasons, he may initiate his own writing tasks, leading to surprising accomplishments.

♦

V.I.P. NAMEPLATES

♦ ACTIVITY

Learning to form the letters that make up one's own name and the names of other family members.

♦ PROPS

Felt-tip pen, poster board, scissors.
Individual photographs of family members (optional).
Tracing paper or onionskin, pencil.

♦ ACTIONS

Every child is eager to write her name—the most important word in her vocabulary. See my name? There I am in black and white, the inner thought whispers.

Cut posterboard into rectangles that are 3 inches by 10 inches, one for each member of the family. Let your child paste a picture of each person at the left of each card. Then write the name of your child in either capital or upper- and lower-case letters, whichever she is learning to write. Print the letters about 1½ inches high. You can letter the nameplates for other family members, too.

Lay tracing paper or onionskin paper over each card and paper-clip it at each corner. Give your child a smooth pen or a soft pencil. Let your child try to follow the contours of each letter. When your child is not practicing writing with them, you can use the nameplates to identify Mom's and Dad's individual piles of mail or hang them on bedroom or study doors.

♦ BENEFIT

Writing one's name is a satisfying form of self-assertion.

TRACING THE HEADLINES

♦ ACTIVITY

Tracing the largest letters on a newspaper's front page or on a magazine cover.

♦ PROPS

Newspapers, magazines, felt-tip pen or pencil of good quality, onionskin paper or tracing paper.

◆ ACTIONS

Your child will probably enjoy working with your periodicals (because they're yours) more than with dime-store workbooks. Cover today's newspaper headline with a see-through sheet of paper and paper-clip it in position. Teach your child how to gently move his hand across the page so as not to move the paper out of its original position and thus distort the letters.

Magazine covers with large-enough titles of articles furnish good practice for beginning writers, too.

Seek some information from a first-grade teacher, elementary school workbook, or early learning book on the correct way to form each letter. Writing workbooks show the route the pencil should travel by printing little arrows beside each letter. Watch that your child starts at the top of the letter and forms the left side of it first, then the right.

◆ BENEFIT

Tracing letters acquaints a child in a kinesthetic way with the differences among them and thereby aids visual discrimination of the alphabet.

DOT-TO-DOT DELIGHTS

◆ ACTIVITY

Mom or Dad forming the pattern of the letters with barely visible dots, and junior scribe fleshing out the letters to make the word appear.

◆ PROPS

Pencil, colored pens, blank paper, ruler (optional).

◆ ACTIONS

Decide together on some letters your child would like to learn to write. Perhaps tackle a hard letter such as the sinuous s. With a ruler draw lines (not too close together) for the top and bottom perimeters of the letter. Form the letter by a series of dots. Create this curvy line of dots several times. Watch your child trying to connect the dots, making sure she starts at the top.

As your daughter becomes more familiar with the letter, use fewer dots for the pattern. One child who eagerly filled whole sheets of paper with the same letter then said, "Here, Mommy, read this to me."

You could make a list of short words that begin with s (sap, sad, sip).

Leave the *s* as dots only and write the other letters properly. As your child fills in each *s,* say out loud the word just formed.

If she has already had practice on individual letters, talk over some words she'd like to write all by herself (see Provocative Words, p. 000). Take some time to write them out, using dots for each letter. Offer different-color pens for bringing each word to life.

PRIZE PEN CEREMONY

♦ ACTIVITY

Creating an aura around the act of writing and a respect for writing tools.

♦ PROPS

Crisp, clean, good-quality paper.
An especially fine pen.

♦ ACTIONS

When you think of the ancient profession of the scribe, the beauty of illuminated manuscripts, or the Oriental art of calligraphy, you begin to realize how nonchalant—and even scornful—we are about penmanship these days. We are infatuated with electric typewriters and computers. Here's an activity to counteract this trend.

Locate in your home, among relatives, or in a store an extra-special pen. It should be very attractive to look at and pleasant to hold. Most important, its point should glide particularly well across paper.

Store this pen in its own box on a high shelf out of your child's reach. Bring it down on special occasions, presenting it as if it were a crown jewel. Offer sparkling white paper. Express delight over your child's strokes with this instrument and the resulting preschooler "scroll."

Make sure he puts the cap back on the point and places the pen in its box. Make a little ceremony of returning it to its storage place.

Fat crayons or markers are often thrust into small hands. In fact, normal-size pens may be a lot easier for little fingers to maneuver.

♦ BENEFIT

A show of appreciation for graphics may elicit more interest in writing skills.

BLANK-PAGE NOTEBOOKS

♦ ACTIVITY

Building a collection of first tries at letters, words, phrases, and pic-ture captions.

♦ PROPS

Blank typing paper stapled together, or a spiral notebook of blank pages.

Ballpoint pen.

♦ ACTIONS

You'll be surprised at how your child's regular entries in this booklet will improve over time. When your child first becomes interested in writ-ing, offer a notebook for her jottings. If you choose to staple blank paper together, keep a series of such booklets.

A little girl who started her booklet with laborious writing lapsed into drawing. She overruled her mom's objections with the firm command, "Don't say that's not writing." To her, drawing and writing were equiv-alents. You won't want to supervise with too many restraints. Spelling errors and other imperfections are inconsequential. It's the joy of self-expression that counts.

Inspired suggestions from you may ignite the desire to write. You may introduce a forgotten letter: "Isn't it funny how capital *H* looks like goalposts?" Or you might dictate to an older preschooler a list of the names of good friends, stuffed animals, or favorite TV characters.

Either you or your child could draw a picture of a day's event, and she could subtitle it: "Justine with supermarket cart." You could paste in a photograph of your house, and your child could practice writing her address four times, once along each side of the picture: "43 Blueberry Lane."

Does your child often repeat a catchy advertising slogan she sees on TV? A four- to five-year-old might enjoy reproducing it in her own hand. Does Grandma use a particular phrase frequently that your child associ-ates with her—for example, Doing things the easy way? That page could be titled "Grandma's Motto." If you have a saying in your family de-signed for encouragement, such as "Up and at 'em" or "Upward and onward," spell that out for your child to write on a page of her notebook.

PICTURES PLUS WORDS

◆ ACTIVITY

Copying the word cards used for learn-to-read games.

◆ PROPS

Picture cards and word cards from reading activities.
Pen and paper.

◆ ACTIONS

You may have made a group of cards with words of special interest on them when following Provocative Words, the activity on page 232. The word printed in your handwriting can be your child's model. Suggest that he copy some of these.

If you rounded up magazine pictures or drew sketches of objects for Words Describe Pictures on page 233, use these now to stimulate writing. "It's your turn now to make labels." Give your son a large piece of paper to practice writing the label for one of these pictures. Then cut out his best-formed word and lay it under the appropriate picture. Perhaps paste his word onto a rectangle of colored construction paper so the word has a pretty frame.

◆ BENEFIT

Writing a word helps reinforce the ability to recognize and read it.

INTERFAMILY MEMOS

◆ ACTIVITY

Grasping the concept that writing is a unique way of communicating, with advantages over talking.

◆ PROPS

Greeting cards, postcards, stationery designed for kids, scrap paper, envelopes.

◆ ACTIONS

The interoffice memo has its domestic counterpart, the interfamily memo. It comes in a variety of forms.

Amelia wanted to know how to spell *Mom, I love you.* She drew the letters in the sand of her sandbox and waited nearby till her mother "discovered" her message. Scrap paper letters with *I love you* messages can be folded, sealed with tape, and popped inside Dad's or Mom's briefcase or delivered to other surprise places.

Holiday greeting cards are an exciting medium for would-be writers. Supply your child with birthday cards for relatives and Mother's and Father's Day cards. So eager are kids to sign their names or add an additional personal message that they don't regard as toil the fierce effort they are sometimes making to write the words.

Even if your child only enjoys writing a very few words, they are enough for a letter to a doting grandparent. Both sender and receiver will enjoy colorful stationery with matching envelopes.

It's never too soon to cultivate the habit of thank-you notes. A scrawled *thank you,* accompanied by a drawing, is enough to send to a caring aunt who put your child up for a night. A birthday gift received in the mail can be answered post-haste with a letter dictated to Mom and written by her but embroidered with drawings or words penned by the birthday girl.

If your child is having trouble making up after a squabble, leave her a card with the word *sorry* spelled out. She can copy it and slip it under the door to a sibling in an effort to reconcile.

Welcome Home or Congratulations signs are wonderful ways one parent can help a child celebrate the other parent's return from a trip or a promotion at work.

♦ BENEFIT

The differentness of communicating to family members in print rather than in conversation spurs a child to practice writing.

INSTANT RECALL

♦ ACTIVITY

Writing down a homemade story that is dictated, and reading it back to your child later.

♦ PROPS

Paper, pen, envelopes.

♦ ACTIONS

Who's the storyteller in your family—Mom, Dad, or your child? If Grandpa or Dad is telling a bedtime story, Mom can write it down word for word, if it's not too long. Then she can read it back to her child the next night. It is interesting to save the story for a week or a month, too.

"Do you remember that story Dad told about your Teddy bear at the Thanksgiving dinner table?" Your child will be quite surprised at this "magic" way of preserving and recalling Dad's tale.

Encourage your child to make up stories, too, helping with the story line now and then. Write them down without correcting or changing anything. Read them back to your child or read them aloud to your spouse with your child present. Save them for future enjoyment. This written record of a personal tale told helps motivate your child to want to learn to write and read.

When your child is able to write several words without a sense of toil, let him write down one of his own stories. Help him boil it down to the fewest number of words: "A boy went fishing. He caught a mermaid who didn't like the sea. He put her in his fish tank. The end."

If your child bogs down with a story of that length, try writing the majority of words yourself and let him write just the key words such as *boy, mermaid,* and *fish tank.*

♦ VARIATION

If your child doesn't like making up stories, she can simply recount an event of her day and make a "story" out of it. You can take that down in diarylike style.

· 22 ·

CURIOSITY ABOUT
COUNTING

"We count a lot. When I top-and-tail the string beans, I say, 'Keith, give me two beans. Now give me five.'" Another mother throws a quick numerical challenge to her son, such as: "Count how many red cars go by in the next ten minutes." These remarks are typical of parents I interviewed.

A tired dad, to escape roughhousing, arrested his child's attention by asking, "How many lamps are there in this room? How many chairs? How many tables? How many chair and table legs?" He whipped out a card from his breast pocket to take notes on his son's calculations.

Bret, when he was not quite two, learned from TV how to recognize all the numerals from 1 to 20. If his mother was near pen and paper, he'd put his hand on his mother's hand to coax her into writing numbers for him to identify. With a certain amount of suspense he'd watch to see which number she was forming.

A child becoming aware of numbers sees them everywhere: on the oven thermometer, on scales, measuring cups, elevators, clocks, and license plates. Your child can become aware of how often you're using numbers if you talk out loud about prices, checks you're writing, mileage, weights, telephone numbers and addresses, and even some figures you deal with at the office.

In this chapter the first several activities involve counting and the last several involve numeral recognition (naming numbers when seeing digits). The final activity reviews some computer games. Before pursuing all of these, you might consider whether you've given your child a chance to explore certain nonnumber ways of thinking that are fundamental to working with numbers. Every child needs experience with classification, seriation, and one-to-one correspondence.

Classification means sorting things and putting them in different classes or categories according to their similarities and differences. When your child unloads the dishwasher, he classifies the flatware by storing the forks, spoons, and knives in their special compartments in the drawer. Give your child sorting tasks with coins, buttons, workbench

266

hardware, and laundry items. Classification ability prepares the way for dealing with arithmetic sets and subsets.

Seriation means arranging things in an orderly sequence. There are many common toys that reinforce this skill, such as stacking doughnuts and graduated cups that fit inside one another. Plan experiences in which your child can arrange objects from smallest to largest, from lightest to heaviest, or in a particular sequence of color or shape. Being able to answer "what comes first" and "what comes next" questions when dealing with concrete objects prepares a child for doing the same thing with abstract number symbols.

One-to-one correspondence means matching objects in a simplistic way to make sure there are the same number of objects in each of two different groups. At a dolls' tea party your child sets a teacup in front of each doll. She doesn't count five dolls and then get five cups. This experience with corresponding objects helps when a child is first learning to count. Then a child "matches" each item she's counting with a number she's saying.

Some preschoolers lean toward letters, others toward numbers. If your child has curiosity about numbers, you can satisfy it with the following activities. If not, perhaps these games will pique such a curiosity.

♦

RINGS ON MY FINGERS

♦ ACTIVITY

Placing numbered rings on cardboard fingers traced from your child's hands.

♦ PROPS

Cardboard (back of legal pad), scissors, felt-tip pen.

♦ ACTIONS

Fingers were the human family's first calculator. Here's a variation on the common game of touching the tips of your child's fingers (or toes) as you count from one to ten.

Have your child place both hands on a rectangle of cardboard about the size of a legal pad. Trace around all his fingers. Leave a bridge of cardboard between the hands to write the name of your child and the date his hands were drawn. Cut around your outline, not separating the hands but leaving them joined by the bridge of cardboard.

Out of the scrap cardboard cut little rings with a hole in the center to enable them to slip over the cardboard fingers. Number the rings from 1 to 10.

Set the cardboard hands in front of you and your child. To reinforce the left-to-right reading skill, arrange the rings as follows: Start with the little finger of the traced left hand. Slip ring number 1 over it. Work toward the thumb of the left hand with rings 2, 3, 4, and 5. Then slip ring number 6 over the thumb of the right hand, slide on rings 7, 8, 9, and 10. As soon as your child recognizes numerals, let him choose the rings.

As you and your child play, he may surprise you by fitting a ring onto one of his real fingers.

The outlined hands, small and chubby, make a nice keepsake. In a year you can compare hand size and remember the fun.

DOMINO AND DICE DOTS

◆ ACTIVITY

Matching a specific amount of objects to a specific number of dots.

◆ PROPS

Ten or more 3-by-5-inch cards, felt-tip pen, large dice, about sixty pennies or poker chips.

◆ ACTIONS

Draw small circles on your cards to make them look like giant dominoes. Each one should have a different number of circles from one to ten. Your child can color in the circles. Have a bowl of pennies nearby. Then let her put a penny on each dot or circle, covering it. On the card with five dots, she will put five pennies. Teachers call this matching of quantities *one-to-one correspondence*.

Later you can organize the cards from left to right starting with the "one" card and ending with the "ten" card. Then you might label them with the appropriate numerals.

◆ VARIATION

Working with dice, even large cubes, is more difficult, as the dots are tiny and close together. But throwing dice is fun, and your son may enjoy the counting exercise it provides. Have him throw one die at first, count the number of dots, and then count out an equivalent number of pennies to place beside the cube. Then remove them before the next throw. When he's mastered this, use two dice.

SMOKESTACKS

♦ **ACTIVITY**

Arranging graduated lengths of paper in order of ascending size.

♦ **PROPS**

Red or black construction paper, scissors.

♦ **ACTIONS**

Cut a dozen strips of paper about the width of a bookmark. Make the first strip one inch long, the second strip two inches long, and continue until the last strip is 12 inches long.

You may start with only three or four strips and ask your child to put down the shortest first, then the next tallest to its right. Line them up against a box or straight edge of some kind so the base of each smokestack is level. Eventually your child should be able to line up all dozen smokestacks in the correct sequence.

♦ **BENEFIT**

Your child will grasp seriation of abstract numbers more easily if given many opportunities to arrange concrete materials in order.

NUMBERED COMPARTMENTS

♦ **ACTIVITY**

Counting from one to twelve, with objects to exemplify each quantity.

♦ **PROPS**

Egg carton, muffin tin, or margarine tubs; marking pen, seventy-eight small objects such as dried beans, paper clips, or pennies.

♦ **ACTIONS**

Let your child watch you mark each compartment of your egg carton or muffin tin, from left to right, with a numeral from 1 to 12. (You might start with half an egg carton so you have only six compartments.)

Take turns dropping into each compartment the corresponding number of beans or paper clips. Count out loud as you do this. Make sure your child touches a bean each time he names a number.

This device is like a "counting box," one of the many Montessori materials designed to ease preschoolers into arithmetic through visualizing and manipulating varying amounts of real things.

♦ BENEFIT

The fact sinks in that numbers your child easily names, perhaps by rote, stand for particular quantities.

HANDS-ON COUNTING

♦ ACTIVITY

Progressing from recitation counting (naming the numerals from one to ten like a rhyme) to counting while touching, one by one, objects in a collection.

♦ PROPS

A variety of small objects such as one pencil, two keys, three jar lids, four coins, five raisins, six straws, seven M & M's, eight stamps, nine toothpicks, ten paper clips.

Three-by-5-inch cards with large numerals on them, or playing cards from ace to 10 in one suit.

♦ ACTIONS

Sometimes children learn from TV or a nursery rhyme to count by rote. They sound as though they're familiar with numbers but they don't have a mental concept of "three-ness" (a few) when they say *three* or "ten-ness" (a lot) when they say *ten*.

Arrange the numbered cards in a row, with 1 at the far left, 10 at the far right. Have your collection of objects in front of you both. Help your child place the right number of objects beside each numeral.

Be sure that every time your child touches an object, she only mentions one number. Also check that whenever she mentions a number, she also picks up an item.

You should have more than the required number of objects available; perhaps a dozen of each item intended for the larger numbers. Then your child can match any item to any number. She learns that eight stamps are the same as eight toothpicks, that the number is a fixed entity that can be applied to a variety of things.

♦ **VARIATION**

Arrange sequenced piles of objects. After counting them together, ask your child to pick the appropriate numeral card for each pile. (See activities later in this chapter for numeral recognition games.)

♦ **BENEFIT**

Touching objects being counted cultivates the ability to associate numbers with quantities.

TELEPHONE TASKS

♦ **ACTIVITY**

Letting your child dial numbers to show the usefulness of numeral recognition.

♦ **PROPS**

Push-button telephone (rotary dials are too hard for preschooler fingers).

♦ **ACTIONS**

This game proves that your child can match a number when he sees it and can point to its printed symbol when he hears it.

Assign your son the task of calling Daddy, Grandma, or a good friend of yours. At first write down the number in fairly large numerals. Oversee his endeavor to match each numeral with a finger-press on the proper push button. There's no hurry. Most telephone systems tolerate a long pause between digits. Be sure he's going from left to right in reading the number you have written.

Later you should be able to give a number verbally. If you know your child is able to visualize the numeral 6 when you say "six," you can give him phone numbers orally and he can "dial" them for you. After practice at such oral dictation, he may be able to retain three or four digits in his mind, and you won't have to pause after saying each individual one.

CONCENTRATION ON NUMBERS

♦ **ACTIVITY**

Getting practice at recognizing numerals, a skill different from counting and not necessarily learned in counting games.

♦ **PROPS**

Three-by-5-inch cards, felt-tip pen.

♦ **ACTIONS**

You and your child may be familiar with the rules of Concentration, a card game, if you tried Animal and Fish Concentration (p. 206) or Concentration on Words (p. 239).

Here you must prepare your cards by writing identical numbers on two cards so that you have at least ten pairs. If your child is a number novice, you will work with pairs of 3s, 6s, 9s, and so forth. If your child is advanced, you can match higher numbers—19, 27, 35.

Place your cards in rows facedown. Each of you takes turns turning up two cards at a time. Put them down in the same spots on the table if the numbers don't match. Remember their locations. Then soon when you draw your first card, perhaps a 6, you'll remember where you put the other 6. You can draw it and make a pair.

Your child may soon earn the title Miss or Mr. Bright Eyes, as a preschooler often "concentrates" on placement better than an adult.

♦ **BENEFIT**

Spatial relationship skills as well as retention of number shapes are exercised here.

CARD SHARK

♦ **ACTIVITY**

Sorting, matching, and sequencing numbers.

♦ **PROPS**

Ordinary deck of cards without picture cards.

♦ **ACTIONS**

Your goal is to lay down four parallel rows of cards with the numbers of each suit in sequence from ace to 10. You can give lots of help or very little depending on your child's current stage.

Ask your child to find 6s. He may have to look through the pack till he finds four of them. If this is too difficult, you join in. "Oh, there's a 6, that sly one. He almost got away!" Next, track down 8s.

To make sequencing easier, remove two suits and let him build from left to right just two rows of cards, 1 through 10. Explain that the A for ace is a substitute for the numeral 1.

Frequently ask questions such as "What comes after 4? Let's see: 1,

2, 3, 4 . . . Yes, 5. So now we'll hunt for 5s." This can phase into first addition problems if you phrase your question this way: "Four and 1 more is what?"

The ordinary card games such as Go Fish and War familiarize a child with numbers. In one family the youngest child teamed up with a parent to play older members in these simple games.

IF YOU HAVE A COMPUTER

♦ ACTIVITY

Becoming familiar with a computer while reinforcing some beginning math concepts.

♦ PROPS

Personal computer disks designed to teach first lessons in arithmetic such as "Learning About Numbers, Volume I" by C & C Software, "Number Match" of Micro School Programs by Bertamax, Inc. (TRS-80 and Atari only), "Stickybear Numbers" by Xerox Education Publications, "Sequence" by Spinnaker, and "Counting Bee" by Edu-Ware. These are available for Apple-compatible computers.

♦ ACTIONS

A four-year-old tackling a disk with math content will need plenty of adult partnering at the terminal. Also counting or adding and subtracting with three-dimensional objects away from the terminal, as in the previous activities, will help her understand the two-dimensional challenges appearing on the screen.

"Learning About Numbers" starts with a kindergarten program called Let's Count and includes next-level math skills in a program called Arithmetic Fun. In the first, your child will be counting colorful objects such as flowers and cars as they materialize on the screen. Later these objects are grouped into sets with boxes drawn around them. When a box with three cars appears, your child types a 3. When the next box with two cars appears, he types a 2. When the box of five apears, he enters the correct number, 5, from the keyboard. Thus the counting game phases into adding and working with sets.

"Number Match" presents on the screen several ways of expressing each of the numbers from one to ten. For instance, the graphics can exhibit five domino spots, five objects or shapes, and the numeral 5. Sometimes your child has to key in the appropriate numeral when shown the domino spots. In another exercise he's asked to press the space bar the right number of times to make the number of objects appear that corresponds with the numeral.

"Stickybear Numbers" with its cartoonlike animation is a good example of software designed to make early learning amusing to a child. One by one, and not too fast for very young counters, exciting objects appear on the screen—spinning hats, flying birds, revolving planets, Stickybears coming out of windows, and many other such wonders.

"Sequence" aids numeral recognition by presenting your child with four sequential numbers and asking her to search the keyboard for the proper fifth.

"Counting Bee" includes weight and measuring exercises as well as counting, addition, and subtraction.

While these programs dress up arithmetic drills in electronic graphics and charming music, they may not give a young child as clear a comprehension of number facts as concrete examples do. Nevertheless, if you're planning to acquaint your child with your home or office computer anyway, these educational disks are more profitable than arcade-game disks.

· 23 ·
A HEAD FOR
FIGURES

I n recent decades consciousness has been raised about the intelligence and abilities of preschoolers. Educational researchers and teachers working with children in nursery schools, day-care centers, and homes have led parents to increase their expectations regarding how much children like to learn and how much they can learn. Both theory and practice support the logic of parents introducing information of a cognitive or academic nature into their one-on-one exchanges with their preschoolers. Kids' minds are often ready to soak up facts and figures, and who better than the loving parent to provide that stimulation!

Any preconception that this would be a dry and dreary pastime should be erased. Parents need to stick to a game format; have a cheerful, nonchalant air; and be consistently kind, never showing annoyance at lack of comprehension on the child's part. Perhaps this educational style is harder to achieve in the area of arithmetic. But a new generation of parents is aiming for it.

Some parents have begun teaching numerical concepts to babies and toddlers as a result of reading *Teach Your Baby Math,* by Glenn Doman (Simon & Schuster, 1980). They achieve amazing results with white flash cards patterned with red dots. Others, who have reproduced Montessori-type materials in the home, have been able to portray numbers tangibly to their child, ranging into the hundreds and thousands. They use cubes symbolizing a thousand, tablets symbolizing a hundred, rods for ten, and single units. The bright tots can add such figures as 1,201 and 2,245 using these concrete representations. Parents who have found Cuisenaire rods in toy stores or libraries bone up in the manual on the math concepts these rods illustrate. Parents continue to buy copies of *Give Your Child a Superior Mind* by Siegfried and Therese Engelmann (Cornerstone, 1981). These authors give detailed instructions to parents of prekindergarten kids on imparting many math concepts ranging from simple to complex.

These methods and early cognitive learning itself are controversial. A casual conversation about them with the average neighbor or nursery school teacher may generate all sorts of negative comments. You'll have to investigate and decide for yourself if these approaches are valid for you and your child. With the math activities that follow, you can get your feet wet.

Those interested in an adventurous math education for their children may be considering a personal computer. Many disks for the home personal computer market are designed for teaching simple arithmetic to preschoolers and primary grade pupils. A review of a few of them immediately precedes this chapter.

Your most interesting route into the world of computer science and mathematics may be achieved through the graphics-based language of Logo. By means of this simple programming language, your child can talk to a computer. Logo is discussed in the last activity of this chapter. Your preschooler can enjoy a bit of its potential now and much more of it through the middle years. You too will enjoy the sophisticated possibilities of programming with Logo.

Following are excellent sources for manipulative math materials. A catalog from the first shows math dominoes, geofix boards, and cubic measuring spoons. A catalog from the second shows attribute blocks, a math balance scale, tangrams and the hundred board. Enjoy establishing your child's foundation in arithmetic at home!

> The Burt Harrison Company
> P.O. Box 732
> Weston, MA 02193
>
> Invicta Plastics, Ltd.
> Educational Aids Division
> Oadby, Leicester, England

◆

CALCULATOR SHINE

◆ ACTIVITY
Familiarizing your child with the world of numbers by playing together with your pocket calculator.

◆ PROPS
Electronic calculator.

◆ ACTIONS
Take your child on your lap and invite her to press the On button. Teach her the name *zero* for the circle that appears. First, you press

buttons and let her watch the illuminated numerals appear. Then it's her turn. Let her press buttons at random and fill the window with numbers. Name them from left to right. Show her how to play magician and make them disappear. Ask her how old she is. Three? Suggest she keep pressing 3s till she has a whole row of them. Make rows of 7s, 8s, 9s.

At another session you can show her how to sequence the numbers. Point to the 1 button and have her press it. Then, without erasing, proceed to 2, 3, et cetera, so that all the numbers from 1 to 8 appear. (Your calculator may show only 8 numerals at a time.) Show her how to reproduce the numbers in reverse by counting backward.

Let her call out numbers at random and you press them. Or you can call out numbers and watch her hunt and peck to bring the digits to the window. If your child's interest lasts, work on a series of numbers, up to 30, perhaps. Help her press each number. Then, after viewing it, remind her to erase before pressing the buttons for the next number.

When you begin teaching your child to add with concrete materials, you can show her how fast the magical calculator performs these functions.

TOY WEIGH-IN

♦ **ACTIVITY**

Noticing that numbers represent the various weights of objects.

♦ **PROPS**

Scales, some small toys, some big toys, pad and pencil, measuring tape.

♦ **ACTIONS**

Let your child place a toy on the scales and read the number. You record the weight and perhaps the name of the item: red bulldozer, 15 ounces. If together you compare a group of lightweight toys and later a group of heavyweight toys, your child will not get too confused about ounces and pounds (i.e., why is 8 ounces a lighter weight than 1 pound?).

♦ **VARIATION**

Measure the toys from one end to another or measure the circumference of each toy. "This car is 3 inches long from front to back. This fire engine is 12 inches long from head to toe. The fire engine is longer, isn't it?"

Use your child's own hands and feet as units of measure. For example, you'll come out with facts such as these: the desk top is 10 hands wide; the book is 2 hands long; the bedroom floor is 36 feet long (36 of John's feet); and the bath mat is 12 feet long (12 of John's, 6½ of Dad's).

♦ BENEFIT

Weighing and measuring give a child a good feel for figures.

HIGH-NUMBER PRACTICE

♦ ACTIVITY

Building familiarity with the numbers from ten to one hundred by counting with shells or peanuts.

♦ PROPS

Drawstring bag of random high numbers on little square pieces of paper: 18, 25, 36, 42, 59, etc.

Pail of shells (or basket of peanuts if you don't make trips to a beach).

♦ ACTIONS

Some three- and four-year-olds advance rapidly beyond beginning number games. For a child who shows an inclination toward figures or is excited about a just-emerging ability to count all the way to one hundred, this exercise will be an intense pleasure that adults may find hard to comprehend.

Shake the bag of numbers. Then have your child draw a number as he would for a raffle. Don't let your own feelings about the tedium of counting out eighty-four shells color your interaction with your child. Reflect back to him his ambitious enthusiasm. Stay with him as he works out this problem, picking shell after shell out of the pail. When he hits twenty-nine, he may need reminding that thirty is the next number. When he reaches thirty-nine, he may skip to fifty unless you're there to prompt him.

♦ BENEFIT

Playing with high numbers feeds a child's natural fascination with bigness.

THE PLUS OR MINUS NECKLACE

♦ ACTIVITY

Getting used to the concepts of adding and taking away by an expanding and shrinking necklace.

♦ PROPS

Large pieces of macaroni or beads; shoelace or string.

♦ ACTIONS

Have handy a basket of macaroni pieces with a center large enough for a shoelace or string to be threaded through. The dice will tell your child whether to add or subtract beads. Explain that the first three throws are "add-on" commands. The next three throws are "take-away" commands.

Ask your child to throw a pair of dice and add up the spots. If there are five, she should count out five beads and string them on her shoelace. Next time she throws, if she gets double sixes, she expands the necklace with twelve beads. After a third throw enlarging the necklace, she should count the total number of beads.

Now the next three throws will dictate how short her row of beads will become. Throw the dice, count the spots, then slide off the same number of beads. You can use the term *equal* occasionally, saying, "There are ten spots on the dice. So take off an equal number of beads."

During the operation you can describe the actions in mathematical terms. "So four *more* beads this time. Now four *less* beads." Get your child used to the terms *more* or *less* accompanying the visible changing quantities. You could introduce the words *plus* and *minus,* also. Sometimes say, "You're adding four more beads. That's plus four." Later say, "You're not going to have many left. Take away five is minus five."

End with addition, so your child will have a decent necklace to wear to dinner that night.

♦ BENEFIT

Mathematical terms are best learned when a child can manipulate materials.

EQUATIONS IN THE CONCRETE

♦ ACTIVITY

Teaching your child the process of addition, subtraction, and multiplication through tangible objects at hand.

♦ PROPS

Three small boxes, a dozen little plastic doll figures or soldiers, colored toothpicks; scrap paper; leaves, dried beans.

♦ ACTIONS

Here you're aiming for a real understanding of what is going on in arithmetic before your child gets to the pen-and-pencil stage. You're going to illustrate simple equations by forming sets of objects inside real boxes and then physically clustering them together in a "total" box. Also you will take away some figures and count the remainder.

Addition   Put your three open boxes in a row. Place toothpicks in the form of a plus sign between the first two boxes. Place toothpicks in the form of an equal sign between the last two boxes. Tell your child that the toothpicks say what to do.

Have your child put one or two figures in the first house or fort (box) on the left and a few more figures in the middle house or fort. Explain that the plus sign asks us to add the first group to the second group. When all the people go into the third house (the answer box), your child should count how many there are all together. (You might make up a story about a family in one house and cousins in the next all going to Grandma's house.)

She can count them one by one as she drops them in the total box, or scoop them all into the box and then count those inside it. Explain that the equal sign means there are the same number of people on each side. They are just grouped differently.

When your child has played this many times, take turns writing sums on strips of paper to place below the houses. Express each new arrangement in numerals: $2 + 3 = 5$.

Multiplication   You can teach this after adding and before subtraction because it is so akin to adding. Ask your child to bring you five leaves or seed pods from outdoors. Then ask for five more. Then go get five yourself. Finally ask her to fetch yet another five leaves or pods. Look at your pile and say, "Let's see. How many times did we add five things? We added five things four different times. How many do we have in our pile? Let's count. We have twenty. So five things brought together four times is twenty."

If your youngster observes an older sibling learning times tables, you might try illustrating the "two times" table in the concrete. You can make two rows of beans arranged in sets or groups going from left to right. Place each set a few inches from the previous one. Place one bean at the left to start the top row and one bean underneath to start the bottom row. Moving a few inches to the right, place two beans side by side in the top row and two beans directly underneath. Point as you say, "There are two sets of two beans, one set above, one set below. How many beans in two sets of two?"

Now farther along to the right, place a set of three beans side by side in the top row and three in the bottom. "Look, now we have two sets of three. Shall we count them?" Proceed to assemble two orderly groups of four beans, then of five. "You see? Two sets of four beans is equal to eight beans."

With slips of paper label each unit 2×1, 2×2, 2×3, and so on. When your child is familiar with the process, go on to the "three times" table and let her build three rows of each progressive set of beans.

Subtraction   With the same boxes you used for the adding game, introduce one toothpick as a minus sign between the first two boxes. Ask your child to put a large group of figures in the "house" on the left. Pretend they are grown-ups at a party. Then invent reasons for why some people leave. The second box can represent the car in which people go away. Tell her each time how many people have to go: "Take away three. They have to go home to baby-sitters." Then have her count how many figures are left, placing them in the answer box as she counts. Write that number on a piece of paper and place it below the answer box.

Eventually you can place long strips of paper underneath the boxes showing sums to dictate how many to put in and how many to take away.

BANKERS AT WORK

♦ **ACTIVITY**
Identifying coins and recognizing equivalent coin values.

♦ **PROPS**
Two rolls of pennies, some nickels, dimes, quarters, a half-dollar, a silver dollar.

♦ **ACTIONS**

Announce that for several nights you are going to play at being bankers. Carry out the instructions that follow only as far as your child currently comprehends. Empty the penny rolls into a bowl. Your child can make a column of the other coins on a tabletop, putting down the nickel first, then under it a dime, under the dime a quarter, and so forth. Explain that a nickel is "the same as" or "equal to" five cents. Have him count out five pennies, placing them horizontally beside the nickel. Then explain that a dime is ten cents and together count out and build a row of ten pennies. Under this row you can also place two nickels and under them a nickel and five pennies. Explain that there are three ways to make change for a dime.

When you come to the quarter, work out the various equivalencies in different rows: twenty-five pennies, two dimes and one nickel, three nickels and one dime, five nickels, two dimes and five pennies, two nickels and fifteen pennies. You can simplify the equivalencies for the half-dollar by building a long row of pennies, and short rows of two quarters, five dimes, and ten nickels. Plotting coin combinations for the shiny silver dollar will be your crowning achievement.

This is a game to play only for brief periods so your child doesn't get overwhelmed. But if you keep it up, he will learn to count out change readily and pay for some purchases by himself.

IF YOU HAVE A COMPUTER

♦ **ACTIVITY**

Teaching your child the Logo language, which will enable her to begin thinking like a mathematician.

♦ **PROPS**

Personal computer; one of the following Logo systems: Apple Logo, Sprite Logo For The Apple II Family, Atari Logo, IBM Logo, Smart Logo (for the Coleco Adam).

♦ **ACTIONS**

According to educators I interviewed, Logo is the most educationally valuable math diskette you can give your child. She can start with it and continue using it for many years. (A parent can also enjoy it at a beginning or sophisticated level.)

At age three or four, with your guidance, your child can begin programming a computer. By talking the Logo language to your computer, she will gradually become exposed to some of the deepest ideas of mathematics. You can read all about what Logo can do for your child in *Mindstorms: Children, Computers, and Powerful Ideas* (Basic Books, 1980; Harper Colophon, 1982), written by the inventor of Logo, Seymour Papert, a professor of mathematics at MIT. In this book he makes a number of predictions about the positive effect on a child of growing up with access through Logo to a home computer. He believes your child will pick up mathematics fearlessly and easily. She will develop a style of learning that will help her with all kinds of problem solving, both in school and in life. She'll also fit with ease into the computer-common world of her future.

Your child's first experiences with Logo involve moving an electronic pet turtle across the screen. The trails it leaves behind are termed *turtle graphics*. Your child presses certain keys to make the turtle act like a pen point, drawing triangles, squares, and other patterns in bright colors. The numbers she types dictate how many steps the turtle will take.

With commands such as *forward 50* and *forward 100*, she can immediately compare lines of two lengths. With a command such as *right 90*, she discovers instantly what a right-angle turn looks like (though she doesn't know it by that name). By typing *forward 50* and *right 90* four times, she causes the magic turtle to execute a square on the screen. By giving the computer a name for a series of commands, such as *square*, she writes a program. If you keep one eye on the Logo manual and the other on your child's typing finger, you can help her invent other programs for different geometric shapes. Playing with Logo would enable your child to grasp basic geometry at least on an intuitive level.

Math has always been taught not only for its practical value (making change, figuring costs) but also because it teaches us to think in a special way—in terms of fixed principles, applied rules, order, and logic. A primary value of Logo may be not in an early introduction to number and spatial relationships but to valuable thinking skills. In order to program a computer, a child has to exercise planning, decision-making, and debugging skills. These are all transferrable to life situations. *Debugging* is an everyday routine in which a programmer detects and removes a flaw in a program. It shields kids from the emotional right/wrong syndrome of classroom arithmetic. It helps them approach a life problem with a more nonchalant air gained from attempting to detect the flaw that is holding back a solution.

Unlike some computer software in which the computer programs the child (drilling her in spelling and math), the Logo language enables the child to program the computer. This feeling of being in the driver's seat bolsters self-esteem. That is perhaps one of the most profound effects of interaction with a computer at the early childhood stage.